Library of
Davidson College

THE SPIRITUALITY OF ERASMUS OF ROTTERDAM

BIBLIOTHECA

HUMANISTICA & REFORMATORICA

VOLUME XL

Engraved title-page portrait of Erasmus, surrounded by two angels and the figures of two unidentified saints, quite possibly St. Augustine (left) and St. Jerome (right), standing in the foreground, and the four evangelists (seated left to right in the background): St. John, St. Luke, St. Matthew, and St. Mark. Reproduced by permission of the Erasmus of Rotterdam Society.

ANNOTATIONES,
OF
AANTEEKENINGEN
OP
'tNIEUWE TESTAMENT;
DOOR
DESIDERIUS ERASMUS van Rotterdam

In 't Latijn beschreven, en, volgens des Schrijvers vijfde en leste vermeerdering, van
J. H. *Glazemaker* uit het Latijn vertaalt, en met D. v. B. overgelezen, en nagezien.

t'AMSTERDAM,
Voor IAN RIEVWERTSZ
Boek-verkoper in Dirk van Assen
steegh in t'Martelaars Boek. 1663.
Met Privilegie voor 12 Iaar.

RICHARD L. DeMOLEN

THE SPIRITUALITY OF ERASMUS OF ROTTERDAM

NIEUWKOOP
DE GRAAF PUBLISHERS
1987

CIP-GEGEVENS KONINKLIJKE BIBLIOTHEEK, DEN HAAG

DeMolen, Richard L.

The spirituality of Erasmus of Rotterdam / Richard L. DeMolen. – Nieuwkoop : De Graaf.
– Ill. – (Bibliotheca humanistica & reformatorica ; vol. 40)
Met bibliogr., index.
ISBN 90-6004-392-8 geb.
SISO 155.2 UDC 165.74+929 Erasmus, Desiderius
Trefw.: Erasmus, Desiderius.

© RICHARD L. DEMOLEN 1987

FOR MY PARENTS:

ON THE OCCASION OF THEIR FIFTIETH WEDDING ANNIVERSARY,
JANUARY 16, 1987

TABLE OF CONTENTS

Preface   xi

Prologue   xiii

1. Erasmus of Rotterdam in Profile   1

2. Erasmus as Adolescent   15

3. The Interior Erasmus   35

4. *Opera Omnia Desiderii Erasmi*: Rungs on the Ladder to the *Philosophia Christi*   69

5. First Fruits: The Place of *Antibarbarorum Liber* and *De Contemptu Mundi* in the Formulation of Erasmus' *Philosophia Christi*   125

6. Erasmus on Childhood   143

7. The Expression of Love in the *Oeuvre* of Erasmus   165

8. Erasmus' Commitment to the Canons Regular of St. Augustine   191

Epilogue   199

Selected Bibliography   205

Index   217

Preface

THIS book is based on a series of essays that were published during a fifteen-year period beginning with a 1969 Ithaca College (New York) quincentennial birthday lecture and concluding with a University of Liège festschrift article commemorating the four hundred and fiftieth anniversary of Erasmus' death in 1986. The common thread that links these articles is the spirituality of Erasmus—a religious transformation that took place in the monastery of the Canons Regular of St. Augustine at Steyn in the 1480's and remained the motivating force behind his public life of scholarship and reform. Erasmus' inspiration came from the *Devotio Moderna* as it seems certain that the acorn did not fall very far from the tree.

Stressing Erasmus' devotion to the classics at the expense of sacred Scripture, Augustin Renaudet declared in *Érasme: Sa Pensée Religieuse* (Paris: Alcan, 1926, pp. 13–14) that "De même que son spiritualisme, au fond, procède de Cicéron plus que de saint Paul, son éthique procède de l'antiquité plus que de l'Évangile." Richard G. Villoslada, S. J., drew the same conclusion in his article on Erasmus in volume IV of the *Dictionnaire de Spiritualité* (Paris: Beauchesne, 1960, c. 933) where he argued that "Cette spiritualité trop *anthropocentrique* est en même temps *moralisante*. La vie spirituelle a moins pour but la conformité à la volonté divine, la croissance en la grâce, l'union au Christ, la filiation de Dieu, que la paix et la tranquillité de la conscience. Le suprême bien, le bonheur par excellence, c'est, pour Érasme, la tranquillité de l'âme." Erasmus emerges as a promoter of humanity but not as a model of piety. Villoslada concluded: "Érasme ne fut jamais vraiment pieux; il ne subit jamais de fortes crises spirituelles . . . . Ce n'etait ni un mystique ni un saint . . ." (c. 931).

In a more recent assessment of Erasmus' spirituality, appearing in volume VII of the preceding work (Paris: Beauchesne, 1969, columns 1006–1028), Jean-Pierre Massaut shared the same view of Erasmus' sanctity, but he also insisted that "Théologique et théologale, la spiritualité d'Érasme ne recèle ni l'adogmatisme, ni le rationalisme, ni le moralisme, ni le psychologisme qui trop de critiques lui ont imputés, en dépit de textes formels" (c. 1026). Drawing on the work of Georges Chantraine, S. J., 'Mystère' et 'Philosophie du Christ' selon Érasme (Namur and Gembloux: DuCulot, 1971), Massaut argued "Pas plus qu'elle ne neglige de dogme, la spiritualite d'Erasme ne meconnait les sacrements; elle est intensement baptismale, et aussi eucharistique, quoique de facon moins appuyee" (c. 1026). Erasmus' spirituality is firmly rooted in Scripture and pre-Augustinian patristics, but there is no place in Massaut's analysis for the Augustinian tradition nor the spirit of the *Devotio Moderna* which, in the words of the *Imitation of Christ,* exhorted the reader to "Study, therefore, to withdraw the love of your soul from all things that are visible, and to turn it to things that are invisible" (I, 19). Though he recognized Erasmus as a *Christian* humanist, Massaut concluded his essay with the observation that "Il avait beau citer saint Paul, il pensait comme Cicéron!" (1028).

I am grateful to the following publishers and journals for permission to reprint previously published material: Twayne Publishers (1971), *Renaissance Quarterly* (1973), *Bibliothèque d'Humanisme et Renaissance* (1976), Yale University Press (1978), *Erasmus of Rotterdam Society Yearbook Two* (1982), Susquehanna/Associated University Presses (1984), and the University of Liège. I also wish to thank the Editorial Board of the *Erasmus of Rotterdam Society Yearbook* for reading the manuscript and for offering helpful suggestions. Professors Clarence H. Miller (Saint Louis University), John C. Olin (emeritus, Fordham University), Albert Rabil, Jr. (S.U.N.Y. at Old Westbury), and James D. Tracy (University of Minnesota) have earned my heartfelt gratitude since the founding of the Erasmus of Rotterdam Society in 1980.

Prologue

THE premise of this book is that Erasmus of Rotterdam was born in 1469 and that he entered the monastery of the Canons Regular of St. Augustine in 1485/86 at the age of sixteen. Those scholars who have argued for a birth year of 1466 or 1467 or 1469 have based their position on a wide range of secondary evidence: Ernst-Wilhelm Kohls and John B. Gleason argue for 1466, A. C. F. Koch for 1467, and R. R. Post for 1469.[1] Erasmus himself offers the best challenge to the arguments of Kohls, Gleason, and Koch when he insisted throughout his life that he was compelled by his guardians to join the religious life even though he was still a boy. If Erasmus had been born in 1466, for example, he could not possibly have convinced his readers that he was too young to profess vows in 1487 when he would have been about twenty years old. But if he were only seventeen years old at the time of his first profession, the majority of his readers would have supported his contention that he was far too young to commit himself to a life-long obligation in the religious life.

Moreover, Erasmus' ordination to the priesthood at the age of twenty-two on April 25, 1492, after some six years of residence in the monastery at Steyn, would have been in keeping with contemporary practice. It is instructive to note, for example, that John Fisher, later bishop of Rochester, who was born in 1469, was ordained in 1491 at about the same age, and that Martin Luther, who was born on 10 November 1483, was twenty-three when he was ordained to the priesthood on 4 April 1507. Likewise, Jan (II) Laski was ordained in 1521 at age twenty-two. It is unlikely that Erasmus' superiors at Steyn would have postponed his ordination to the priesthood until 1492 if he had been born in 1466, since he possessed an exceptional intellect and displayed unusual promise. Finally, Beatus Rhenanus, his first biographer, noted that the bishop of Cambrai was delighted with Erasmus' "charm and

---

[1] See Kohls, "Das Geburtsjahr des Erasmus," *Theologische Zeitschrift*, 22 (1966), 91–121 and 347–59; Gleason, "The Birth Dates of John Colet and Erasmus of Rotterdam: Fresh Documentary Evidence," *Renaissance Quarterly*, 32 (1979), 73–76; Koch, *The Year of Erasmus' Birth* (Utrecht: Haentjens Dekker & Gumbert, 1969); and Post, "Quelques précisions sur l'année de la naissance d'Érasme (1469) et sur son education," *Bibliothèque d'Humanisme et Renaissance*, 26 (1964), 489–509, and "Nochmals Erasmus' Geburtsjahr," *Theologische Zeitschrift*, 22 (1966), 319–333.

with the distinction and candor of his youth"[2] Hendrik van Bergen would hardly have described his new secretary as a youth in 1493 if he were approaching his twenty-seventh birthday.

In the pages which follow, I have attempted to present an image of Erasmus which combines elements of the *Devotio Moderna* and Italian humanism. I have tried to clarify his significant role in the Renaissance of the North and, above all, to focus attention on the uniqueness of his contribution. Erasmus was not merely a precursor of religious revolutionaries like Luther and Calvin, nor an early devotee of seventeenth-century rationalism, nor even a man on horseback, caught between two opposing camps. Instead, he was a reformer in his own right. As the proponent and originator of a philosophy of renewal, he sought to bridge two worlds, those of patristic Christianity and sixteenth-century society, in order to effect a new and more humane world order.

Though Erasmus is frequently referred to as the prince of humanists, his concern for humanity was Christ-centered and directed toward achieving a spiritual life that was focused on God. Erasmus defended neither earthly pleasures nor worldly pursuits per se. He directed his own considerable energies as a priest to scholarly endeavors that taught Christians how to become holy in this life in preparation for life eternal.

As if to underscore Erasmus' mysticism, M. A. Screech published *Ecstasy and the Praise of Folly* in 1980. His careful analysis of the concluding lines of *The Praise of Folly* reveals the introspective nature of Erasmus and is fully compatible with his other works of a more orthodox nature and format.

Furthermore, Léon-E. Halkin has demonstrated in *Erasmus ex Erasmo* (1983) that Erasmus purposefully edited his correspondence, selecting for posterity what I believe were those letters that stressed his program of reform and reflected his own interior life of grace. His portraiture, which awaits careful analysis, also complements, I believe, his surviving correspondence and supports Erasmus' insistence that after 1489 he strove to promote studies that would increase the holiness of others. His portraiture draws upon the likenesses of Saints Augustine and Jerome in an apparent effort to add their silent endorsement to his *philosophia Christi*.

---

[2] "The Life of Erasmus by Beatus Rhenanus" in *Christian Humanism and the Reformation: Selected Writings,* trans. and ed. by John C. Olin (New York: Harper and Row, 1965), p. 34.

PROLOGUE

In *Erasmus' Annotations on the New Testament: From Philologist to Theologian* (1986), Erika Rummel tries to persuade her readers that Erasmus underwent a "'conversion' from philologist to biblical scholar" in 1501 (p. 3). It seems to me that although Erasmus acquired many scholarly skills during his lifetime, he never discarded any of them. He could just as wisely be termed a philologist after 1501 as before. The focal point in Erasmus' life was not 1501 but 1489. It was at Steyn that Erasmus vowed to write only of holy men and holiness itself. The accomplishment of his resolution was realized in the remaining years of his life and found expression in his pursuits of classical philology, biblical exegesis, children's textbooks, *spiritualia,* and patristics. Erasmus never ceased being a philologist any more than he ceased to advance his *philosophia Christi.* Although Erasmus did not use the expression *philosophia Christi* until 1516 when he published the *Paraclesis,* one can trace its origins to Steyn. It is only when we recognize that Erasmus became a philologist, exegete, grammarian, editor, and spiritual writer as a result of his 1489 resolution that his life takes direction. Erasmus taught and pursued a spiritual way of life which owed its inspiration to the *Devotio Moderna,* but he was also indebted to classical writers and the Church Fathers.

It seems clear that Erasmus drew wisdom from the ancient philosophers and recognized, for example, that Stoicism advocated the cultivation of both virtue and knowledge. But he was also aware that it was not Christ-centered; that it was not divinely inspired; and that its certitude paled in comparison with sacred Scripture.

Far from viewing him as a spiritual mentor during his residence at Steyn, Rummel insists that Erasmus appeared to be a poet in search of worldly ambition. She concludes: "Although the literary output of the years 1489–92 offered evidence of a subtle change in Erasmus' thinking and showed him diverting his creative efforts to spiritual themes, the image he projected was still that of a man more devoted to secular literature than was deemed compatible with his profession, a man of literary ambitions striving to be a poet after the classical fashion" (p. 6). That Erasmus had little chance of success as a classical poet is evident from the quality of his surviving poetry. To Hector Boece he confided in 1495: "Please consider how unfair it is of you to insist upon having something which I do not even own myself. I swear to you most solemnly that for a long time now I have not been engaged in the pursuit of poetry and if I wrote verse as a boy, I left it in my native land" (*CWE,* 47, 5–9).

THE SPIRITUALITY OF ERASMUS

Erasmus spent the years 1489 to 1492 at Steyn studying holy men and holiness. It was only when he realized that a majority of his fellow canons were unpersuaded by the compatibility of *bonae litterae* and church dogma that he sought release from the monastery. It was the hostile environment at Steyn that led him to seek the patronage of the bishop of Cambrai. The bishop's later misfortunes resulted in Erasmus' pursuit of theological study at Paris where he planned to acquire the background necessary to realize his 1489 goal. When the scholastic disputations of his mentors failed to lead to his desired end he abandoned his studies and sought reassurance from the contacts he made in England between 1499 and 1500. John Colet's invitation to lecture on specific books of the Old Testament convinced Erasmus to master classical Greek before devoting his energies to Scripture. Philology was the necessary handmaiden of exegesis, and both men saw these skills as indispensable complements. Erasmus would end his career in the pursuit of the *philosophia Christi*, mastering many skills that were secondary to the goal itself. His 1489 resolution had been nurtured in the monastery at Steyn and found full expression in the monastery without walls, the world of the sixteenth century.

II

The following book consists of eight chapters. Chapter one provides an overview of the life of Erasmus of Rotterdam, underscoring his program of reform (*philosophia Christi*) and his own efforts to imitate Christ during his life.

Chapter two concentrates its focus on the adolescence of Erasmus, the reasons surrounding his choice of the religious life as a vocation, the rejection of friendship by his brother, and his adaptations to the emotional crises of his youth. It is based largely on the Steyn correspondence which records events between 1486 and 1493. Erasmus' spirituality was formed during these critical years of his life. When he emerged from the monastery at Steyn in 1493, he pursued a life of holiness patterned on that of the rule of St. Augustine, but without having to endure the pressures of community life which he confessed was unsuitable to his nature.

Chapter three draws attention to the rich interior life of Erasmus which was nurtured at Steyn by the *Devotio Moderna* and found expression in his *philosophia Christi*. Erasmus was indebted to the *Imitatio*

PROLOGUE

Christi which was composed in the fifteenth century by a fellow Augustinian canon, Thomas à Kempis. 1489 was the turning point in Erasmus' life. It was at Steyn that Erasmus "decided for the future to write nothing which does not breathe the atmosphere either of praise of holy men or of holiness itself." Erasmus' public life outside the monastery at Steyn was devoted to the fulfillment of this promise. Conscious of his mission he was careful to protect his reputation for piety and integrity of character so that his nascent *philosophia Christi* would not be rejected by a critical public. Erasmus also sought canonical dispensations for his new mode of life from the papacy so as not to give offense to fellow Christians. Erasmus' spirituality was formed internally before he left Steyn and was made public through the printed page. His study of classical Greek, sacred Scripture, and the Church Fathers; his authorship of textbooks for boys; his religious and devotional treatises are all reflections of Erasmus' commitment to promote holiness. But hostile critics, such as Guillaume Budé, found fault with his concern for lay piety and the education of schoolboys in learning and virtue. Such pursuits, Budé reasoned, drained precious time away from the study of sacred Scripture. At the request of a distraught wife, Erasmus delayed his studies once again and wrote a handbook for holiness, the *Enchiridion,* in 1501 which was later published in 1503. Prayer and knowledge of Scripture and the Church Fathers would become the weapons that would secure true spirituality for all, whether prince or schoolboy. Erasmus also urged his readers to reject the material riches of this life for an interior life of contemplation even if they were living a cloistered religious life. Erasmus insisted that an elaborate habit could be as much of a deterrent to true piety for a nun as great wealth for a merchant.

Chapter four surveys twenty major works by Erasmus and demonstrates that all of them attempt to preach the message of his *philosophia Christi*. Letters, defenses of classical studies, adages, and colloquies sought to direct the reader to a richer spiritual life. In the words of Erasmus, "untaught virtue dies with its author unless it is handed down to posterity in writings" (see p. 82). Even the satirical *Praise of Folly* seeks to direct the reader to a life of interior holiness expressed through deeds of piety. When his life-long labors were attacked by critics, Erasmus rebounded with a series of apologies. He sought to allay charges of heresy and blasphemy. Conservative defenders of the church saw his efforts at reform as attacks on church dogma and tradition. The appearance of the *Novum Instrumentum* in 1516 was criticized because of

Erasmus' pretentious presumption of authority to improve upon the work of St. Jerome's Vulgate. Critics failed to note that Erasmus' works and letters serve as rungs on the ladder to his *philosophia Christi*.

Chapter five seeks to establish the thesis that Erasmus originated his *philosophia Christi* while living at the monastery of the Canons Regular of St. Augustine at Steyn, influenced by the *Devotio Moderna* and the works of St. Augustine. It was during the years between 1489 and 1493 that Erasmus composed his two earliest works, the *Antibarbarorum Liber* and *De Contemptu Mundi*, in which he urged his readers to imitate the life of Christ.

In Chapter six I attempt to show that Erasmus' great concern for childhood grew out of the unfortunate circumstances that characterized his boyhood. Erasmus sought to convince his readers that a child's character can be patterned after that of the child Jesus, providing that he is exposed to piety and good behavior from the earliest years.

Chapter seven discusses two themes: how Erasmus succeeded at Steyn in fulfilling the biblical injunction to "love your neighbor as you love yourself" and how he applied his concept of love to those with whom he came in contact while living outside the monastery. It was while at Steyn that Erasmus attempted to dispense the Christian charity which integrates the rule of St. Augustine to his fellow canons; and when such efforts failed to materialize, he looked to the world beyond for a successful application of his concept.

Finally, chapter eight places the religious life of Erasmus in perspective by underscoring his commitment to the Canons Regular of St. Augustine, even though he lived outside the monastery after 1493 and was not subject to the authority of the prior at Steyn after 1517. Papal dispensation allowed him to live the life of a secular priest while remaining technically a canon regular. Erasmus tried to use the example of his own life to demonstrate that religious life was not confined to monasteries. By imitating Christ all mankind could acquire holiness and continue to live in the world. Erasmus became the first reformer of the sixteenth century to perceive a life of dedication to Christ either inside or outside monastic walls, and his *philosophia Christi* remains a blueprint of holiness for all.

CHAPTER ONE

*Erasmus of Rotterdam in Profile**

DESIDERIUS Erasmus is without question one of the most eminent figures of the sixteenth century. His life was one of periodic movement and controversy, and his fame, which was established in his own lifetime, has never suffered from critical appraisal. The reasons for Erasmus' popularity are not far to seek. In the words of Peter Gay, "Erasmus was a true classical spirit in his search for clarity and simplicity, a modern in his complexity, an ancestor of the Enlightenment in his critical temper and pacific cosmopolitanism. But, above all, he was a Christian intellectual, striving, as he himself said, to establish a *philosophia Christi*."[1] Erasmus was in search of a new way of life, a code of behavior which would combine the best of Christianity and Renaissance humanism. And in this quest for truth and human understanding, he produced a copious array of practical and scholarly works. Together, they offered the Renaissance reader both a critical standard of composition and comparison and brilliant insights into intellectual and social progress. Great, indeed, were his services to posterity; but his origins, by contrast, were most inauspicious.

On the eve of October 28, probably in 1469, Erasmus was born in Rotterdam, the son of Gerard and Margaret.[2] Because of the scandal attached to his parents' illicit relationship, Erasmus bore the scars of illegitimacy throughout life. Sensitive and introspective by nature, he must have been sorely humiliated when he accidentally witnessed the retelling of those unpleasant circumstances which surrounded his birth.[3]

At the age of four, Erasmus, along with his older brother Pieter, was sent to a privately conducted elementary school in Gouda. Later on he spent a year in Utrecht as a chorister in the cathedral. When he was about nine, Erasmus began his studies at Deventer where he came under the influence of the Brethren of the Common Life and where he learned to

---

* This chapter was originally delivered as a lecture at the Erasmus Quincentennial Symposium, Ithaca College, 1969.

[1] Peter Gay, *The Enlightenment: An Interpretation* (New York: Alfred A. Knopf, 1967), p. 274.

[2] The date of Erasmus' birth has been the subject of considerable debate. For a discussion of the controversy, see Prologue, note 1.

[3] Johan Huizinga, *Erasmus of Rotterdam* (London: Phaidon Press, Ltd., 1952), p. 5.

master the elementary rules of Latin grammar. Following the untimely death of his parents in 1484, Erasmus was left in the care of indifferent guardians who, in an effort to rid themselves of their charge and, at the same time, to benefit from the meager trust fund which his father had established, sent him to the Brethren's school at 's Hertogenbosch. After three years in residence, Erasmus joined the Order of Canons Regular of St. Augustine and entered their monastery at Steyn in 1487. He seems to have entered the religious life without really having considered the consequences. He himself suggested later on that his vocation had been promoted under pious pretenses by greedy guardians, and, therefore, doubted that he had a true calling.[4] But even in the face of these doubts, Erasmus professed solemn vows and was ordained to the priesthood. Following his ordination on April 25, 1492, the young priest remained at Steyn, leading the life of a choir canon and digesting selected morsels from the monastery's library. For at least one more year, he seemed satisfied with the Augustinians. He read widely in the classic and the patristic literature and developed a special appreciation of St. Augustine and St. Jerome, the compiler of the Latin Vulgate edition of the Bible. Inspired by his confreres, he even wrote a treatise in defense of monasticism, which he called *On the Contempt of the World*. As an Augustinian canon, Erasmus reflected the piety of his former teachers in Deventer and 's Hertogenbosch. These members of the Brethren of the Common Life were disciples of Christ who sought to imitate the Prince of Peace and to cultivate a spirit which we have learned to call the *Devotio Moderna*.[5] Yet, at the same time, Erasmus also came under the spell of Renaissance humanism. At Steyn, especially, he perfected a fluid and lucid style of writing. Torn between the piety of the *Devotio Moderna* and the humanism of Italy, he set his confused mind to work on *The Book of the Antibarbarians*. Written in the form of dialogues, the tract expresses Erasmus' continuing respect for the religious life, but reveals a much stronger attraction to humanism. Later on, he was to rewrite certain sections of the treatise in an effort to expose the evils of the church and of the monastic life in particular.[6] But in 1492, Erasmus was very much

---

[4] *Ibid.*, pp. 8–9.

[5] For an account of the origins and history of the *Devotio Moderna*, see Albert Hyma, *The Christian Renaissance*. Second ed. (Hamden, Connecticut, 1965).

[6] A. Hyma, *The Youth of Erasmus*. Second ed. (New York: Russell & Russell, 1968) pp. 167–204.

under the influence of the religious discipline of an Augustinian order and the Brethren of the Common Life. Even so, he soon found the holy rule and the confinement of the monastery to be exceedingly onerous and longed for a glimpse of the Italian setting of which he had only a reader's imperfect knowledge.

A year after his ordination, Erasmus discovered an episcopal patron who was willing to free him from the monastic cell and from the responsibilities of community life. Moreover, since this princely bishop promised him a year's residence in Rome and future opportunities for study, how could he resist? In the face of such tempting prospects, Erasmus accepted an appointment in 1493 as Latin secretary to Hendrik van Bergen, the bishop of Cambrai. But only disappointment followed his decision. Within a month, the bishop's proposed trip to Italy, where he had hoped to be invested as a cardinal, failed to materialize and Erasmus feared that he would be required to return to Steyn and there resume the monastic life for which he had developed an aversion. But his fears were groundless. The worldly Hendrik van Bergen took pity on the brooding cleric, who had been temporarily assigned to routine duties, and assured his deliverance by eventually sending him off to France for advanced study in theology. Filled with enthusiasm, Erasmus enrolled at Montaigu College within the august University of Paris in 1495.

Like graduate students everywhere, Erasmus found his living conditions unbearable at Montaigu and sought relief by offering vivid and unsolicited descriptions of his surroundings to sympathetic but powerless correspondents. His health soon deteriorated. Racked by pain and subject to fainting spells, he was forced to return to Steyn for a period of recuperation.[7] Who could have foreseen such a disaster? But his demoralizing confinement did not endure. When forced to choose between Steyn with its moribund silence and self-effacing canons and Paris with an inexhaustible supply of books and inspiration, Erasmus spontaneously regained his health and set out again for Paris. This time, however, he took up residence outside the cloisters of Montaigu. He rented a nearby flat so he could rest when he chose, eat whatever and whenever he liked, and study late into the night, unencumbered by custom and stifling protocol. At long last, Erasmus almost began to enjoy the academic life of the university. He now concentrated on questions of scholastic

---

[7] Preserved Smith, *Erasmus: A Study of His Life, Ideals and Place in History* (New York: Harper & Brothers, 1923), pp. 25–26.

theology and language without having to endure the austerity of the university's residence halls. Poverty, however, soon restricted his earlier enthusiasm. Short of funds, he found it necessary to tutor young men in Latin grammar and rhetoric. As a tutor, Erasmus began to experiment with educational methods. He devised a number of textbooks which he hoped would stimulate learning among his students. The most famous of these popular texts is the delightful collection of dialogues entitled the *Colloquies,* some of which were written at this time but not published until much later. Other works in this pedagogical series dealt with exposition and matters of curriculum.[8] Moreover, mindful of the economic advantages which might accrue, he preferred to teach only the affluent. It was in this way that Erasmus struck up a lifelong friendship with the English nobleman William Blount. What wisdom there was in his selection of that particular student! For Blount fell almost immediately in awe of the gifted teacher and soon extended an invitation to him to visit England. By 1497 Erasmus had acquired a distaste for his Parisian colleagues and the formal methods of scholastic instruction which they promoted. He, therefore, looked forward to an opportunity to set aside his studies and to escape from the restrictive atmosphere of Paris.[9] Thus, before the fifteenth century drew its last breath, Erasmus settled at Oxford where he met such notables as John Colet, later dean of St. Paul's, William Grocyn, and Thomas Linacre, two eminent classical scholars, and the gifted London barrister Thomas More.

The turn of the century added a new dimension to Erasmus' life. He became a cosmopolite—a citizen of the world.[10] Indeed, throughout the first decade of the sixteenth century Erasmus was on an almost continuous journey. He traveled in France, Italy, and the Low Countries, forming friendships with the leading humanists of the age and promoting his own special interest in educational reform. During the course of his travels Erasmus published the earliest version of the *Enchiridion* or *Handbook of the Christian Soldier.* Addressed to the layman, this guide to moral behavior first appeared in 1503 and sketches Erasmus' concept of the philosophy of Christ. He encouraged the sixteenth-century Christian

---

[8] Margaret Mann Phillips, *Erasmus and the Northern Renaissance* (London: Hodder & Stoughton Ltd., 1949), p. 6.

[9] J. Huizinga, *Erasmus of Rotterdam,* p. 22.

[10] Craig R. Thompson, "Erasmus as Internationalist and Cosmopolitan," *Archiv für Reformationsgeschichte,* 46 (1955), pp. 167–95.

to cultivate those virtues which are in keeping with the spirit of the Gospel. By so doing, the individual strengthens his will and fortifies himself against the temptation to sin.

Moreover, in these formative years Erasmus acquired an appreciation of exegesis and intensified his study of Greek. He soon mastered the critical method of Lorenzo Valla and sought to apply the rigorous philological standards of his Italian humanist to biblical and patristic literature. Following the publication of Valla's *Annotations on the New Testament* in 1505, Erasmus issued Latin editions of numerous Greek authors, including Lucian, Euripides, and Plutarch.[11] In addition, Erasmus continued his studies and accepted a doctorate in theology from the University of Turin. While in Italy he also formed a profitable association with Aldus Manutius, the scholar-printer. Many of Erasmus' earliest works were to be issued by this Venetian: an enlarged edition of the *Adages* and new editions of Seneca, Plautus, and Terence are but four examples.[12]

With the appearance of the second edition of the *Adages* in 1508, Erasmus became the most celebrated teacher and promoter of humanism in Renaissance Europe.[13] At thirty-nine he was regarded by contemporary literati as the Prince of Humanists. They admired him for his erudition and sagacity and especially for his ability to write elegant Latin compositions. Indeed, nothing was more dearly prized in the sixteenth century than a holograph by Erasmus, and it is to his praise that Erasmus frequently employed the pen to write letters encouraging young, aspiring minds to adopt humanism and to cultivate intellectual tastes. His correspondence, which includes some three thousand surviving items,[14] brought the humanists of Europe together. Acknowledging Erasmus as its leader, the movement drew its strength and vitality from the Latin prose of this Dutch savant.

But by 1509 Erasmus had developed an aversion to traveling. The peripatetic inquirer now longed for the security of a permanent position. Encouraged by Henry VIII's ascension to the English throne and by the urgings of a former student, Lord Mountjoy, it is no surprise, therefore,

---

[11] M. M. Phillips, *Erasmus and the Northern Renaissance*, pp. 32–33.
[12] J. Huizinga, *Erasmus of Rotterdam*, pp. 64–65.
[13] M. M. Phillips, *Erasmus and the Northern Renaissance*, pp. 60–61.
[14] P. S. Allen, *Opvs Epistolarvm Des. Erasmi Roterodami* (Oxford: Clarendon Press, 1958), vol. 12.

that Erasmus returned to England; and through the influence of More, Archbishop William Warham, and Bishop John Fisher, he was appointed Lady Margaret Professor of Divinity at Cambridge and a lecturer of Greek in 1511.[15] While en route from Italy to London, Erasmus devoted the idle hours to composing an early draft of his best remembered work, *The Praise of Folly*. Generally regarded as a literary masterpiece, this biting satire was written in the form of an extended declamation. The principal speaker, Folly, embodies the author's conception of human nature. As a humanist, Erasmus believed in man's innate goodness, but he also acknowledged man's predisposition to evil, suggesting that human error and transgression were frequently due to an imperfect understanding of God's law. Erasmus focuses attention on this concept of human nature in the course of his book. "You would never believe," Folly argues, "what sport and entertainment your mortal manikins provide daily for the gods. These gods, you know, set aside their sober forenoon hours for composing quarrels and giving ear to prayers. But after that, when they seek out some promontory of heaven and, setting there with faces bent downward, they watch what mortal men are doing. There is no show like it. Good God, what a theater! How various the action of fools! . . . Here is a fellow dying for love of a sweet young thing, and the less he is loved in return the more helplessly he is in love. . . . Here is a man in mourning, but mercy me, what fool things he says and does! Hiring mourners as if they were actors, to play a comedy of grief!"[16]

In the sweeping satire that followed, Erasmus criticizes man's indulgence in self-love, laziness, sensuality, and intemperance. Society manages to go on day after day believing that its very existence somehow depends on perpetuating these vices. Erasmus holds all men responsible for this deplorable state of sixteenth-century society, but he reserves the sharpest satire for the academicians, monks, and those "scientists, reverenced for their beards and the fur on their gowns, who teach that they alone are wise while the rest of mortal men flit about as shadows. How pleasantly they dote, indeed, while they construct their numberless worlds, and measure the sun, moon, stars, and spheres as with thumb and line. They assign causes for lightning, winds, eclipses, and other

---

[15] J. Huizinga, *Erasmus of Rotterdam*, p. 67.

[16] D. Erasmus, *The Praise of Folly*, ed. by Hoyt H. Hudson (Princeton University Press, 1941), p. 68.

inexplicable things, never hesitating a whit, as if they were privy to the secrets of nature, artificer of things, or as if they visited us fresh from the council of the gods. Yet all the while nature is laughing grandly at them and their conjectures."[17] Underlying the severity of his criticism, Erasmus reveals extraordinary compassion. He possessed both a humanitarian spirit and an instinct for social reform. He directed his attention to corruption wherever it might be detected: in the church, government, the family, the university. As Erasmus perceived it, institutional decay was simply a manifestation of a general disorientation. Sixteenth-century society was caught up in the selfish pursuit of pleasure because it had lost its perspective. Failing to understand the purpose of human existence, man was foolishly pursuing vanity and vice instead of perfecting human nature. But he did not despair. Drawing upon an earlier expression of faith in man, Erasmus saw a solution to man's dilemma in the adoption of a new Christian philosophy—a way of life based on virtue and love. If only man would imitate Jesus Christ. If only he would replace moral depravity with integrity of character and selfishness with sacrifice, mankind would begin an unparalleled ascent. Since society possessed the capacity to improve itself, all that was needed was an emphasis on humanity and a deemphasis on individual gratification. And what better way to restore human society than by recovering Christian unity. Indeed, the restoration of *Christiana Respublica* loomed always in the background of this reformer's mind.

For nearly three years, Erasmus remained at Cambridge. He enjoyed the English countryside and was inspired by the enthusiasm and goodwill of English humanists. In partial appreciation for all that had been given to him, he dedicated a textbook in 1512 to his friend and admirer John Colet, who had only recently refounded London's St. Paul's School.[18] Conceived as a thesaurus, *On Copia of Words and Ideas* is a collection of Latin phrases and idioms, culled from the classics, which offered the Renaissance learner an opportunity to enrich and enlarge his vocabulary. But even in the face of all this activity, he still felt incomplete. Perceiving the need for critical editions of the New Testament and the works of St. Jerome, Erasmus supervised the publication of these works at the press of Johann Froben in Basel. Although many

---

[17] *Ibid.*, pp. 76–77.

[18] Donald B. King and H. David Rix, eds., *Desiderius Erasmus . . . On Copia of Words and Ideas* (Milwaukee, Wisconsin: Marquette University Press, 1963), p. 2.

printed versions of the New Testament were circulating in Europe at this time, there had been no edition available to the educated bourgeoisie in as pure a format. Erasmus, therefore, filled an immensely important vacuum in 1516 when he completed a Greek version of the New Testament. It included both the Greek text and a Latin translation as well. As Margaret Mann Phillips has recorded: "Erasmus' greatest contribution to his time [now] lay before the world."[19] *The Novum Instrumentum* had a revolutionary effect on biblical exegesis. Not only did Martin Luther consult it in preparing his translation of the New Testament but the work itself contributed to a general movement espousing Church reform and a return to early Christianity. Erasmus enjoyed this period of respite. He loved scholarship and the smell of printer's ink! But restlessness soon gripped him once more. Yearning to travel, he returned to Holland and Germany, and even managed trips to England in 1515 and 1517.

Shortly after his third trip to England, Erasmus produced *The Education of a Christian Prince* (1516). In this work he suggests that the purpose of government is to secure the advancement of human society rather than to promote the selfish ambitions of individual princes. This humanitarian and moralistic orientation offers sharp contrast to the statecraft of Machiavelli's *Il Principe*. Erasmus also promoted the idea of man's educability, and ultimately preferred an elective system of monarchy to a hereditary one.[20] Erasmus mistrusted most deeply dynastic politics that permitted princes to rule over people who were totally foreign to him. In an effort to reform society, he wanted to instruct ecclesiastical and secular leaders in how to govern wisely and to instill in them the importance of acquiring peaceful methods of persuasion. Above all, he wanted them to rely more on arbitration than on weapons of war. Erasmus expressed his deep concern for peace in a second treatise, entitled *The Complaint of Peace* (1517). An avowed pacifist, the Prince of Humanists condemned warfare in general and suggested some practical ways on how to avoid future wars. The moral tone of Erasmus' two political treatises served as an introduction to one of the truly great classics of the Renaissance, the *Colloquies*. First published in 1518, these pungent dialogues were, as we have indicated, originally intended as a handbook to learning Latin, but their combined impact was considerably

---

[19] M. M. Phillips, *Erasmus and the Northern Renaissance*, p. 73.
[20] C. R. Thompson, "Erasmus as Internationalist and Cosmopolitan," pp. 176–177.

greater. They offered the inquiring student both a running commentary on contemporary events and an exposé on social, political, and religious corruption. Erasmus' wit and common sense appealed especially to the middle class, which now stuffed its conversation with quotations from the *Colloquies* and soon entered the arena of humanistic debate. Combining travel and scholarship, Erasmus roamed about the Low Countries for seven years in search of men and ideas. But at last the wandering ceased. It was now time to set in print the many thoughts which had occupied him during the past two decades. With this in mind, he accepted an invitation from Froben and took up residence in Basel. Here from 1521 to 1527, he acted as the general editor of Froben's press and produced a steady stream of religious tracts. Certainly, the most important of these publications is the one which was directed to Martin Luther. Entitled *Discourse on Free Will*, this calm restatement of scholastic theology grew out of a heated exchange of letters between the "Wittenberg gladiator" and his supporters.[21] By 1524 Erasmus and Luther had adopted such entrenched positions that no amount of sagacity or correspondence could resolve their differences. And something of the width and depth of that growing chasm is revealed in Erasmus' treatise on free will. Since errors in judgment may be caused by man's intellectual limitations, Erasmus cautioned Luther against accepting with certitude matters of an interpretive nature. Only clearly revealed truths can be accepted unconditionally.

As a reformer, Erasmus was a moderate. He generally preferred compromise and scholarly dialogue to revolt and public debate. Through his philosophy of Christ, he envisioned a new world committed to the exercise of Christian virtue and individual responsibility. At the same time, he tried to restore primitive Christianity and to encourage inward spirituality. Erasmus' concept of Christian piety was offended by weekend pilgrimages and public processions. Such hollow displays of religious fervor seemed hopelessly out of step with the image of the historical Jesus. Pleading for more belief but fewer beliefs, he was willing to trim down the Credo in favor of a limited number of basic truths. Since Christ represented the best of all models, and his life had been dedicated to interior holiness and public service, the sixteenth century, and centuries to come, would do well to imitate him.

At the height of his career, such eminent artists as Albrecht Dürer,

[21] P. Smith, *Erasmus*, p. 341.

Hans Holbein the Younger, and Quentin Metsys recorded for posterity the engaging profile of Erasmus.[22] All these artists exhibit much in common, but of the many portraits of Erasmus which have been produced, the most compelling one is by Metsys. Completed in 1517, this extraordinary painting exists in two versions: one now at Hampton Court Palace and the other in the Galleria Nazionale in Rome. The subject appears recollected, clothed in the *vestimentum clausum* of the cleric-academician. Lined with fur, his outer cloak appears almost luxurious on close examination. A gold ring, which is worn on the right index finger, accentuates this quality and acknowledges his doctor of divinity status. The head of Erasmus, wearing a biretta, is seen in three-quarter view, turned slightly to the viewer's left. Attached to his waist is a black purse, conspicuous for its gold trim.

Standing in front of an open book, Erasmus rests his left hand on a page of his *Paraphrases* and, with his other hand, composes an inscription on the opposite leaf. The room in which he is working is starkly simple. Even the subdued colors of the painting, mostly browns and oranges, emphasize the introspective pose of the subject. But the focal point of Metsys' portrait is the haunting visage of the scholar and bibliophile. Our eyes are immediately drawn to his dignified and delicate features. Stamped with mental acuity, the face is both serene and infectious. Yet it is the downcast eyes, those small, dark, penetrating beacons of light which somehow add depth and intensity to his thin and pale countenance. The high cheek bones, angular nose, and pursed lips, on the other hand, make him appear almost dour. But even in this gloomy setting, his silent looks and carriage betray an inward feeling: Erasmus loved humanity.

Although this portrait and those by Holbein and Dürer may convey the impression that Erasmus was an icy and sober introvert, who was immersed in his scholarship and in himself, such was not the case. Far from being shy or reserved, Erasmus possessed an extraordinary ability to make friends, and this gregarious side of his personality gives abundant testimony to a warm and compassionate disposition. He loved many men deeply and frequently expressed his affection by years of faithful correspondence. The names of Jacob Batt, Thomas More, Boniface Amerbach, Peter Gillis, and Beatus Rhenanus are but a few

---

[22] Roland H. Bainton, *Erasmus of Christendom* (New York: Charles Scribner's Sons, 1969), pp. 236–37. Bainton incorrectly dates Metsys' portrait of Erasmus as 1519.

representative examples of persons who reciprocated Erasmus' comradeship with pride and gravity.[23]

In these letters and in his major publications Erasmus wrote with both flexibility and grace; and, yet, very little of what he wrote can be classified as purely literary. Except for a few poems, all of his writing had a very practical purpose: problems of morality or social and political questions were uppermost in his mind. And no matter what point of view or position he assumed in his various works, Erasmus' faith remained unshaken. For him it was the interior life of grace that really mattered. Fortified with unswerving confidence, he was able to launch his testy barbs and to withstand the expected but explosive reactions. Erasmus was truly the archetype of the sixteenth-century intellectual. Although born in embarrassing obscurity, he rose to undisputed heights by means of his publications.

1524 was another watershed in Erasmus' career. To maintain his independence, Erasmus declined the gifts of popes and princes, avoided royal courts, and lived in Switzerland, far away from the Netherlands, France, England, Italy, and Germany where he had lived so fully in the past and had earned so many honors and so much praise. Despite his self-imposed exile, however, he lived to see his works condemned, his admirers dispersed, and his dreams unfulfilled. Erasmus was torn between two extremes. For his refusal to support Luther and the cause of Protestant reform he had been condemned as a coward. But his refusal to take sides, his refusal to join either camp, was a mark of courage and dedication to principle. There was no temerity in his silence. Even though Erasmus sympathized with Luther's criticism and saw the need for reform, he did not think that Luther offered a better alternative. Erasmus was committed to Christendom. Above all, he wished to preserve the unity of an institutional Church—a church founded by Christ and protected by the Holy Spirit. Hating war, he saw a solution to the vexing choice between compromise or revolt in the *philosophia Christi*. Though at times, Erasmus was caught between principle and practicality, and was buffeted by indecision and by forces and events beyond prophecy and control, he never lost sight of his goal. With reassuring élan, he condemned fanaticism, dogmatism, and pride, upheld personal independence, applauded compromise, and sought to unite mankind.

[23] P. Smith, *Erasmus*, pp. 203–208.

After eight years in Basel, Erasmus was forced to leave. The city which had offered him a haven for nearly a decade now closed its mind and accepted intolerance as a deterrent to liberal thought.[24] Beginning in 1529, he lived in Freiburg, during which time the city fathers and the university showered him with honors. But somehow, his vitality had been sapped. Europe was then at war and he saw his life-struggle for universal brotherhood and human progress degenerate into mindless chaos. Even England with its circle of brilliant humanists had given itself over to fratricide. What comfort was there now in thinking about England's future when that country's barbaric king had taken the lives of two of mankind's most humane personalities, Sir Thomas More and the saintly bishop of Rochester, John Fisher?[25]

Something of Erasmus' dolefulness and despondency can be detected in a series of later portraits. Hans Holbein, especially, succeeds in revealing a sense of abject resignation and a public expression of failure. This artist's 1531 portrait of Erasmus is a great deal different from the relatively flattering image produced by Metsys in 1517. And, indeed, Erasmus had changed during the fifteen years which separated the two paintings. By the middle of the thirties, he was filled with uncontrollable ennui. Bent toward death, the withering sage almost pleaded for his deliverance. Only the grave could spare him from further unpleasantness and disappointment. What a relief it would be to rejoin those departed friends who had been snuffed out by intolerance and inhumanity. Apparently sensing Erasmus' melancholy, Holbein preserved it on canvas in an oval-shaped portrait which can be found in the print room of the Öffentliche Kunstsammlung in Basel. Now that he had grown gray, now that his strength had begun to diminish, Erasmus stands helpless, imprisoned within an oval frame. He appears disillusioned, gaunt, and ailing. Even the cruel scars of old age have by this time parched his tired face. During the past forty years, Erasmus had spent a life dedicated to scholarship and human welfare, but in proceeding along this lonely path, it finally became clear to him that he had, at last, reached an impasse. A scholar to the very end of his life, Erasmus, nevertheless, made a final visit to Basel in 1535 in order to edit the works of Origen. While at work on this new edition, he died at the age of sixty-six in the

---

[24] J. Huizinga, *Erasmus of Rotterdam*, pp. 174–75.
[25] P. Smith, *Erasmus*, pp. 417–19.

home of Jerome Froben, the son of his old friend. Death found him as it had found his great Italian precursor, Petrarch, in study and in prayer.

Erasmus of Rotterdam is a unique example among Renaissance writers of an intellectual whose earthly role was essentially public, but whose everyday life was primarily withdrawn. Somehow, Erasmus found strength for his public responsibilities in the hidden life of a scholarly recluse. And, yet, without that incomparable face and ethereal voice, Erasmus on the printed page was never to inspire in later generations what the magnetism of his personal presence had created in his own day. Erasmus, as a subtle critic, was face to face a living myth—the appointed leader of a generation who arrives at the beginning of a new age, sounds a collective hope and purpose, and before fading into the background conveys spiritual strength to others.

The greatness of Erasmus, however, lies in the conviction that truth, spoken with love and patience, to say nothing of wit and grace, is a more potent instrument of reform than force or invective. Trusting always in the love of God, Erasmus believed that every man could promote human progress by becoming an imitator of Christ and an inheritor of heaven. In his learning and candor, Erasmus is without equal in the Northern Renaissance. Behind every faint smile and twinkling eyelid there is both brilliance and clarity of expression. As a writer, he is among that small group of elite men who succeed in winning our admiration and affection. Erasmus also impresses us with his rare critical powers and intuitions. We might well join him in deploring the dichotomy existing between pure thought and experience and the lack of critical scholarship which leads to a heavy dependence on authority. The spontaneity, vigor, and independence of mind which characterize this complex man emerge from even the most casual reading of the record. Highly critical of formalism and bureaucracy, Erasmus sought truth in the word of the Gospel. He also sought personal freedom, not through revolt or isolation, but through involvement. And he ended his life in the conviction that the way he lived was in imitation of Christ.

Erasmus' life was private and was lived simply. Since he looked upon political institutions as a threat to his security as well as an affront to his faith in Christianity, he jealously guarded his own personal freedom. In living, he sought few acquisitions. He prized love and morality above all else. And, although the satisfaction which he sought through love could not be fully realized in his own lifetime, he was able to create a life of partial fulfillment by writing. Indeed, writing was his one great instrument of reform. By means of his pen he produced a pulsating prose that always took the form of personal experience. His rapier wit and laconic style made even the shortest of his colloquies worth more than a hundred syllogisms. The admiring reader cannot help but respond to the compelling emotion in his pages—his impatience with authority, his natural vagabondage, his ability to remain true to his soul and to the social world about him. This sense of commitment is what is most vital and vivid in the man and his work. Erasmus lived a full life of the mind and knew how to share his hidden thoughts. He knew the value of joy. And those who were close to him knew it too.

CHAPTER TWO

*Erasmus as Adolescent: "Shipwrecked am I, and Lost, 'Mid Waters Chill'"**

Erasmus to Sister Elisabeth

THIS succinct description of his condition in about 1486 (shortly after he entered the monastery of the Canons Regular of St. Augustine at Steyn) ought to remind us that Erasmus suffered a series of misfortunes during the period of his adolescence.[1] Though Erasmus has been accused of adjusting dates to suit his purposes and of chronological inconsistency, it may be unfair to accuse him of forgetting how old he was when a particular event in his life took place, especially when the event itself is of major consequences. For a gifted and sensitive boy it should not be surprising that the death of his parents, his departure from schools at Deventer and 's Hertogenbosch, and his entrance and profession in the religious life should have made a lasting impression. To associate one's age with a specific year may be difficult to accomplish after thirty years has elapsed but to identify one's age with a major event in life, even when one is about 55 years old (i.e. in 1524), should not be regarded as unlikely or unique.[2]

Though there has been considerable debate over the exact year of Erasmus' birth, it seems safe to assume that Erasmus was born in 1469. Moreover, if we can accept as accurate certain statements of Erasmus that were made concerning his age at a particular event in his life, this writer cannot insist too vigorously that Erasmus' state of mind in 1486 had been conditioned by the following factors:

(1) the death of his mother (from the plague) when he was 13 years old;

(2) his departure from Deventer because of the plague that claimed the lives of twenty of his schoolmates; (3) the death of his father (from the

---

* This paper was delivered originally to the faculty and students of the School of Hellenic and Roman Studies at the University of Birmingham in 1975. The writer wishes to thank Dr. J. W. Binns for his gracious hospitality. *CWE*, 1, 3.

[1] Erasmus to Elisabeth [Gouda? 1487?] in P. S. Allen (ed.), *Opus Epistolarvm Des. Erasmi Roterodami* (Oxford, 1906), 1, 75 [hereafter referred to as *Allen*]. Trans. by R.A.B. Mynors and D. F. S. Thomson in *The Correspondence of Erasmus* (Toronto, 1974), 1, 3 [hereafter referred to as *CWE*].

[2] For a discussion of Erasmus' age, see Prologue, note 1.

plague); (4) his forced admission into the school of the Brethren of the Common Life at 's Hertogenbosch—all at the age of 14;

(5) the decision of his brother Pieter to enter the monastery of the Austin Canons at Sion (thus separating Erasmus from his only sibling); and (6) the financial circumstances that required Erasmus to enter the monastery of the same order at Steyn at the age of 16, and to profess vows as an Austin Canon at the age of 17.[3]

Thus within a period of five years (ages 13 to 17), Erasmus was confronted with six major crises, and in 1487, the year of his profession, he expressed anguish over the continuing misfortunes in his life in a letter to his brother:

. . . and as you did not fail me at the hardest crisis of my life, so please now again lend me support in circumstances that are less harsh even if not exactly favourable.[4]

Moreover, it could be maintained that Erasmus' unhappiness persisted until he emerged finally from the monastery at Steyn, having secured the position of secretary to the bishop of Cambrai about 1493; and that having once escaped the confinement of the religious life, he resisted every attempt to compel him to return.[5] It will be the purpose of this chapter to argue that Erasmus' perapatetic nature was itself conditioned by a series of events that occurred during his adolescence and that his earliest letters, occasional poetry, and his *De contemptu mundi* (ca. 1488) all reflect his efforts to find, as he himself expressed it: "tranquillity, liberty, and concord."[6]

Thirty-two letters, twenty-eight written by Erasmus and four written

---

[3] The chronology of Erasmus' early life is as follows: 1473/74: began school at Gouda at age 4 ("Compendium Vitae Erasmi," ca. 2 April 1524, *Allen*, 1, 48, 1. 30); 1478/79: began school at Deventer at age 9 (*ibid.*, 48, 1. 32); 1480/81: saw Agricola at age 11 (Erasmus to John Botzheim, 30 January 1523, *Allen*, 1, 2, n. 26); 1482/83: death of mother when Erasmus was 13 ("Compendium Vitae Erasmi," *Allen*, 1, 48, 1. 41); 1483/84: left Deventer because of the plague at age 14 (Jean LeClerc, ed., *Desiderii Erasmi Roterodami Opera Omnia* (Leiden, 1703–06), 1, 347E); 1484/85: returned to Gouda at age 15 (Erasmus to L. Grunnius, August 1516, *Allen*, 2, 297, 11. 156–7); 1485/86: entered the monastery at Steyn at age 16 (*ibid.*, 299, 11. 241–2); 1486/87: professed first vows as Austin Canon at age 17 (Erasmus to Servatius Roger, 8 July 1514, *Allen*, 1, 566, 1.35).

[4] Erasmus to Pieter Gerard [Steyn 1487?], *Allen*, 1, 76. Trans. by Mynors and Thomson, *CWE*, 1, 5.

[5] See Erasmus' letter to Servatius Roger, 8 July 1514, in *Allen*, 1, 565–573.

[6] Erasmus to Lambertus Grunnius, August 1516, in Allen, 2, 300. Translated by John J. Mangan, *Life . . . of . . . Erasmus . . .* (New York, 1927), 1. 17.

to him by Cornelis Gerard, have survived the period between 1484 and 1490, when Erasmus would have been between the ages of 15 and 21.[7] In spite of the fact that none of these letters is actually dated or include the place of origin, P. S. Allen has assigned dates and places of origin to them in his edition of the correspondence. He believed that the first two letters of Erasmus were composed at Gouda in 1484 and 1487 respectively and that all of the other letters that Erasmus wrote before 1493 originated at Steyn. Wallace K. Ferguson has adopted Allen's findings with two exceptions, but fails to indicate why he has differed from him: Ferguson assigns the date circa 1487 to the tenth letter instead of following Allen's date of circa 1488 and he neglects to add "July" to the year 1489 in dating the twenty-fourth letter, as does Allen.[8] Most other scholars are also in full agreement with Allen on the dates and places of origin.[9] This writer, however, finds fault with the traditional dating of the first two letters: those to Pieter Winckel and Sister Elisabeth. There is no internal or external evidence nor any valid reason why Allen should have assigned either one of these letters to Gouda and have dated them as 1484 and 1487 respectively. With regard to the so-called 1484 letter to Winckel, Erasmus refers deliberately to Winckel as his "former guardian" in the salutation, which implies that Erasmus must have been living at Steyn and have been admitted as a novice to the order of Austin Canons.[10] Certainly Winckel's duties as a guardian did not end until Erasmus had

---

[7] See *Allen*, 1, 73–127. Trans. by Mynors and Thomson, *CWE*, 1, 2–62.

[8] See W. K. Ferguson, *CWE*, 1, pp. 15 and 41. For Allen's final statement on Erasmus' boyhood, see his "The Young Erasmus" in Gedenkschrift zum 400, Todestages des Erasmus von Rotterdam (Basel, 1936), pp. 25–33.

[9] Henry de Vocht, in "Erasmiana I and II," *Anglia*, 79 (1962), 319–337, argues unconvincingly that "the first sixteen or seventeen letters" belong "to the years of his studies at Deventer, 1475–1484" (p. 326). He assumes that these letters could not have originated at Steyn because they contain ideas incompatible with the religious life of the Austin Canons. For a rebuttal of De Vocht's position, see James D. Tracy, "On the Composition Dates of Seven of Erasmus' Writings," *Bibliothèque d'Humanisme et Renaissance*, 31 (1969), 355–6. De Vocht also insists that Pieter was born to his mother Margaret and her first husband about 1463, thus making him the half brother of Erasmus, *op. cit.*, pp. 319–325. Erasmus, on the other hand, asserts that his mother's children shared the same father: "While they [i.e. Peter and Erasmus] were still boys they lost their mother; and their father, dying soon after, left a property." See Erasmus to Grunnius, August of 1516, in *Allen*, 2, p. 294; trans. by Mangan, 1, p. 11.

[10] *Allen*, 1, 73: "Erasmvs Roterodamvs Magistro Petro Winckel, Tvtori Qvondam Svo S."

been safely delivered into the religious life.[11] Thus the date of this letter to Winckel should be circa 1486 instead of at the "end of 1484." A second reason which suggests a later date for this letter is Erasmus' reference to the settlement of his father's estate. He refers to it in these words: "I am very much afraid that the end of this brief period [i.e. his novitiate] may find our affairs not yet safely taken care of, though they should have been settled long since—belatedly even then."[12] If Erasmus' father had died in 1484, would this complaint of Erasmus be appropriate in the very same year? It seems more likely that the settlement of his father's estate had dragged on for several years and thus prompted this letter. In connection with the date of the letter to Sister Elisabeth, it seems clear from the Grunnius letter of 1516 that Erasmus was living at Steyn at the outset of 1487. Furthermore, it can be conjectured from this letter that he actually entered the monastery as a postulant as early as 1485/86 and did not begin his novitiate until 1486/87.[13]

Since it is fairly important for my thesis to establish with some certainty that Erasmus' letter to Sister Elisabeth was actually composed at Steyn rather than at Gouda in 1486, there will be a fuller treatment of the evidence at this point in the chapter. In his letter to Grunnius, an imaginary papal official, Erasmus indicated that he had left Deventer at the age of 14; entered the school of the Brethren of the Common Life at 's Hertogenbosch at the same age; returned to Gouda when he was 15; and entered the monastery at Steyn when he was 16 years of age. Assuming that Erasmus was born in 1469, we can arrive at the following dates for these events: Erasmus would have been 14 in 1483/84, when he left Deventer and entered the school at 's Hertogenbosch; he would have been 15 in 1484/85 when he returned to Gouda and, according to him, composed his first letter; and he would have been 16 in 1485/86 when he entered the monastery at Steyn. With this documentation as evidence, we can be reasonably certain that Erasmus' letter to Sister Elisabeth was written at Steyn after 1485 but

---

[11] Erasmus to Grunnius, *Allen*, 2, 301–302; trans. by Mangan, *Life of Erasmus*, 1, 18: "Thus were several months spent without serious reflection; but when the day was at hand when he must put off the secular and put on the religious habit, Florentius [i.e. Erasmus] came to his senses, and began to sing the old song; and sending for his guardian, began to treat about his freedom."

[12] *Allen*, 1, 73. Trans. by Mynors and Thomson, *CWE*, 1, 2.

[13] Erasmus to Grunnius, *Allen*, 2, 299 *et seq*. Erasmus would have been sixteen in 1485/86. See footnote 3.

before he professed his first vows in 1487/88 (at the age of 17).[14] It might be more accurate, therefore, to suggest that this letter was composed about 1486—that is during the period of his postulancy when he was still deciding whether or not to enter the novitiate—rather than in 1487 as Allen has suggested. Erasmus himself described his admission to the monastery at Steyn as follows:

> Besides, he [i.e. Erasmus] had not betaken himself thither with the intention of joining the Order, but only that he might for a little while escape the clacking tongues, until time itself might bring forth something better. . . .
> Thus were several months spent without serious reflection; but, when the day was at hand when he must put off the secular and put on the religious habit, Florentius [i.e. Erasmus] came to his senses, and began to sing the old song; and sending for his guardian, began to treat about his freedom. Once more were harsh threats used, once more was the desperate state of his finances pointed out to him unless he continued in what was well begun.[15]

And thus could Erasmus write to the sympathetic Sister Elisabeth about his "present misfortune" in 1486:

> So my joy is great in the knowledge that there are still those who care for me even in my present misfortune, and who are sorry for it. I think it is all the more welcome since I am aware that it seldom comes the way of the unfortunate . . . . But I can see more clearly than the sun, as the saying goes, that you, dearest Elisabeth, are no member of that company, for in all the chaos of my affairs and the miseries of my condition I know that you both remain and have ever remained one who kept your affection for me undimmed.[16]

It can also be argued that Allen should not have dated the letter to Sister Elisabeth as 1487 because of the contents of Erasmus' letter to his brother Pieter which he also dated 1487.[17] In the latter letter Erasmus describes his present circumstances with less pessimism than in his earlier letter to Sister Elisabeth. The difference in tone is unmistakable:

> . . . and as you did not fail me at the hardest crisis of my life, so please now again

---

[14] Erasmus to Servatius Roger, 8 July 1514, *Allen*, 1, 566; trans. by Mangan, *Life of Erasmus*, 1, 362. Allen notes that the constitution of the congregation of Sion provided that a novice could not make his profession until he had completed his sixteenth year and had passed at least a year and a day in probation. See *Allen*, 2, 1, 566, n. 33.

[15] Erasmus to Grunnius, *Allen*, 2, 301; trans. by Mangan, *Life of Erasmus*, 1, 18.

[16] Erasmus to Elisabeth, *Allen*, 1, 74; trans. by Mynors and Thomson, *CWE*, 1, 3.

[17] Erasmus to Pieter Gerard, *Allen*, 1, 76; trans. by Mynors and Thomson, *CWE*, 1, 5.

lend me support in circumstances that are less harsh even if not exactly favourable.[18]

By 1487 Erasmus had begun to accept the religious life with resignation. Though not fully compatible with its philosophy and discipline, he was adjusting somewhat to its routine. Finally, a third argument can be made for Erasmus' entrance into the monastery at Steyn in about 1485/86. In his letter to Servatius Roger (dated 1489) Erasmus states that "four years have gone by" since the two of them have been together in the religious life.[19] Simply by subtracting four years from 1489 one would arrive at the date 1485—a date which agrees with the claim that Erasmus may have entered the monastery at Steyn as early as 1485/86.

In attempting to assess the meaning of the letters that Erasmus composed at Steyn, Roland Bainton has concluded that death figures as a major theme. Bainton explains it in these words:

> We have the letters of Erasmus from the monastery period. These enable us to see that during his six years at Steyn the Devil was not quiet. Erasmus went through both an interior and an exterior crisis. The interior was set up for him, as for Luther, by the fear of death. Erasmus testified that in his youth he had trembled at the very mention of the name of death.[20]

Bainton's position on Erasmus' emotional crisis at Steyn seems too generalized. Surely, one can be far more specific in accounting for his psychological behavior at Steyn. As an adolescent, Erasmus may have had a special fear of death (and even the devil) but it was only one facet of his personality. More important to his emotional situation than the fear of death was the fact that the plague had taken the lives of his parents within a year of one another. In a 1487 letter to his brother, Erasmus recalled that Pieter had helped him "at the hardest crisis of my life" and that he had displayed "fraternal feeling for me, which long ago was attested by countless proofs."[21] It is not too farfetched to believe that

---

[18] *ibid.*

[19] Erasmus to Servatius Roger [Steyn, c. 1488], *Allen*, 1, 89; trans. by Mynors and Thomson, *CWE*, 1, 21. Allen argues that "this does not necessarily imply that Erasmus had then been four years at Steyn." See Allen, 1, 585. Yet if we read on in the letter, Erasmus also states that "whereas if you had heeded my warnings at the outset you would by this time have turned into one who could not only rival me in literature but even school me in turn." It is clear from this letter that Erasmus and Servatius had been living together in the same monastery for some time.

[20] Roland H. Bainton, *Erasmus of Christendom* (New York, 1969), 17.

[21] Erasmus to Pieter Gerard, *Allen*, 1, 76; trans. by Mynors and Thomson, *CWE*, 1, 5.

Erasmus was here recalling the untimely deaths of his parents. The loss of his mother and father must have been especially painful for Erasmus since he had been haunted as a child by the illegitimacy of his own birth. Following their deaths in 1484, he must have agonized over the possibility that his parents may have been condemned to eternal damnation for their indiscretion. In seeking a papal dispensation from the disabilities of his illegitimate birth in 1516, Erasmus disclosed to Pope Leo X that he had been born "of an unlawful and, as he feared, a sacrilegious union."[22]

Searching for solace in 1484, Erasmus found a compassionate widow, Berta de Hegen, who lavished attention on him. Upon her death about 1487, he wrote to her daughters, recalling the acts of kindness that Berta displayed during his bereavement:

> You, dear sisters, will understand my suffering. When I was left an orphan she consoled me. She lifted me out of my faint-heartedness. She guided me with her counsel. She cared for me as if I had come from her own womb.[23]

In addition to obtaining comfort from the widow De Hegen, Erasmus turned to his brother for consolation. Since they had been raised and educated together from their infancy, it was only natural that these two boys should be close to one another as adolescents. Even when they had been sent to the preparatory school at 's Hertogenbosch, Erasmus and Pieter remained devoted to each other and entered into a pact that they would resist the pressures of their guardians to join the religious life by attending the university instead.[24] When Pieter did in fact succumb to outside pressures and entered the monastery of the Austin Canons at Sion, Erasmus felt betrayed and rejected. He went so far as to describe his faithless brother in August as a Judas Iscariot:

> He [i.e. Pieter] was always his brother's evil genius. Not long afterwards he played the part among his companions that Iscariot played among the Apostles. When, however, he saw his brother [i.e. Erasmus] miserably entrapped, his conscience stung him, and he deplored bitterly that he had ruined him by drawing him into the snare.[25]

---

[22] Leo X to Andrea Ammonio, 26 January 1517, *Allen*, 2, 434, 1. 8: "ex illicito et, vt timet, incesto damnatoque coitu genitus. . . ."

[23] Erasmus, "Oratio . . . Bertae de Heyen. . . ," in Jean Le Clerc (ed.), *Opera Omnia*, 8, 551–560. Trans. by Bainton, *Erasmus of Christendom*, 18.

[24] Erasmus to Grunnius, *Allen*, 2, 297–298; trans. by Mangan, *Life of Erasmus*, 1, 13–14.

[25] *Ibid.*, *Allen*, 2, 298; trans. by Mangan, 1, 15.

But in his letter of 1487, Erasmus' judgment was less severe, even conciliatory:

> Have you so completely rid yourself of all brotherly feeling, or has all thought of your Erasmus wholly fled your heart? I write letters and send them repeatedly, I demand news again and again, I keep asking your friends when they come from your direction, but they never have a hint of a letter or any message: they merely say that you are well. Of course this is the most welcome news I could hear but you are no more dutiful thereby. As I perceive how obstinate you are, I believe it would be easier to get blood from a stone than coax a letter out of you! Where is your early good will towards me and the ardent brotherly affection which you once had for me? . . . . If—and I can scarcely contain my anger at the thought—you do not think our mutual love merits the little time spent on writing a letter, it must be that either I am of no importance in your eyes or else you have quite forgotten about me. If you wish to relieve me of this suspicion, if you care for your brother at all, if there is any vestige of fraternal spirit left in you, be sure to write to me at the earliest possible moment. If you do this, then, Pieter, I shall be glad some time soon to see you in health, and for my part will think nothing more desirable or precious than a letter from you . . . .[26]

In this letter from Steyn, Erasmus poured out his love for his brother, pleading with him in the strongest language not to abandon him nor to end their relationship by failing to write; but it appears that Pieter was a better canon than a brother, and, in the end, he did indeed sever the relationship with Erasmus that had meant so much to the younger boy. It may be for this reason that Erasmus revised his earlier opinion of his brother in 1516 and spoke so harshly of him in his letter to Grunnius. Nonetheless the excessiveness of the language betrays an inward, emotional conflict. To the informed reader Erasmus' description suggests that he was someone who cared a great deal for his brother. How else can we account for the passion and bitterness of the language concerning circumstances that had taken place some thirty years previously?

Having lost his parents to the plague and his brother to the religious life, Erasmus now turned for attention to his fellow canons. The monastery became a substitute family and home. He enjoyed for the first time a family life that had been denied him because of his illegitimate status. It was in search of a brother-substitute that Erasmus lavished so

---

[26] Erasmus to Pieter Gerard, *Allen*, 1, 75–76; trans. by Mynors and Thomson *CWE*, 1, 4–5.

much affection on his "fellow countryman" Servatius Roger of Rotterdam and cultivated a number of other close relationships as well. Far more important to his intellectual and spiritual growth than the friendship with Servatius was Erasmus' relationship with Cornelis Gerard, a fellow Austin canon, who was resident in the monastery at Lopsen. Erasmus composed eleven surviving letters to Cornelis in the year 1489 alone.[27] In one of these letters (No. 20), he wrote with tender affection that

> as, in a charming proof of your good will towards me, you have put together a single Apologetic out of your verses and mine, so, admitting the possibility that we may find anything divided between friends, may the hearts of both be linked by a single bond of mutual love to the end that, just as your verses have been woven into the fabric of my poem and mine into yours, so your spirit may ever dwell in me and mine in you . . . .[28]

Even at the age of 20, Erasmus had not lost his youthful capacity for loving men deeply. He combined it, as before, with his passion for classical literature. As if to illustrate this point, Erasmus recalled his boyhood love of literature and his admiration for men of letters in another letter (No. 23) to Cornelis Gerard:

> However, leaving all else aside, suffice it to say that you could not have sent me a more welcome present than this, since from boyhood I have loved literature, and still love it, so much that it seems to me rightly to be preferred even to all the treasures of Arabia . . . . And in proportion to the intensity of my love for literature is the delight I take in the pursuits of literary men. So, my dear Cornelis, if you love me, as you surely do, pray let me always have some share in your own studies.[29]

Erasmus was clearly more in love with literature, scholarship, and the minds of writers than with individuals per se.

Owing to Cornelis' urgings Erasmus decided in 1489 to devote his pen to the praise of saints and sanctity. He expressed it in a letter to Cornelis (No. 28) as follows:

---

[27] Erasmus to Cornelis Gerard [Steyn 1489?], *Allen*, 1, 93–122; trans. by Mynors and Thomson, *CWE*, 1, 24–57.

[28] Erasmus to Cornelis Gerard [15 May 1489?], *Allen*, 1, 98; trans. by Mynors and Thomson, *CWE*, 1, 29.

[29] Erasmus to Cornelis Gerard [June 1489?], *Allen*, 1, 104; trans. by Mynors and Thomson, *CWE*, 1, 37.

But, since you kindly remind me of this, I have decided for the future to write nothing which does not breathe the atmosphere either of praise of holy men or of holiness itself.

At the same time, he admitted that many of the poems that he had sent to Cornelis in times past had been composed during his early adolescence and had reflected self-indulgence:

Yet if any of the poems I am sending to you seems more self-indulgent than is proper you will readily forgive this in consideration of the time of life at which I wrote them; for, apart from the lyric ode which I was writing when your letter arrived, and the funeral speech . . . and that one solitary satire, all the rest of the poems were written by me when I was a youth and virtually still a layman.[30]

One suspects that both his love for letters and human affection were responses to the tragedies that occurred during his youth and helped to sustain his equilibrium. Erasmus reflected on the reason for his attachment to literature in his *Catalogus Lucubrationum* (1523): "As a boy I was carried off by enthusiasm for *bonne litterae* as if by some hidden force of my nature." To the study of poetry especially "I was as a boy so inclined that I could only with painful difficulty turn my attention to the language of prose."[31] Is it any wonder then that Erasmus made slow progress in his studies at Deventer and 's Hertogenbosch, where undoubtedly the emphasis was on composing prose rather than poetry.[32] Since Cornelis Reedijk has described his *Carmen Bucolicum,* written at about the age of fourteen, as "essentially correct as to form" and at the same time that it reflects an "essentially cosmopolitan mind," we should not be surprised that Erasmus found his confinement at Steyn to be oppressive and sterile.[33] Poetry, no doubt, helped Erasmus to weather some traumatic experiences and to find comfort amid surroundings which he regarded as parochial, but it was temporary relief only and he knew it was no substitute for the freedom to pursue his scholarly tastes. Erasmus' later poetry from Steyn, especially two poems in praise of the Blessed Virgin and St. Gregory, the patron of the monastery at Steyn, displays his

---

[30] Erasmus to Cornelis Gerard [1489?], *Allen,* 1, 118; trans. by Mynors and Thomson, *CWE,* 1, 51–52.
[31] See *Allen,* 1, 2, 1. 30 and 3, 1. 1.
[32] Erasmus to Grunnius, *Allen,* 2, 295–296.
[33] Cornelis Reedijk, *Poems of Desiderius Erasmus* (Leiden, 1956), 113–114 and 131–35.

deeply religious nature and is proof that Cornelis' influence was real and lasting.³⁴

Most scholars have neglected the influence of Cornelis and have concentrated their attention on the correspondence between Erasmus and Servatius during the years between 1487 and 1488. As Ferguson has noted: "Taken at their face value, though with considerable allowance for rhetorical exaggeration, the nine letters to Servatius indicate that Erasmus had become involved in an emotional attachment to his young friend, which Servatius seems at first to have reciprocated, but then found irksome."³⁵ At the same time, Ferguson should have emphasized the point that Servatius was only one of several young canons to whom Erasmus was attracted during these years. In the letter to Grunnius, for example, Erasmus wrote of his affection for a certain religious named Cantelius [i.e. Cornelis Gerard] whom he admired even before he had entered the monastery at Steyn and continued to do so after he was admitted. Erasmus reminds us that

> Florentius [i.e. Erasmus] loved this Cantelius with intense boyish ardor, due to the candor of his nature (especially since he had found him again beyond his expectation after so long a time), as is customary with those of his years, who are likely to conceive violent affections for certain acquaintances. For he had not yet learned to judge men's minds, but from his own feelings estimated others.³⁶

Erasmus lavished his attention on many persons throughout his life. Indeed before he began his relationship with Servatius, he has formed deep attachments with his brother, Cornelis Gerard, Willem Hermans, and Sister Elisabeth.³⁷ Thus one must not be misled by the intensity of Erasmus' language to Servatius and conclude that his relationship with this young canon was radically different from his other relationships during this trying period of his life. While it is true that Erasmus did refer

---

³⁴ *Ibid.*, 174–186; 172–173.

³⁵ W. K. Ferguson (ed.), *CWE*, 1, 6, See also R. H. Bainton, *Erasmus of Christendom*, 18: "Erasmus craved the support of others and fastened his affections upon a fellow monk, Servatius Rogers." D. F. S. Thomson argues unconvincingly that Erasmus' earliest letters (4 to 9) and poems to Servatius Roger point "clearly to literary imitation as a motivating force." See Thomson, "Erasmus as a Poet in the Context of Northern Humanism," *De Gulden Passer*, 47 (1969): 187–210.

³⁶ Erasmus to Grunnius, *Allen*, 1, 301; trans. by Mangan, *Life of Erasmus*, 1, 17.

³⁷ Though the surviving correspondence between Erasmus and Willem Hermans does not begin until circa 1493, these two canons knew each other from boyhood and were residents of the monastery at Steyn. See *Allen*, 1, 128.

to Servatius as "the half of my soul," he also used the same description in a letter to Franciscus Theodoricus.[38] Moreover, in a letter to Cornelis Gerard, he remarked:

> What a propitious day it was, a day to be marked with a pure-white stone, on which Fortune brought me to you in friendship and you were added to my soul—and as no small part of it either.[39]

In response Cornelis wrote:

> But, to avoid tarnishing your distinguished character with my foolish compliments, let it suffice me to say that I ardently hope to have a bond of brotherhood with you, a single enthusiasm for common pursuits, and, in short, a single basis for enduring affection.[40]

Cornelis emphasized the good character of Erasmus deliberately. He was aware that his relationship with Erasmus, and Erasmus' relationship with him and others, was purely platonic. Erasmus himself maintained in a letter to Servatius:

> Indeed, you would have some reason to excuse yourself, if what I were asking of you were something arduous or difficult or wrong. But you yourself are surely aware what it is that I beg of you, inasmuch as it was not for the sake of reward or out of a desire for any favour that I have wooed you both unhappily and relentlessly. What is it then? Why, that you love him who loves you. What is easier, more pleasant, or more suited to a generous heart, than this? I would repeat: only love me, and it is enough for me.[41]

Erasmus thought of his relationship with Servatius, Cornelis, and Franciscus as a revival of a similar practice that had been maintained between St. Jerome and St. Augustine. To Cornelis, he wrote:

> It was by such means that the two famous Fathers of the church, Jerome and Augustine, prevented as they were by enormous temporal and spatial distances from being together and enjoying each other's embrace as they would have wished, still managed never to lack each other's presence; and each was ever aware of the other's feelings of good will. Let us accordingly, my sweet Cornelis,

---

[38] Erasmus to Franciscus Theodoricus [Steyn ca. 1488], *Allen*, 1, 88.

[39] Erasmus to Cornelis Gerard [Steyn 1489?], *Allen*, 1, 94; trans. by Mynors and Thomson, *CWE*, 1, 24.

[40] Cornelis Gerard to Erasmus [Lopsen, May 1489?], *Allen*, 1, 96; trans. by Mynors and Thomson, *CWE*, 1, 27.

[41] Erasmus to Servatius Rogerus [Steyn, ca. 1487], *Allen*, 1, 81; trans. by Mynors and Thomson, *CWE*, 1, 12.

be careful to ensure that frequently something of yours is on the wing to me or something of mine to you. This will enable us to compensate for separation and to fulfill the duties of a perfect affection.[42]

Several scholars have sought other reasons to explain why Erasmus surrounded himself at Steyn with men of letters. Otto Schottenloher, for example, has argued that following Servatius' rejection of his friendship, Erasmus organized a coterie of literati who became in effect substitutes for Servatius.[43] Reacting to this thesis, James D. Tracy has observed:

> Whether or not the hypothesis of 'sublimation' is accepted Erasmus clearly did change from an ardent friend to a literary mentor. After Letter 9 he no longer pressed his case with Servatius. In Letter 13 he gave up hope, 'since you remain harder than adamantine in the same frame of mind.' Beginning with Letter 10, he emerged as a teacher of the Muses to Servatius and several other young men, not all of whom were monks . . . .[44]

Though Tracy has found something in letters 9 to 12 that justifies his claim that "After letter 9 he no longer pressed his case with Servatius," I cannot find any such supporting evidence. Instead it is clear that Erasmus remained committed to Servatius throughout 1488. In letter 13, for example, he confided:

> My dear Servatius, as there is nothing on earth more pleasant or sweeter than loving and being loved, so there is, in my opinion, nothing more distressing or more miserable than loving without being loved in return . . . . Perhaps you will already guess that I have drawn up this preamble so that I may reconcile you to me again and repair afresh the interrupted good will between us . . . . I have left untried no means by which the youthful heart could be affected . . . . Am I to make

---

[42] Erasmus to Cornelis Gerard [Steyn, June 1489?], *Allen,* 1, 104; trans. by Mynors and Thomson, *CWE,* 1, 36.

[43] Otto H. Schottenloher, *Erasmus im Ringen um die Humanistische Bildungsform.* Reformationsgeschichtliche Studien und Texte, 61 (Münster, 1933), 44–45.

[44] James D. Tracy, *Erasmus: The Growth of a Mind* (Geneva, 1972), 38. Tracy also confuses Erasmus' postulancy with his novitiate on p. 47: "While he [i.e. Erasmus] was still a novice the monks slyly indulged his penchant for spending time with books and did not require him to follow the daily regimen. But when he had taken the habit, after renewed hesitation, he discovered he had been 'pushed into a type of life to which I was most alien in soul as in body.'" It must be pointed out that Erasmus did not formally begin his novitiate until after he had received the habit of the Austin Canons. Before then he was simply a postulant.

up my mind to live bereft of the companion I deserted? But life without a friend I think no life but rather death . . . .[45]

Certainly this letter does not sound as though Erasmus had abandoned his attempts to secure the affection of Servatius.

At the same time, this reader finds fault with another of Tracy's conclusions. The latter insists that "Beginning with Letter 10 he [i.e. Erasmus] emerged as a teacher of the Muses to Servatius and several other young men . . . ."[46] Before then, he assumes that Erasmus was too occupied with his relationship with Servatius to interest himself in teaching others. But the letters themselves offer no support for this position. It is important to keep in mind that six of the nine letters (i.e. Nos. 4, 5, 6, 7, 8, and 9) to Servatius were composed about 1487 and that the other three (Nos. 11, 13, and 15) were written about 1488.[47] Thus within a year, Tracy wants us to believe that Erasmus transformed his strong emotional attachment for Servatius into something paternalistic; that he changed from a friend and admirer to a pedagogue. It would seem more reasonable to surmise that Erasmus was both a friend and teacher of Servatius throughout their relationship. In suggesting to Servatius in 1488 (letter No. 15) that "already four years have gone by" since the two of them began the religious life together, Erasmus was actually admitting that he had been striving from the beginning to persuade Servatius to apply himself to classical studies. Erasmus writes:

> Look, I beg you, and see how much time has already slipped between your fingers, as the saying goes . . . whereas if you had heeded my warnings at the outset you would by this time have turned into one who could not only rival me in literature but even school me in turn.[48]

It also seems clear that Erasmus' failure to establish a lasting friendship with Servatius had nothing to do with his intention to form a coterie of literati. He began to pursue literary studies and to enlist a following immediately upon arriving at Steyn, spending sleepless nights reading Terence with Willem Hermans and Cornelis. Erasmus describes his nightly revelry with Cornelis in his letter to Grunnius:

---

[45] Erasmus to Servatius Roger [Steyn, ca. 1488], *Allen*, 1, 86; trans. by Mynors and Thomson, *CWE*, 1, 17.

[46] Tracy, *Erasmus*, 38.

[47] See Erasmus' letters to Servatius Roger in *Allen*, 1, 77–88.

[48] Erasmus to Servatius Roger [Steyn, ca. 1488], *Allen*, 1, 89–90; trans. by Mynors and Thomson, *CWE*, 1, 21.

Meanwhile Cantelius [i.e. Cornelis] eagerly enjoyed his good fortune, taking advantage of the good nature and simplicity of his companion. For Florentius [i.e. Erasmus] frequently and secretly by night would read to him a whole comedy of Terence, so that in a few months, as a result of their secret nocturnal sessions, they had finished the principal authors . . . .[49]

Erasmus formed friendships easily with those canons who shared an interest in literature. His relationship with Servatius ended, no doubt, when the latter rejected Erasmus' efforts to convert him to classical studies. Servatius was aware that Erasmus' scholarly tastes were at variance with the regulations of the congregation of Sion.[50]

In adjusting to the religious life at Steyn after 1487, Erasmus conceived of it in a wholly new light. He found that he could convert a segment of the monastery into a literary salon and pursue his studies actively, though clandestinely, through correspondence and conversations with religious and laymen of like disposition. Tracy has observed that Erasmus' "craving the intimacy, thwarted by his fellow monks, led him to propose a community of affection among devotees of the Muses as the goal of study."[51] Moreover, Schottenloher had concluded, sometime before Tracy, that Erasmus sought a quiet and secure place to live a virtuous life of study rather than the combination of asceticism and religious exercises which is the distinguishing characteristic of monasticism.[52] In composing

---

[49] Erasmus to Grunnius, *Allen*, 2, 301; trans. by Mangan, *Life of Erasmus*, 1, 18.

[50] For the history of the Canons Regular of St. Augustine in the fifteenth and sixteenth centuries, see Alois van Ette, *Les Chanoines réguliers de Saint Augustin: Aperçu historique* (Cholet, 1953), Gebhard Koberger, *Kurzgefasste Geschichte der Augustine Chorherren* (Klosterneuburg, 1961/62), 3, and Eelcko Ypma, *Het Generaal Kapittel van Sion* (Nijmegen, 1949). As Hyma has pointed out in *The Youth of Erasmus* (p. 150): "It has been stated, though without any justification, that the chapter of Sion used to belong to the chapter of Windesheim and later withdrew from it, or at least shaped its rules after those of Windesheim. None of these assumptions is correct. . . . They each led an independent existence, and none of the sources give any clue to intimate relationship, nor to substantial dependence of Sion on Windesheim." Bainton, on the other hand, continues to confuse the two congregations in his 1969 biography, when he states that Erasmus "did not break with the Brethren [of the Common Life, i.e. the Windesheim congregation] . . . who ordained him to the priesthood in 1492." Erasmus was neither a member of the Windesheim congregation nor of the Brethren of the Common Life. He was clearly an Austin Canon, subject to the rule of St. Augustine and the regulations of the congregation of Sion. See Bainton, *Erasmus of Christendom*, 25–26.

[51] Tracy, *Erasmus*, 31.

[52] Schottenloher, *Erasmus im Ringen um die Humanistische Bildungsform*, 45–51.

his *De contemptu mundi,* Erasmus rejected the monastic ideals of St. Bernard for a life of uninterrupted scholarship: "The monastic life affords liberty, for Cicero said that liberty is the ability to live as you wish. If, then, you wish to be a monk, you have liberty. But above all, monastic life offers the highest felicity. . . . And to a man of learning what felicity the monastery affords! Here he may read and ruminate and write books. Delights never cease, since books are so varied."[53] Erasmus defied the rule of his congregation on the grounds that he had been tricked into the religious life and that his vows, in effect, were not binding. Sensing the objections of his religious superiors, Erasmus summarized their position in his letter to Grunnius as follows:

> "But, puberty," they say, "gives the power of discriminating between good and evil."[54]

Erasmus rejected this view of adolescence with contempt. Puberty was too volatile a period of life in which to expect persons to make lifelong commitments. Erasmus reasoned:

> But someone will say, "What about the year of probation (as they call it) and the age of maturity?" That is ridiculous. As if one should demand that a boy in his seventeenth year, especially educated to literature, should know himself, which is a great thing in an old man; or as if he would learn in one year what many grey-haired men do not yet understand.[55]
>
> All bodies do not mature at the same age, much less minds. It matters not that perchance puberty has rendered them mature for marriage; they may not be mature enough to enter a religious life; for many indeed have entered therein, men of about thirty years of age otherwise well experienced in the ways of the world, who have withdrawn before their profession, saying "I had not thought."
>
> But I do not intend to attack these Orders: providing this or that kind of life is suitable to this or that man, or even necessary, let the vow be irrevocable; but the holier and more exacting the life, then the more circumspectly, the more slowly, and the more seriously ought it to be embraced, and sufficiently early if just previous to forty. Other vows are not binding, unless it is evident there is a sound mind, clear intelligence, and an absence of fear or apprehension.[56]

Erasmus maintained the view that a seventeen year-old adolescent was

---

[53] Erasmus, *De contemptu mundi,* trans. by R. H. Bainton, *Erasmus of Christendom,* 15.

[54] Erasmus to Grunnius, *Allen,* 2, 309; trans. by Mangan, *Life of Erasmus, 1, 25.*

[55] Erasmus to Servatius Roger, 8 July 1514, *Allen* 1, 566; trans. by Mangan, *Life of Erasmus,* 1, 362. Servatius was now prior of the monastery at Steyn.

[56] Erasmus to Grunnius, *Allen,* 2, 309; trans. by Mangan, *Life of Erasmus,* 1, 25–26.

still a boy. Thus in two 1489 letters to Cornelis Gerard, he felt justified in describing himself as a boy, when he would have been about nineteen.[57] Fear based on an inability to take care of himself in 1486/87 finally forced Erasmus to accept the religious habit of the Austin Canons, when he was sixteen years of age, and it was pride and coercion that led him to profess vows a year later. He explained his profession as follows:

"Now it is too late to retreat," said they. "You have put your hand to the plough; it is wrong to turn back; if you put aside the habit which you assumed before many witnesses, you will always be the common talk of everybody." . . . "Where will you turn?" said they. "You will never be able to come into the presence of good men; you will be execrated by the monks, and hated by the common people." Now the youth had a mind which felt dishonor keenly, and feared death less than disgrace. On the other hand, he was urged on by his guardians and friends, some of whom had lessened his property by theft. In a word, they conquered by villainy. The boy, with abhorrence in his soul and reluctance in his words, was compelled to put his head into the halter, just as captives in war stretch forth their hands to the victor to be bound, or as men overcome by protracted torments are wont: they do, not what they wish, but what their conqueror wishes.[58]

The Grunnius letter vindicates Erasmus, though Hyma, who has devoted a good deal of attention to the youth of Erasmus, doubts its reliability. He insists that

Few readers of this second account by Erasmus, which was composed in the year 1517, will be able to keep from their minds a certain amount of suspicion; they are inclined to doubt the sincerity of Erasmus. In the year 1517 he was trying to obtain a dispensation which would free him for ever from the monastic vows and from the monastic habit. It was to his interest to describe his entrance in the monastery of Steyn in such a way as to prove that he had been fairly compelled to enter against his will.[59]

---

[57] Erasmus to Cornelis Gerard, *Allen*, 1, nos. 26 (pp. 112–115) and 29 (119–120).

[58] Erasmus to Grunnius, *Allen*, 2, 303–304; trans. by Mangan, *Life of Erasmus*, 1, 20.

[59] Albert Hyma, *The Youth of Erasmus*, 148. In writing to his prior at Steyn, Servatius Roger (on 8 July 1514), who was familiar with the circumstances surrounding Erasmus' entrance into the monastery at Steyn, Erasmus disclosed: "You know that by the pertinacity of my guardians and by the bad advice of others, I was compelled rather than persuaded to adopt that kind of life, and bound to it thereafter by the reproaches of Cornelius Woerden, and by a certain boyish shame, although I knew that that sort of life was not in any way suitable for me . . . ." See *Allen*, 1, 565: trans. by Mangan, *Life of Erasmus*, 1, 361. Tracy adopts Hyma's thesis and argues that Erasmus "did, in order to

But Hyma is not justified in questioning Erasmus' motives. Since he does not refute the evidence that Erasmus and his brother had been deprived of their parents and inheritance and were now subject to the authority of greedy guardians, why is it so difficult for him to believe that Erasmus was telling the truth when he insisted that cohersion and financial exigencies were the principal reasons behind his entrance into the religious life? Where else could he and his brother have gone without parents or an inheritance? More important, perhaps, for questioning Hyma's thesis is the fact that it now seems clear that Erasmus was not "trying to obtain a dispensation which would free him forever from the monastic vows and from the monastic habit." As this writer has tried to demonstrate in a previous article, Erasmus obtained permission to live outside the cloister and to wear a modified religious habit, but he was not dispensed from his vows nor from the obligation to wear part of the habit of an Austin canon.[60] Indeed Erasmus remained a member of the Canons Regular to the end of his life. In seeking permission to live outside the cloister and to wear a modified religious habit, Erasmus did not need to invent a wholly fallacious story. By 1517 he was a scholar of eminence and Pope Leo X would have granted his request without question. This pope knew only too well that Erasmus no longer belonged exclusively to the monastery of the Austin Canons at Steyn. He belonged to Christendom instead.

Hyma also contends that Erasmus accepted the religious life of a canon regular at the outset but in time came to dislike it. He reasons:

> Since he [i.e. Erasmus] arrived during the winter of 1486/87 and left about six years later, one may assume that from 1487 to 1490 he was fairly content with monasticism, but became more and more dissatisfied with every passing month.[61]

It is this writer's opinion that Erasmus developed just the opposite attitude. He disliked the religious life intensely in the beginning (1486 to 1487), adapted to it gradually (after 1487), and, after obtaining a position

obtain a papal dispensation, releasing him from his obligation to live as a monk, deliberately falsify the circumstances of his birth and his entrance into the monastery in the letter to Grunnius." See Tracy, *Erasmus*, 21. The letter to Servatius, in my opinion, vindicates Erasmus of duplicity.

[60] See R. L. DeMolen, "Erasmus' Commitment to the Canons Regular of St. Augustine," *Renaissance Quarterly*, 26 (1973), 437–443.

[61] Hyma, *The Youth of Erasmus*, 163.

with the bishop of Cambrai in 1493, felt genuine pride in his order, even if he could not physically and emotionally accept its strict discipline. Writing to Jan Mombaer, a fellow Austin Canon, in 1497, he observed:

> For though you and I have never been closely associated, I still somehow feel strongly drawn to you. I am by nature extremely prone to form friendships of all kinds, but so strong is the attraction I feel towards enthusiasts for good literature that I can even love my rivals. Yet I am bound to regard you as especially precious in view of our bond in the higher studies which, as Cicero perceived, is by far the most reliable means of cementing good will and besides which, even without this link, your modesty and kindness, friendliness and honour are enough to make me love you. Then there is our common Order and its habit and what I take to be a considerable similarity in our dispositions, except that you are more inclined to virtue.[62]

Erasmus' friendship with Mombaer was thus based on three considerations: their mutual regard for classical letters, his friend's virtues, and the fact that the two men were members of the same religious order. Nevertheless Erasmus could never resign himself to return to the semi-cloistered monastic life at Steyn. In a 1498 letter to Arnoldius Bostius he reflected:

> You ask me to share my thoughts with you; I will tell you one thing: I have long since lost all interest in the world, and find no merit in my own hopes. I only ask to be given leisure to live a life entirely devoted to God alone, in lamentation for the sins of my rash youth, absorption in holy writ, and either reading or writing something continually. This I cannot do in a retreat, or under a monastic regime, for I am the most sensitive man alive. My health can never, even at its best, tolerate vigils or fasting, or hardships of any kind. Even in my present circumstances, living in the midst of such luxury, I sometimes fall ill; what should I do among the toils of a monkish life?[63]

While living outside the walls of his monastery, Erasmus developed an interior religious life. He conformed in general to the rule of St. Augustine but without having to endure the pressures of community life or to follow a strictly regulated schedule. He pursued this life of holiness, as he himself explained, "in lamentation for the sins of my rash youth."

---

[62] Erasmus to Jan Mombaer, 4 February [1497], *Allen*, 1, 167; trans. by Mynors and Thomson, *CWE*, 1, 108–109.

[63] Erasmus to Arnoldius Bostius [ca. April 1498], *Allen*, 1, 202; trans. by Mynors and Thomson, *CWE*, 1, 151.

Adolescence left its mark on the interior Erasmus just as it helped to shape his exterior life.

In conclusion, the life of Erasmus from 1469 to 1490, when he would have reached the age of majority, is largely hidden from view since only the barest outlines of it have survived. Yet it is obvious from Erasmus' letters and other writings that his adolescent years were marked by tragedy and personal grief. The life he led as an Austin canon was largely forced upon him by the death of his parents by 1484 and by financial contingencies. Sensitive and introspective by nature, Erasmus found the semi-cloistered life of the monastery to be beyond his capabilities. Yet he felt a commitment both to his order and to those religious vows that he professed for the first time in 1487. When he emerged from the monastery at Steyn in 1493, he was embittered by the hardships of the religious life and by efforts to thwart his scholarly interests. A series of fortuitous circumstances gave him his life's ambition, however, and within twenty years he became Europe's most admired man of letters. Just as the trappings and ceremonials of the monastic life left him unresponsive, so the offer of a cardinal's hat by Pope Paul III in 1535 was rejected out of hand. As Erasmus himself put it: he would be like "the proverbial cat in court dress."[64] It was the freedom of the cat that Erasmus cherished most of all. Indeed one may conclude that posterity itself has come to admire Erasmus not only for his feline independence of mind but for his fidelity to his Master under the most trying circumstances in his youth.

---

[64] Erasmus to Bartholomew Latomus, 24 August 1535, *Allen,* 11, 217: "Feli aiunt crocoton."

CHAPTER THREE

The Interior Erasmus

Though our outward man is corrupted, yet the inward man is renewed day by day.

2 Corinthians 4:16

HAILED as a classicist, humanist, theologian, and reformer, Erasmus of Rotterdam has for nearly five centuries attracted the attention of scholars of every Christian persuasion. What is lacking, however, in this four-dimensional view of the prince of humanists is his own deep spiritual life—an interiorization of his philosophy of reform, *philosophia Christi,* which grew out of his contacts with the *Devotio Moderna* and was activated in the monastery of the Canons Regular of St. Augustine at Steyn in about 1489 when Erasmus underwent a spiritual awakening of enormous consequences. Marjorie O'Rourke Boyle, on the other hand, has argued recently that the commonplace view that holds that Erasmus was "spiritually formed under the tutelage of the "Brothers of the Common Life" can no longer be supported. She goes on to insist that Erasmus' theological method of imitation "is grounded in the pedagogy of classical rhetoric more probably than in the piety of the Modern Devotion as scholars have previously insisted"; that Erasmus was more clearly indebted to the works of Cicero than to those of Thomas à Kempis. Boyle sees "very distinct theological tonalities" in the works of Erasmus that make it impossible for him to have based his *philosophia Christi* on the *Imitatio Christi* of Thomas à Kempis, a fellow Augustinian canon.[1] It will be one of the purposes of this chapter to argue

---

[1] Marjorie O'Rourke Boyle, *Erasmus on Language and Method in Theology* (Toronto, 1977), 233 n. 244, and 101. The following writers have adopted a different point of view by maintaining that Erasmus' religious ideas were in harmony with the *Devotio Moderna:* Louis Bouyer, *Erasmus and His Times,* trans. Francis X. Murphy (Westminster, Md., 1959); Lewis W. Spitz, *The Religious Renaissance of the German Humanists* (Cambridge, Mass., 1963); E. E. Reynolds, *Thomas More and Erasmus* (New York, 1965); and John Payne, *Erasmus: His Theology of the Sacraments* (Richmond, Va., 1970).

that the language of the *philosophia Christi* is identical to the undogmatic spirituality of the *Devotio Moderna* and that Erasmus proposed a way of life rather than a method of learning. The classics were no more than tools that were used by Erasmus to prod others to adopt his *philosophia Christi*. Like the dust jacket of a book, the classics helped to sell his reform program, but they were secondary to the program itself.

All of the portraits of Erasmus that were painted during his lifetime have one thing in common: they show an introspective subject. Albrecht Dürer, Hans Holbein the Younger, and Quentin Metsys have captured the spirit of Erasmus by revealing his reflective nature. Even the presence of a money pouch, a fur-lined gown, and rings does not detract from the preoccupation with the nonphysical world that is etched on Erasmus' visage. The extensive correspondence of Erasmus, on the contrary, gives a different view of the man. He appears gregarious, industrious, at times peevish and even sarcastic in the pages of his letters. The correspondence shows a man of the world.[2] Reacting to this image, writers have tended to liken Erasmus to a peripatetic scholar in pursuit of honors and revenues or, somewhat more disparagingly, to the offshoot of "a long line of maiden aunts."[3] It is doubtful if very many authors of works about Erasmus would suggest that he was, above all, a man of God or would go so far as to acknowledge that he not only proposed a plan for holiness but actively pursued it as well. In the following pages I hope to show that this two-sided image of Erasmus was deliberately effected in an effort to demonstrate to mankind that sanctity grows out of a persistent struggle with sin and imperfection. Erasmus conveyed through his correspondence and literary labors the image of an adolescent

---

[2] Important biographical information about Erasmus can be found in numerous letters written by him. Especially important are his letters to Servatius Roger (8 July 1514) in *The Correspondence of Erasmus* (Toronto, 1974), 2:294–95, and to Lambertus Grunnius (August 1516), *The Correspondence of Erasmus*, 4:8–32. (Hereafter the Toronto edition of Erasmus' correspondence cited as *CWE*.)

[3] Preserved Smith, *Erasmus: A Study of His Life, Ideals and Place in History* (New York, 1923), 440. Christopher Hollis went even further and accused Erasmus of being non-Christian: "Any pretense that he ever made that he tried to regulate his own conduct by that of Christ was the most patent insincerity, and on its most fundamental ethical teaching he was at issue with Christian theory." See Hollis, *Erasmus* (Milwaukee, Wis., 1933), 265. Albert Hyma offered another negative view when he insisted that "He [Erasmus] gave no expression to any amount of love for Christ. . . . The Cross, which saves through pain and death, seems to have had practically no significance for Erasmus at Steyn. See Hyma, *The Youth of Erasmus* (New York, 1968), 18.

and, later on, of an adult who not only possessed human weaknesses but also committed transgressions against God and man. And yet it was the very same man who would transcend his physical frailties and faults and submerge his personality in the love of Christ.

Writing to Wolfgang Faber Capito at the height of his career, 1517, Erasmus of Rotterdam was profoundly aware that *l'uomo universale* possessed not only a sound mind in a sound body but also a noble character that reflected inner goodness:

> Aulus Gellius tells us how long ago a good and acceptable proposal was rendered futile by the bad character of its proposer; and in the same way the fruits of study are quite rightly made more attractive by the reputation of the man who recommends it.[4]

During the last quarter of his life Erasmus suffered from the stings of critics who sought to discredit his *philosophia Christi* by attacking his character. In spite of the severity of these attacks, Erasmus maintained pious practices during his lifetime as a demonstration of his Christian commitment and as a testimony to the integrity of his program of reform.[5] He emphasized that devotion must show itself in acts or else it is false:

> Perhaps you are wont to venerate the relics of the saints. . . . No veneration of Mary is more beautiful than the imitation of her humility. No devotion to the saints is more acceptable to God than the imitation of their virtues. Say you have a great devotion to St. Peter and St. Paul. Then by all means imitate the faith of the former and the charity of the latter.[6]

The emphasis on imitating virtue remained a consistent theme throughout Erasmus' writings. In his work on Christian marriage, Erasmus observed: "The fact is that from the best of parents the worst of children may be born and on the contrary we sometimes see admirable

---

[4] Erasmus to Wolfgang Faber Capito (26 February 1517) in *CWE*, 4:266.

[5] For example, in 1501, he sent his patroness, Anna van Borssele of Veere, a gift of some prayers to the Blessed Virgin and a poem in praise of St. Anne. See *CWE*, 2:17. Moreover in 1523 he composed a Mass in honor of Our Lady of Loreto at the request of Theobald Bietricius. Both sets of devotion are an indication of Erasmus' fidelity to the mother of Christ. Erasmus also dedicated his *Commentarius in duos hymnos Prudentii* in 1523 to Margaret More Roper, who reciprocated by translating his *Precatio Dominica* into English.

[6] Erasmus, *The Handbook of the Militant Christian*, trans. and ed. John P. Dolan in *The Essential Erasmus* (New York, 1964), 66.

men born from illicit unions."⁷ No doubt Erasmus was here thinking of his own parents and the sordid conditions that surrounded his birth. Even in the face of adversity he insisted on the pursuit of virtue.

During his adolescence Erasmus endured physical as well as emotional crises. He lost both of his parents in his early teens and was separated from his only brother when the two boys, Pieter aged 19 and Erasmus aged 16, were required to enter the religious life for lack of independent finances. It was probably during this time that Erasmus became aware of those circumstances that surrounded his birth. In Leo X's letter to Andrea Ammonio (26 January 1517), Erasmus was described as "de illicito et, ut timet, incesto damnatoque coitu genitus." Writing in the sixteenth century, J. C. Scaliger spoke of Erasmus as "incesto natus concubitu, sordibus parentibus, altero sacrificulo, altera prostituta." Having been born to unmarried parents, Erasmus faced a debilitating awakening during his formative years.⁸

From an early date, Erasmus reacted strongly to personal attacks on his character. As Jacopo Sadoleto observed in 1530:

> There is one thing, I repeat, that I desire and which I vehemently urge upon you to do, that is, that you restrain yourself from entering into every sort of recrimination and that in your writing you avoid saying things which, although they may not be contrary to true piety, yet are not in accordance with the long-received opinions of the people and aggravate the zeal of certain men and even certain orders whom I deem it of the greatest importance not to oppose. What makes you, a man who excels in the highest degree in all kinds of learning, fight with persons who are not your equal in these altercations and quarrellings of yours?⁹

Though a personal friend, Sadoleto could not understand the importance of a good reputation in furthering the program of reform that Erasmus had clearly developed before he left the monastery at Steyn; nor could he

---

⁷ Erasmus, *Opera omnia*, ed. Jean LeClerc (Leiden, 1703–06), 5: col. 669B. It was first published at Basel in 1526.

⁸ Leo X to Andrea Ammonio (26 January 1517), *CWE*, 4:190: "an unlawful and (as he fears) incestuous and condemned union." J. C. Scaliger's accusation is discussed by Christopher Hollis, *Erasmus* (Milwaukee, Wis., 1933), 3. See J. C. Scaliger, *Contra Desid. Erasmum Roterodamum Oratio II* (Paris, 1537). For a discussion of Erasmus' adolescence, see R. L. DeMolen, "Erasmus as Adolescent," *Bibliothèque d' Humanisme et Renaissance*, 38 (1976): 7–25.

⁹ Jacopo Sadoleto to Erasmus (12 February 1530), *Opus Epistolarum Des. Erasmi*, ed. P. S. Allen et al. (Oxford, 1906–47), 8:360. Hereafter cited as *Allen*.

understand that Erasmus was more than a scholar with a reputation. He was the architect of a spiritual life in Christ. In the words of *The Imitation of Christ:* "The life of a good religious man should shine in all virtue and be inwardly as it appears outwardly."[10]

It was while in residence at the monastery of the Augustinian Canons Regular at Steyn that Erasmus, encouraged by Cornelis Gerard, "decided for the future to write nothing which does not breathe the atmosphere either of praise of holy men or of holiness itself."[11] This was in 1489. And for the rest of Erasmus' life—some forty-seven years—he remained true to his promise: an extraordinary achievement indeed! Since Erasmus was pursuing studies for the priesthood at the time, he owed his life's ambition to a spiritual awakening among the Augustinian canons—an indebtedness that recalled his childhood contacts with the Brethren of the Common Life at Deventer and 's Hertogenbosch. At the outset of Book 1 of *The Imitation of Christ,* Thomas à Kempis offered a similar dedication:

> Let all the study of our heart be from now on to have our meditation fixed wholly on the life of Christ, for His holy teachings are of more virtue and strength than the words of all the angels and saints. And he who through grace has the inner eye of his soul opened to the true beholding of the Gospels of Christ will find in them hidden manna.[12]

Although Erasmus spoke disparagingly of the teaching abilities of the Brethren of the Common Life at 's Hertogenbosch, as well as of their zeal in promoting religious vocations, he praised them for their attitude toward religious vows: "For men of this persuasion have one exceptional advantage, which is a vestige of the early days of religion: they are not bound by indissoluble vows."[13] In 1493 Erasmus accepted a secretaryship with the bishop of Cambrai in order to escape the monastic life at Steyn and to pursue a particular goal.

Soon after Erasmus left Steyn, admiring colleagues were aware of the program of reform that this newly ordained priest had initiated. The learned Robert Gaguin, writing in 1495, insisted that

---

[10] Thomas à Kempis, *The Imitation of Christ,* ed. Harold C. Gardiner (New York, 1955), bk. 1, chap. 19, 53.
[11] Erasmus to Cornelis Gerard (1489?), *CWE,* 1:51.
[12] Kempis, *Imitation of Christ,* ed. Gardiner, 1. 1. 31.
[13] Erasmus to Lambertus Grunnius (August 1516), *CWE,* 4:12.

I do not write this with the intention of teaching you, for you are fit to be the teacher of others. I only wish to show what hope of glory lies in the journey you have undertaken. For I have come to believe of you that you combine piety with integrity of character. . . .[14]

Those scholars who claim that Erasmus' *philosophia Christi* owed its origins to John Colet ignore the fact that Erasmus had undergone a spiritual renewal before his arrival in England in 1499.[15] He came to England as a committed disciple of Christ as well as a reputable scholar. Colet himself summarized the opinion of English humanists concerning this "truly virtuous man":

You have already been recommended to me by your reputation and by the evidence afforded by certain of your writings. At the time when I was in Paris the name of Erasmus on the lips of scholars was one to conjure with. . . . But what above all recommends you to me is the fact that the reverend father with whom you are staying, the prior of the house and congregation of Our Lord Jesus Christ, only yesterday described you to me as one who was, in his judgment, a truly virtuous man, uniquely endowed with natural goodness. . . . I hope you may like our country as much as I think you are capable of benefiting her by your scholarship; while for my part I regard you, and shall continue to regard you, as a person whom I consider to be eminently virtuous as well as eminently learned.[16]

It is clear from this passage that Colet believed that the presence of Erasmus would stimulate English scholarship and spirituality. In 1499 Erasmus was more than a classical scholar in search of a research project. He was a man of deep religious commitment and considerable virtue. Moreover, as a sign of his dedication to Christ, he chose as his friends men of like disposition: John Colet, Sir Thomas More, and Bishop John Fisher[17]—all of whom nurtured and gave direction to his preconceived plan of holiness in the century that followed.

When first applying for a dispensation to hold ecclesiastical offices and to live outside of the cloister at Steyn in 1506, Erasmus acknowledged his

---

[14] Robert Gaguin to Erasmus (24 September 1495?), *CWE*, 1:85.

[15] Douglas Bush, *The Renaissance and English Humanism* (Toronto, 1939), 64.

[16] John Colet to Erasmus (October 1499), *CWE*, 1:198–99.

[17] After More's death Erasmus confessed: "I feel as if I had died with More so closely were our two-souls united." See E. E. Reynolds, *Thomas More and Erasmus* (New York, 1965), 238.

illegitimacy but did not refer to the clerical status of his father.[18] Later on he acknowledged the possibility that his father was in holy orders at the time of his birth when he applied for a dispensation from Leo X to hold more than one benefice, to live outside the monastery at Steyn, and to adopt a modified form of the Augustinian habit. The letter granting the dispensation sets forth as the reasons that led the pope to grant it: Erasmus' uprightness of life and character, his exceptional learning, and his outstanding virtues—all of which had been commended to the pope in letters from Henry VIII and Charles V.[19]

In defense of his new mode of life, Erasmus wrote to his superior at Steyn that "I have always regarded as the worst of my misfortunes the fact that I had been forced into the kind of profession which was utterly repugnant to my mind and body alike: to my mind because I disliked ritual and loved freedom, and to my body because, even had I been wholly satisfied to live such a life, my bodily constitution could not tolerate its hardships."[20] The key words are "I disliked ritual and loved freedom." In essence it is a summary of the religious life that Erasmus envisioned not only for himself but for all Christians. Freedom from ritual and dogmatism would enable men to reach the ultimate heights in their progress toward union with Christ—a theme common to *The Imitation of Christ*.

Unable to endure the rigors of community life at Steyn because of physical disabilities, Erasmus followed legal channels in arranging his release from the monastery and its obligations. One is struck by his zeal in effecting the change from the formal religious habit of the canons regular, which resembled that of a bishop, to that of a secular priest. In doing so he sought simplicity. The garb of the canons regular, with its

---

[18] Julius II to Erasmus (4 January 1506), *CWE*, 2:105–06.

[19] Leo X to Erasmus (26 January 1517), *CWE*, 4:197. Indeed, Erasmus was held in high esteem by all the pontiffs between Julius II and Paul IV. Julius II praised Erasmus' zeal for religion, his integrity of life and character, and his uprightness and virtue. See *CWE*, 2:105. In a letter dated 31 May 1535, Paul III wrote to Erasmus: "We especially exhort you, our son, whom God has adorned with so much talent and learning, to help us in this pious work, which is so much in keeping with your ideals, to defend the Catholic religion both in word and writing before and during the Council. In so doing you will not only crown in the best fashion possible a life of religion and literary productivity, you will also refute your accusers and rouse your admirers." See John P. Dolan, ed., *The Essential Erasmus* (New York, 1964), 23.

[20] Erasmus to Servatius Roger (8 July 1514), *CWE*, 2:295.

rochet and train, was far too ostentatious for his tastes and contradicted his call for simplicity in dress. Having decided to follow a life of commitment to Christ, he felt certain that his external image had to testify to his interior disposition. Leo X's letter to Andrea Ammonio insists that Erasmus, "through no desire of his own but under pressure of events at first concealed and later altogether abandoned the habit which the said canons do customarily wear and went about for several years and still goes about in the habit of a secular priest . . . and now wishes for the peace of his soul and the avoidance of greater scandal to continue in the said secular habit.[21]

Erasmus proposed a life style for himself that would be in keeping with his relaxed status as a canon regular:

> I have searched for the kind of life in which I should be least bad; and indeed I believe I have found it. During this time I have lived among men of sobriety, and among literary studies which have kept me away from many vices. I have been able to enjoy the society of such as have the true flavour of Christianity and have been improved by their conversation.[22]

Erasmus here resolved to live the life of a priest-scholar in pursuit of Christ. Furthermore, in a letter to an unnamed monk dated 1527, Erasmus gives us a capsule summary of the kind of life he was actually living then:

> What kind of liberty is that where it is not allowable to say prayers, where it is not permitted to say Mass, where it is not proper to fast, where it is not licit to abstain from meat? Think what could be more wretched than such things even in these times.[23]

Though scholars have frequently cited the importance of liberty or freedom in his life, Erasmus carefully qualified and centered it around those practices which were in keeping with his clerical status. Thus as late as 1527 he pursued a priestly life by offering prayers, saying Mass,

---

[21] Leo X to Andrea Ammonio (26 January 1517), *CWE*, 4:191. In the words of *The Imitation of Christ:* "I am He who teaches all the people to despise earthly things, to loathe things that are present, to seek and savor eternal things, to flee honors. . . . See Kempis, *Imitation of Christ*, ed. Gardiner, 3, 43, 166.

[22] Erasmus to Servatius Roger (8 July 1514), CWE, 2:295. Thomas à Kempis also cautioned his readers to "Keep company with the humble and the simple in heart, who are devout and of good deportment, and treat with them of things that may edify and strengthen your soul." See Kempis, *Imitation of Christ*, ed. Gardiner, 1.8.39.

[23] Erasmus to an unnamed monk (15 October 1527), *Allen*, 7:200.

fasting, and abstaining from meat. For him pious practices had to involve the whole person, not just the mind.[24] Continuing his advice to the monk referred to above, he reminded the reader:

> May I die if I should not prefer to dwell with you there than to be the highest bishop in the palace of the Emperor, provided that this poor weak body of mine had strength to live there. . . . If with all your heart you will despise the false attractions of this world; if you will give yourself to sacred literature and to mediating on the heavenly life, believe me, you will find more than abundant solace, and this little weariness of which you speak will vanish like smoke.[25]

It seems certain that by 1527 Erasmus had learned to reject the attractions of this life and had given himself wholly to the cause of sacred literature and to mediating on the heavenly life. The solace that he was offering the monk was already his. He had earned it from a life of withdrawal from the earthly realm and from a life of commitment to spiritual pursuits.

Separated from the monastery at Steyn, Erasmus was forced to seek patronage from a variety of sources. Indeed, subsistence was an almost constant preoccupation with him at the start of his public career. In a gentle admonition Colet cautioned him in 1511 not to be so active in pursuing patrons but to rely more on Divine Providence; and at the same time he observed how much Erasmus hated to act as a beggar for himself.[26] In time Erasmus became far more selective. Though numerous offers of patronage came to him from France, Germany, and Rome, he refused most of them.[27]

In declining the offer to come to the French court, Erasmus remarked that the generous opinion that others had of him laid upon him the burden of a reputation that he could not accept without gross egoism nor

---

[24] One finds a similar attitude in *The Imitation of Christ:* "The religious habit and the tonsure help little; the changing of one's life and the mortifying of passions make a person perfectly and truly religious." See Kempis, *Imitation of Christ*, ed. Gardiner, 1. 17. 50.

[25] Erasmus to an unnamed monk (15 October 1527), *Allen*, 7:200–201.

[26] John Colet to Erasmus (end of September 1511), *CWE*, 2:175.

[27] In declining the offer of a cardinalate from Paul III, Erasmus wrote to Latomus that "I have a friend in Rome who is particularly active in the business: in vain have I warned him more than once by letter that I want no cures or pensions, that I am a man who lives from day to day, and every day expecting death. . . ." Erasmus to Bartholomew Latomus (24 August 1535) in Johan Huizinga, *Erasmus and the Age of Reformation*, trans. Barbara Flower (New York, 1957), 253. Earlier, in 1516, Erasmus had declined a bishopric. See *CWE*, 4:95–96.

live up to without being a different sort of man.²⁸ Erasmus chose not to mix court politics with his pursuit of holiness. Near the end of his life he observed that "the glory [of an immortal name] moves me not at all, I am not anxious over the applause of posterity. My one concern and desire is to depart hence with Christ's favour."²⁹

Following the appearance of *The Praise of Folly* in 1509, which was soon criticized by Maarten van Dorp and other theologians at the University of Louvain, Erasmus confessed that he regretted its attacks on theologians and its apparent mockery of sacred subjects:

> I am almost sorry myself that I published my *Folly*. That small book has earned me not a little reputation, or notoriety if you prefer; but I have no use for reputation coupled with ill will. . . . In all the books I have published my sole object has always been to do something useful by my exertions or, if that should not be possible, at least to do no harm.³⁰

Erasmus also reminded Dorp that he had never singled out any theologians by name and that his discussion of faults did not imply a criticism of any particular individual. The real intent of his work was to offer guidance, to show men how to become better. He also sought comfort from the fact that not all theologians reacted so unkindly to his *Folly*:

> how many theologians I could list for you, renowned for holiness of life, eminent for scholarship, and of the highest station, some of them even bishops, who have never given me such a warm welcome as since the publication of my *Folly*, and who think more highly of that small book than I do myself.³¹

Nor was Dorp Erasmus' only critic. Guillaume Budé complained to Erasmus that he wasted his talents on trivial school boys. Erasmus responded with reference to his program of reform:

> Again, the risk you display before me that by publishing so many minor works I shall get myself a bad name does not move me in the least. Whatever in the way

---

²⁸ Erasmus to Etienne Poncher (14 February 1517), *CWE*, 4:219.

²⁹ Erasmus to Bartholomew Latomus (24 August 1535) in Huizinga, *Erasmus and the Age of Reformation*, 252.

³⁰ Erasmus to Maarten van Dorp (end of May 1515), *CWE*, 3:112. Beatus Rhenanus expressed the same point: "I do remember him often saying while he was alive that if he had foreseen such an age arising as ours, he would not have written many things or would not have written them in the way he did." See John C. Olin, ed., *Christian Humanism and the Reformation* (New York, 1965), 49.

³¹ Erasmus to Maarten van Dorp (end of May 1515), *CWE*, 3:123.

of notoriety rather than glory has been won for me by my publications, I would peacefully and willingly dispense with, if I could. . . . For my own part, these superficial subjects are the field in which it suits me to philosophize, and I see in them less frivolity and somewhat more profit than in those themes which the professional philosophers find so pre-eminent. Finally the man whose sole object is not to advertise himself but to help other people, asks not so much Is it grand, my chosen field? as Is it useful?[32]

Erasmus' defense of his reputation was based not on self-conceit but on a desire to protect his reform program, which was directed to every Christian, from schoolboy to king.[33] He was convinced that both the minds and hearts of the young could be soundly molded and directed by good teachers. The wise mentor could teach the intellect and will to know and choose good and the spirit to savor virtue and love God. Of the prince, Erasmus insisted that he be reared "in such a manner that from the example of his life all the others (nobles and commoners alike) may take this model of frugality and temperance."[34]

Later on, Luther launched his barbs at the unyielding reformer. Responding to Luther's 1526 letter of apology, in which he begged Erasmus not to take the abuse that had been piled on his head too seriously (Luther had earlier described him as "Christ's most bitter enemy"), Erasmus retorted:

I am not so simple as to be appeased by one or two pleasantries or soothed by flattery after receiving so many more than mortal wounds. . . . it is *this* that distresses me, and all the best spirits with me, that with that arrogant, impudent, seditious temperament of yours you are shattering the whole globe in ruinous discord.[35]

He insisted on civility and refused to be drawn into an untenable position of friendship when Luther's reform produced only confusion in Christendom. Erasmus saw Christ as the prince of peace and not as the advocate of violent change.[36]

---

[32] Erasmus to Guillaume Budé (28 October 1516), *CWE*, 4:104.

[33] Erasmus to Paul Volz (August 1518) in Olin, *Christian Humanism and the Reformation*, 112.

[34] Erasmus, *The Education of a Christian Prince*, trans. and ed. Lester K. Born (New York, 1936), 210.

[35] Erasmus to Martin Luther (11 April 1526) in Huizinga, *Erasmus and the Age of Reformation*, 240–41.

[36] In a letter to Archbishop Albert of Brandenburg (1519), Erasmus insisted that he had

In his *philosophia Christi,* Erasmus stressed the importance of interior spirituality rather than external observances; of the ways of the spirit rather than the letter of the law. Writing to Servatius Roger, he observed:

> We make Christianity and piety consist in place, dress, diet, and a number of petty observances. . . . How much more consonant with Christ's teaching it would be to regard the entire Christian world as a single household, a single monastery as it were, and to think of all men as one's fellow-canons and brethren, to regard the sacrament of baptism as the supreme religious obligation, and to consider not where one lives, but how one lives.[37]

Erasmus found fault with the monastic life at Steyn because it placed so much emphasis on ritual and form that it ignored the interior spirituality of the canon. It was the quality of one's interior life that truly mattered to Christ, and Erasmus refers to it over and over again.[38]

Erasmus composed his blueprint for holiness in 1501 as the result of a request from a woman who sought help for her wayward husband. He made it very clear at the outset that he wished "to describe a way of life, not a method of learning."[39] Titled *The Handbook of the Militant Christian,* it served as "a shortcut . . . to Christ." It was designed for all Christians. Erasmus was anxious to recall theology, which had fallen into squabbling, to its original simplicity. In the spirit of the *Devotio Moderna,* Erasmus wished to interiorize religion and to bridge the gap between God and man that had been ossified by ritual and structure. Indeed, as he himself stated, he proposed a "path to perfection."

Since Erasmus viewed life on earth as "a type of continual warfare," he armed the Christian who sought true spirituality with the weapons of war. Prayer and knowledge were the two major ones:

---

never been involved in Luther's reforming efforts; that he preferred to have Luther's criticisms of the church corrected but not crushed. He himself stated that "I shall never knowingly teach error or cause confusion; I would endure anything sooner than provoke dissension." Erasmus to Albert of Brandenburg (1519) in Olin, *Christian Humanism and the Reformation,* 145.

[37] Erasmus to Servatius Roger (8 July 1514), *CWE,* 2:296–97.

[38] Kempis made a similar observation about withdrawal: ". . . whoever intends to come to an inward fixing of his heart upon God and to have the grace of devotion must with our Saviour Christ withdraw from the world." Kempis, *Imitation of Christ,* ed. Gardiner, 1. 20. 56.

[39] Erasmus, *The Handbook of the Militant Christian,* trans. and ed. John P. Dolan in *The Essential Erasmus* (New York, 1964), 38–9. Erasmus also insisted that "It is my plan to propose a number of fundamental rules or norms that will guide us through the labyrinth of this world into the pure light of the spiritual life." Ibid., 51. 2.

Pure prayer directed to heaven is able to subdue passion, for it is, as it were, a citadel inaccessible to the enemy. Knowledge, or learning, fortifies the mind with salutary precepts and keeps virtue ever before us.[40]

Armed with these weapons, the Christian is prepared for battle with the devil, the world, and himself: "Christ alone grants that peace that the world cannot give. There is but one way to attain it; we must wage war with ourselves. We must contend fiercely with our vices."[41]

Erasmus also insisted that the true Christian must dedicate himself entirely to the study of Scripture. But in order to understand these writings, he was advised to read the classics, where there are countless examples of right living:

So pick out from pagan books whatever is best. In studying the ancients follow the example of the bee flying about the garden. Like the bee, suck out only what is wholesome and sweet; reject what is useless and poisonous.[42]

The only purpose of the classics was to aid the Christian in his search for Christ. By imitating examples of "right living," the militant Christian would be led to the imitation of Christ Himself. Closer contact with Christ was the object of one's reading.

Moreover, Erasmus recommended the Church Fathers, whose deep piety would help the reader to penetrate some difficult passages in sacred Scripture. What was needed for religious growth was a spiritual rather than literal understanding of the Scriptures. Too many monks, according to Erasmus, failed to understand the word of God because of its hidden meaning: "They [the Church Fathers] will lead you to an inner penetration of the word of God, to an understanding of the spiritual worth it contains."[43] Once the learner had acquired a true knowledge of Scriptures, Erasmus advocated the imitation of spiritual values.

Though Erasmus warned his reader of the evil inclinations inherent in man, he also argued for the efficacy of reason as a means of restraining vice and redirecting the will toward virtue. He saw man as a tripartite creature, composed of spirit, which has the capacity of making men

---

[40] Ibid., 28, 35.
[41] Ibid., 40.
[42] Ibid., 39.
[43] Ibid., 64. Likewise, Thomas à Kempis praised the works of the Church Fathers: "... do not disdain the parables of the ancient Fathers, for they were not spoken without great cause." Kempis, *Imitation of Christ*, ed. Gardiner, 1. 5. 37.

divine, the flesh, and the soul, which distinguishes men from all other creatures. Of the three parts, Erasmus considered the spirit of man to be the most important:

> It is the spirit that gives us the qualities of religion: obedience, kindness, and mercy. The flesh makes us despisers of God, disobedient, and cruel. The soul, on the other hand, is indifferent, neither good nor bad in itself.[44]

According to Erasmus, it was the spirit in man that produced virtue.[45] Virtues that proceeded entirely from natural inclinations had no merit. It was only when the spirit overcame an evil inclination that one acquired true virtue. It was at this point that Erasmus criticized those Christians who out of self-satisfaction or because they believed it would enhance their reputation presumed that they were practicing virtue when they attended daily Mass or made novenas in honor of one of the saints. Divine service was profitable only when it was entered into in the right spirit. If man attended Mass because he loved God and despised his sins, he was practicing virtue. "Leading a virtuous life is accompanied by a certain discipline that the Holy Spirit breathes into those who sincerely aim at godliness."[46]

For entering into "the pure light of the spiritual life," Erasmus proposed a number of fundamental rules or norms that would guide the reader through the labyrinth of this world. These included studying the Scriptures, pursuing the virtue of perseverance, and making Christ the goal of one's life. Erasmus was convinced that there was not a single item in Holy Scripture that did not pertain to man's salvation. Moreover, he was equally convinced that the allurements of this world (whether family, riches, health, or reputation) must not deter one from his goal. Man must "realize that in Christ is the fulfillment of all things."[47]

Erasmus was seen by many of his contemporaries as the supreme teacher and by a few as the "lodestar of all humane studies."[48] As is

---

[44] Erasmus, *The Handbook of the Militant Christian*, ed. Dolan, 50.

[45] For a fuller discussion of this theme, see Georges Chantraine, *"Mystere" et "Philosophie du Christ" selon Erasme* (Gembloux, 1971).

[46] Erasmus, *The Handbook of the Militant Christian*, ed. Dolan, 52.

[47] Ibid., 54. *The Imitation of Christ* offers a similar reflection: "How great a vanity it also is to desire a long life and to care little for a good life; to heed things of the present and not to provide for things that are to come; to love things that will shortly pass away and not to haste to where joy is everlasting." See Kempis, *Imitation of Christ*, ed. Gardiner, 1. 1. 32.

[48] Ludwig Baer to Erasmus (12 November 1516), *CWE*, 4:127.

apparent from his prefatory letter in the *Novum Instrumentum* of 1516, he regarded himself as a teacher of true Christianity. In making the Bible available to the public in a purer form, he wished to draw all men to a more pious life in Christ.

Much of the spirit of the *Imitatio Christi* appeared in the *Enchiridion*. In one passage Erasmus insisted not only that his readers should reject the things of this world but also that they "must be crucified to this world."[49] His outline of a spiritual life was designed for all men, whether lay or religious or cleric: "If you are in the world, you are not in Christ."[50] For those of little fortitude, Erasmus reasoned:

> Even though all of us cannot reach this goal, cannot attain the perfect imitation of the Head, all of us must aim for this goal with all our efforts.[51]

Like the *Imitatio Christi*, the *philosophia Christi* appealed to all Christians and offered a formula for spiritual perfection that was compatible with a career in the world.

Although Erasmus drew upon the ideas of classical philosophers, he christianized their wisdom and made it conform to his *philosophia Christi*. Transforming a Stoic model into something compatible, for example, Erasmus categorized the principal goals in life and placed them under three headings: (1) actions that are intrinsically evil; (2) actions that are indifferent, morally speaking, such as health, beauty, learning; and (3) Christ-centered actions. No doubt speaking of himself, Erasmus cautioned:

> If you are interested in learning, certainly this is a fine quality, provided you turn your knowledge to Christ. If, on the other hand, you love letters only for the sake of knowledge, you have not gone far enough. . . . Let your study bring you to a clearer perception of Christ so that your love for Him will increase and you will in turn be able to communicate this knowledge of Him to others. You

---

[49] Erasmus, *The Handbook of the Militant Christian*, ed. Dolan, 55. Kempis reinforced the same theme: "My son, it is profitable to you to be ignorant in many things and to think of yourself as dead to the world and one to whom all the world is crucified." Kempis, *Imitation of Christ*, ed. Gardiner, 2. 44. 167.

[50] Erasmus, *The Handbook of the Militant Christian*, ed. Dolan, 55. The *Imitation of Christ* underscored a similar message: "Study, therefore, to withdraw the love of your soul from all things that are visible, and to turn to things that are invisible." Kempis, *Imitation of Christ*, 1. 1. 32.

[51] Erasmus, *The Handbook of the Militant Christian*, ed. Dolan, 55.

can do this rather easily if you accustom yourself to admiring nothing that is outside yourself, namely things that do not pertain to the inner man.[52]

Despite this quotation, Edmund Colledge has insisted that Erasmus was poles apart from any of the founders or leaders of the *Devotio Moderna*. He turned for support to a quotation from Lubbert ten Busch, a foundation member and procurator of the house at Deventer, on the intellectual life. It is well worth requoting here because of the similarity to the *Enchiridion* in language and objective:

> You should never study anything which does not nourish the soul, for the fruits of study are the strengthening of the soul and the acquisition of virtues. To study for the sake of knowledge, in order to teach others, or for any other end than the sake of the soul does not strengthen but sickens it.[53]

Erasmus' goal in life was the perfection of the "inner man." He came to this realization in the monastery at Steyn. Here he decided that henceforth he would pursue only studies that would lead to greater piety. He rejected the study of literature for its own sake and aimed all of his scholarship at bridging the gap between God and man:

> There are certain detractors who think that true religion has nothing to do with good literature. Let me say that I have been studying the classics since my youth. For me a knowledge of Greek and Latin required many a long, hard hour. I did not undertake this merely for the sake of empty fame or for the childish pleasures of the mind. My sole purpose was that, knowing these writings, I might the better adorn the Lord's temple with literary richness.[54]

The pursuit of the classics and the study of Scripture and the Church Fathers were useful because they gave man a better understanding of Christ and his message to mankind. Erasmus' spiritual awakening shaped his program of reform and gave special direction to his life. Aware of his

---

[52] Ibid., 58. In the *Imitatio Christi,* Kempis cautioned the reader against misguided learning: "Well-ordered learning is not to be belittled, for it is good and comes from God, but a clean conscience and a virtuous life are much better and more to be desired. . . . On the day of judgment we will not be asked what we have read, but what we have done; not how well we have discoursed, but how religiously we have lived." Kempis, *Imitation of Christ,* ed. Gardiner, 1. 3. 35.

[53] Edmund Colledge, "Erasmus, the Brethren of the Common Life, and the Devotio Moderna," *Erasmus in English* (1975), 7:3.

[54] Erasmus, *The Handbook of the Militant Christian,* ed. Dolan, 93.

own infirmities, he exuded confidence in his quest toward greater perfection:

> Our determination to imitate Christ should be of such a nature that we have no time for these [worldly] matters . . . I suffer from infirmity and weakness, but with St. Paul I show forth a more excellent way.[55]

Erasmus' voluminous correspondence is full of examples of his frailties and weaknesses. They are visible testimony to the fact that he was born with many afflictions. But the important thing to keep in mind is that Erasmus sought to overcome these limitations spiritually and to show others that human failings are not a deterrent to sanctity but serve as incentives or spurs: "A pious man who overcomes great sin is all the more pious. What makes a man evil is not that he sins but that he *loves* his sin."[56]

According to Erasmus the figure of Christ was the "only complete example of perfect piety." For this reason he urged all mankind to imitate Him. At the same time he called forth the examples of Christ's saints and advised his readers to "emulate them in such a way that each of them prompts you to eradicate one or another vice, and practice their particular virtues."[57] It was the practice of virtue that constituted the imitation of Christ and the imitation of His saints.

Erasmus also insisted that external acts of penance ("manual works") have little or no value unless they are accompanied by internal piety. God as a Spirit "is appeased by spiritual sacrifices." To the religious, Erasmus directed this advice:

> Of what advantage to you is a body covered by a religious habit if that same body possesses a mind that is worldly?[58]

The true Christian lives inwardly. He rejects the attractions of this world so that he can concentrate his efforts on knowing and pleasing God:

---

[55] Ibid., 59, 61.

[56] Ibid., 80. Kempis offered a similar reflection on temptation: "And He [God] brings about occasions for such battles so that we may overcome and win the victory, and in the end have the greater reward." Kempis, *Imitation of Christ*, ed. Gardiner, 1. 11. 42–43.

[57] Erasmus, *The Handbook of the Militant Christian*, ed. Dolan, 66.

[58] Ibid., 69. *The Imitation of Christ* made the same point: "If we place the end and perfection of our religion in outward observances, our devotion will soon be ended." Kempis, *Imitation of Christ*, ed. Gardiner, 1. 11. 43.

"Blessed are they who hear the word of God internally. Happy are they to whom the Lord speaks inwardly, for their salvation is assured."[59]

As early as 1503 Erasmus had committed himself to an internal life of holiness. He would reject the physical attractions of this world in order to love God more fully. At the same time, he vowed to communicate his own concept of greater perfection by composing works specifically for this purpose, works that were in harmony with the spirit of the *Devotio Moderna*. It was the silence of God that Erasmus sought:

> if you make a sincere effort to escape from the chains of blindness with which the love of sensible things has bound you, He will come to you, and you, no longer chained to the things of earth, will be enveloped in the silence of God.[60]

This thought is repeated in the *Imitatio Christi:* "My son, says our Lord. . . . My words are spiritual and cannot be comprehended fully by man's intelligence. Neither are they to be adapted or applied according to the vain pleasure of the hearer, but are to be heard in silence, with great humility and reverence. . . ."[61]

Erasmus chose as his friends men of singular piety and goodness. There is a long list of men of personal holiness who were regular correspondents of his. This fact is not coincidental. Erasmus corresponded with men of sanctity because he wanted to make himself better:

> If people do not think along lines that would make you better, withdraw yourself as much as possible from human companionship and take for companions Christ and His prophets and Apostles.[62]

It was the evil in the world that led Erasmus to speak out so harshly against war in his *Complaint of Peace* and *Dulce bellum inexpertis*.[63] He hated war precisely because it violated Christ's injunction to love one another. But the "war" of which he spoke was not confined to the battlefield. It took place in cities, courts of kings, halls of justice, universities, religious houses, and private homes. Such conflict between human beings was just as un-Christian as military combat because it rejected the example of Christ:

---

[59] Erasmus, *The Handbook of the Militant Christian*, ed. Dolan, 70.

[60] Ibid., 71.

[61] Kempis, *Imitation of Christ*, ed. Gardiner, 3. 3. 105.

[62] Erasmus, *The Handbook of the Militant Christian*, ed. Dolan, 92–93.

[63] See also Erasmus' eloquent expression of abhorrence of war in his letter to Antoon van Bergen (14 March 1514), *CWE*, 2:280.

Consider the whole of his [Christ's] life; what is it, but one lesson of concord and mutual love? What do his precepts, what do his parables inculcate, but peace and charity?[64]

For Erasmus the distinguishing mark of a Christian was charity. Christ will be able to recognize his followers only if they practice charity. Neither religious habits, nor harsh diets, nor special prayers count for anything if one lacks charity.[65]

Erasmus did not confine his blueprint for holiness to the *Enchiridion* but advocated it in all of his works. Take, for example, the following passage from *The Praise of Folly,* which is generally regarded by its critics as a work of satire:

what is this future life of heaven toward which the pious aspire with so much endeavor? It consists in the first place of an absorption of the body by the spirit, accomplished the more easily as the spirit is now in its own kingdom and is furthermore by reason of its purgations during life adapted to this transformation. Then the spirit will be in a marvelous manner absorbed by the Highest Mind, more powerful than the infinity of its parts. In this way the entire man will be outside of himself, and his happiness will be due to no other fact than that, so placed, he will share in the Highest Good which draws all to Itself. . . . In this mortal life there is, for the pious, a meditation and foreshadowing of this. . . . Even though this is but an infinitesimal drop by comparison with the flowing fountain of eternal happiness, yet it surpasses all corporeal pleasures. . . . And this is why those who are permitted to have a foretaste of this, and they are very few, suffer from something akin to madness. . . . When they return to themselves, they admit they have no knowledge of where they have been, whether in the body or out of it, whether waking or sleeping. They have no memory of what they heard or saw or did. . . . They regret this return to their senses and prefer nothing more than going back to this state of madness. And this is but a small sampling of the future happiness. It seems that I have forgotten myself and transgressed the bounds.[66]

---

[64] Erasmus, *The Complaint of Peace. Translated from the Querela Pacis (A.D. 1521)* (La Salle, Illinois, 1974), 16.

[65] Kempis made a similar reference to charity: "The outward deed without charity is little to be praised, but whatever is done from charity, even if it be ever so little and worthless in the sight of the world, is very profitable before God." Kempis, *Imitation of Christ,* ed. Gardiner, 1. 15. 48.

[66] Erasmus, *The Praise of Folly,* trans. and ed. John P. Dolan in *The Essential Erasmus* (New York, 1964), pp. 172–73. For a fuller discussion of the *philosophia Christi* in the works of Erasmus, see R. L. DeMolen, "*Opera Omnia Desiderii Erasmi:* Rungs on the Ladder to the

Without question Erasmus was referring to himself in the concluding lines of this quotation. It seems certain that in the guise of Folly the real Erasmus speaks of his own spiritual life with compelling force. Erasmus had by this time experienced an intimate union with God through contemplation.

Moreover, in *The Education of a Christian Prince,* Erasmus repeated his program of reform: "Who is truly Christian? Not he who is baptized or anointed, or who attends church. It is rather the man who has embraced Christ in the innermost feelings of his heart, and who emulates Him by pious deeds."[67]

Some two-and-one-half years before his death in July of 1536, Erasmus composed a treatise at the request of Thomas Boleyn, Viscount Rochford and the Earl of Wiltshire and Ormonde, "teaching how a man ought to prepare himself for death."[68] Erasmus was at the time living in Freiburg. The thought of death was a recurring theme throughout his life. His poor health occasioned much concern. In many ways the specter of death conditioned Erasmus' life.[69]

In teaching others how to die in the arms of Christ, Erasmus reinforced the idea that he actively followed a Christ-centered life of detachment. As he himself observed:

For if with our whole heart we believe the things that God has promised us by his son Jesus, all the delectations of this world should soon be little regarded, and death which sets us ever unto them with a painful (but yet a short) passage, should be less feared.[70]

In a subsequent passage Erasmus carefully clarified the point that "the delectations of this world" included not only material riches, but "honors, pleasures, a wife, children, kinsfolk, friends, beauty, youth, good health." The sincere Christian had to place such earthly goods in

Philosophia Christi," in *Essays on the Works of Erasmus,* ed. R. L. DeMolen (New Haven, Conn., 1978), 1–50.

[67] Erasmus, *The Education of a Christian Prince,* trans. and ed. Lester K. Born (New York, 1965), 153.

[68] Erasmus, *Preparation to Death,* anonymous trans. (London, 1538), [A$_2$]. The English translation has been modernized by this writer both here and elsewhere in the essay.

[69] Roland H. Bainton, *Erasmus of Christendom* (New York, 1967), 17–18, 87.

[70] Erasmus, *Preparation to Death,* [A$_4$].

perspective and recognize the point that the "more fervently we love a thing, the more painfully we are plucked from it."[71] In rejecting the allurements of physical pleasure for all Christians living in the world, Erasmus was in effect opening up the cloistered cells and bringing into the world what were then regarded as characteristics of the religious life. In calling all men to follow Him, it was assumed that Christ was asking Christians to leave the world and to join a religious community. For Erasmus it was possible to imitate Christ and remain in the world.

To ease the transition from the life of sensual pleasure to that of spiritual growth, Erasmus proposed an interior life of contemplation—an emphasis on things eternal and heavenly rather than temporal and earthly. Erasmus viewed life on earth as "a dark and painful prison."[72] Human life, he suggested, was a series of unpleasant experiences: Birth, infancy, childhood, youth, and old age were painful reminders of man's progression from cradle to grave:

> I stand in doubt whether a man can find any one person so happily born that if God would grant unto him to begin and come up again by the same steps . . . would take this offer.[73]

The unpleasantnesses that he associated with life came not only from without but also from within.[74] As a corruptible entity, man's body habitually encumbered the soul while his earthly habitation depressed the mind. To place life in proper perspective, Erasmus urged his reader to "contemplate and praise his Maker, Redeemer, and Governor."[75] Though physically tied to earth, men of such disposition will learn how to bridge two worlds and enjoy an intimate conversation with God in heaven.

Erasmus' meditation on death had as one of its objects to enrich and extend the faith of the reader. The more frequently the Christian contemplated the life and death of Christ, the easier would be his

---

[71] Ibid. Thomas à Kempis would have agreed with Erasmus: see Kempis, *Imitation of Christ*, ed. Gardiner, 1. 11. 43.

[72] Erasmus, *Preparation to Death*, [A$_6$].

[73] Ibid., [B$_6^v$].

[74] Kempis underscored the same observation: "And truly, to live in this world is but misery, and the more spiritual a man would be the more painful is it to him to live, and the more plainly he feels the defects of man's corruption." Kempis, *Imitation of Christ*, ed. Gardiner, 1. 22. 61.

[75] Erasmus, *Preparation to Death*, [A$_6^v$].

preparation for death. Faith, together with the virtues of hope and charity, would arm the Christian soldier for battle with the devil and the forces of evil.

Not only did Erasmus counsel frequent meditation on the life of Christ, but he urged his reader to examine his conscience daily and to confess his sins to a priest three or four times a year. Consistency in facing one's shortcomings and faults throughout life would bring much tranquillity to that life and alleviate the fear of a final confession, which was often accompanied by scrupulosity.

After one had confessed his sins to a priest, Erasmus commended to him the frequent reception of the Eucharist, which leads one to spiritual growth: "This shall be if we, our conscience being purged from all affection of sinning, often receive the mystical bread and drink of the mystical cup."[76] According to Erasmus, participation in Communion had two effects: It drew the participant into closer contact with Jesus Christ, the head of the church, and with the other members of the Christian community.[77] It is the participation itself in the mystical body of Christ that conveys goodness to the recipients of Communion.

Erasmus stressed again and again the importance of the individual Christian's relationship to the mystical body of Christ. It should take the form of a lifelong spiritual exercise. In referring to a common practice of requesting prayers for the sick at one of the monasteries of the Carthusians or Friars Observants, he urged the reader to dwell instead on one's spiritual relationship with the whole Christian church and to recognize the enormously beneficial results that can come when an entire church asks God to help a sick man who is approaching the end of life: "The church cannot be poor which is joined to so rich a head . . . nor the member cannot be destitute which is sustained of so many thousands of saints."[78] According to James K. McConica, Erasmus emphasized the active role of the Holy Spirit in maintaining unity—consensus—among Christians as a community of believers. Though Erasmus saw good in

---

[76] Ibid., [D$_3^v$]. It is interesting to note that the entire fourth book of *The Imitation of Christ* commends the reception of communion, especially chap. three, titled "That it is very profitable to receive Communion often." See Kempis, *Imitation of Christ*, ed. Gardiner, 4. 3. 209.

[77] Erasmus, *Preparation to Death*, [D$_4$].

[78] Ibid., [D$_4^v$].

Luther's message of reform, he refrained from joining the cause because of its disruptive effect on the ongoing work of the Holy Spirit.[79]

Erasmus saw all baptized men as incorporated members of the church of Christ. The bond of incorporation was enriched and strengthened by the sacraments of penance and Communion. He also recommended the reading of the Book of Hours, "which parted the history of our Lord's death into certain hours."[80] Since, according to Erasmus, examples have great virtue and strength to move men's minds, the actions preceding Christ's passion and death on the cross should serve as the ideal preparation for death:

> But there shall no example be found more perfect than that which the Lord expressed unto us in Himself. For when that last night approached, against the storm of temptation, which was at hand, he armed his disciples with the food of His most holy Body and Blood, monishing us that so often as we fall unto casualty or disease, which threatens death, forthwith should purge our affections with confession, like as our Lord washed the feet of His disciples, and that done that we take reverently the Body of our Lord, which meat may make our minds strong and unvanquishable against our spiritual enemy. . . . Last of all we must with our Lord all naked ascend upon the cross far from all earthly affections; lift up to the love of the heavenly life that with Saint Paul we may say: "The world is crucified unto me, as I to the world." And there nailed with these nails—faith, hope, charity—we must constantly persevere, fighting valiantly with our enemy the devil, until at last, after we have vanquished him, we may pass into eternal rest through the aid and grace of our Lord Jesus Christ.[81]

The second part of the above passage reveals a side of Erasmus that has been frequently ignored by scholars. Erasmus was more than a humanist or a classical scholar, or even a reformer and theologian. He was an imitator of Christ's life. And as such, he was a man of great interior holiness. It might be useful to draw attention, once again, to his specific language to demonstrate his mystical nature:

> Last of all we must with our Lord all naked ascend upon the cross far from all earthly affections. . . . And there nailed with these nails—faith, hope, charity—we must constantly persevere.[82]

---

[79] See McConica, "Erasmus and the Grammar of Consent," *Scrinium Erasmianum*, ed. Joseph Coppens (Leiden, 1969), 2:77–99.

[80] Erasmus, *Preparation to Death*, [D$_5$].

[81] Ibid., [H$_2$^{v}–H$_4$].

[82] Ibid. Kempis also emphasized the importance of Christ's passion: "And if you flee

If there is one virtue that stands out in the life of Erasmus of Rotterdam, it is that of perseverance to the *philosophia Christi*.

After serving as a priest for thirty-two years, Erasmus composed a treatise on the *Manner and Form of Confession* in 1524. He dedicated it to François Du Moulin. The contents of the tome were based not only on wide reading but on the reflections of an experienced confessor. This may surprise some readers, since many biographers of Erasmus have claimed that he was an inactive priest who enjoyed all the perquisites of the celibate state but shunned saying Mass or performing other priestly duties. But the record speaks for itself. With regard to his role as confessor, Erasmus interjected this personal account:

> For though I do pass over and speak no word, how grievous and how painful a thing it is to a good and well learned priest to spend so much time in hearing the filths and sins of man's life . . . even with the jeopardy of his own integrity, chastity, or health, and to suffer and abide the stinking and unwholesome breaths of them that favor and smell of garlic or which be infected with sickness and disease, namely, seeing that many are diseased and combed with leprosy, which are not yet kept apart, or with the French pocks, which is a spice or kind of leprosy, considering there is no way more sure and undoubted to take infection by than by taking in the breath of the person diseased; so that beside the pain and grief, there is not a little jeopardy also joined thereunto.[83]

Only an experienced confessor could have given us such a detailed account of the hazards of the confessional. And despite the burdens of the confessor, he praised the importance of confession as a means to greater piety.

During the year before this manual on confession was completed, Erasmus suffered from two attacks of gall stones, one in July and the other, more critical, in December. He viewed such rendezvous with death as trial runs for the ultimate meeting with his Maker. As a result of recurring illnesses, Erasmus continually prepared himself for his final end: "I do now diligently and heartily give heed and provide that death may not come upon me, and take me unprepared and unready."[84] One

---

devoutly to the wound in Christ's side, and to the marks of His Passion, you will feel great comfort in every trouble." Kempis, *Imitation of Christ*, ed. Gardiner, 2. 1. 76.

[83] Erasmus, *A Little Treatise of the Manner and Form of Confession*, anonymous translation (London, 1535?), [F$_4^v$–F$_5$]. The English translation has been modernized by this writer both here and elsewhere in the essay.

[84] Ibid., [A$_3^v$].

must conclude from this passage that Erasmus remained always in the state of grace so that he would not necessarily need to make a deathbed confession. Thus as early as October 1518 Erasmus could write to Beatus Rhenanus and declare that he was becoming free of the fear of death and of the desire for physical life.[85]

With regard to the sacramental nature of confession, Erasmus was not certain that it had been instituted by Christ or the apostles and therefore it was not absolutely necessary for salvation. Nevertheless he advocated the frequent use of confession because it had been recommended by the popes and prelates of the church "not without the inspiration of the Holy Spirit."[86] Erasmus himself admitted that when he committed a serious sin he confessed to a priest "according to the most common usual custom of the church."[87]

For Erasmus confession was useful because it taught humility. Pride, on the other hand, obstructed the path to sanctity: ". . . the first degree or step unto godliness shall be a mind utterly misliking itself and submitting itself unto God."[88] Having achieved humility, the penitent was prepared to acquire additional virtues. Erasmus pictured Christ as "that mild Spirit" who, being diametrically opposed to "that proud spirit" in man, cannot communicate love without prior submission on the part of the penitent. In the act of confessing one's sins to another man, the penitent acknowledges his dependence on God and the role of the priest as mediator.

In addition to teaching humility, confession led the penitent away from future error, offered comfort, and disentangled doubtful from real evil: "And this thing is never done in better or more convenient season than in sacramental confession."[89] For Erasmus never doubted that confession was a sacrament. He simply did not have enough evidence from Scripture or the Church Fathers to certify to its institution by Christ, though he stood prepared to be shown otherwise.

Erasmus went on in the treatise to elaborate on seven other beneficial

---

[85] Thomas N. Tentler, "Forgiveness and Consolation in the Religious Thought of Erasmus, *Studies in the Renaissance,* 12 (1966): 110–33.

[86] Erasmus, *Manner and Form of Confession,* [A_6^v].

[87] Ibid.

[88] Ibid., [B_4]. *The Imitation of Christ* offered a similar view on humility: "What avail is it to a man to reason about the high, secret mysteries of the Trinity if he lack humility and so displeases the Holy Trinity?" Kempis, *Imitation of Christ,* ed. Gardiner, 1. 1. 31.

[89] Erasmus, *Manner and Form of Confession,* [D].

results of confession. The third utility concerned ridding the penitent of notions of either rejoicing or despair. Erasmus identified the first group of sinners as those who took special delight in describing every detail of their sin (e.g., "the defiling of a fair and beautiful maiden"), and the second group of sinners as despondents who out of misinformation have despaired of the mercy of God. He cited as an example the fear that nocturnal emissions were in themselves sinful. Criticizing Jean de Gerson for "creating a climate of scrupulosity," Erasmus argued that such emissions were sinful only if they were the result of a "vicious occasion."[90] In the section on the fourth benefit of confession (overcoming scrupulosity), he describes his view of a truly virtuous man:

> A man that is verily virtuous and godly wishes and desires the perfect integrity and cleanness of his body, which he hopes to have in the general resurrection, and therefore he is sorry that his vessel is polluted and defiled with unclean dreams; but it follows not, because it grieves him, and he is sorry for it, that it is therefore straight-away sin. For so good a virtuous man is grieved also, and sorry, that with hunger, with thirst, with sleeping, with fainting or weariness of the body, he is fain to break up the continual fervor of prayer. He is sorry for the rebellious motions of the members against the mind. He sorrows that the flesh does lust against the spirit. But these things are so far off from being sins that they be rather matter and occasion of virtue, if a man does strive against them to the uttermost of his power.[91]

For Erasmus, then, the weaknesses of the body were occasions of virtue. His own frailties of body were prods to virtue and reminders to others that sanctity was not inherited. At the same time, the scrupulous sinner must be taught by the priest how "to love and to fear less," how to distinguish between the occasion of sin and sin itself.

The fifth through the ninth benefits of confession can be condensed below in a single paragraph: sin must be detested and avoided in the future if the penitent expected forgiveness; the shame of having to confess sins was itself beneficial; confession revealed the inner man; the priest in confession prayed that the penitent would receive the grace of the Holy Spirit so that he could resist the devil; and penance restored the individual to fellowship in the mystical Body of Christ. Confession was

---

[90] Ibid., [D₄]. Kempis also warned against scrupulosity: "Sometimes excessive scrupulosity over a sense of devotion or too much doubt about making Confession greatly hinder this holy purpose." Kempis, *Imitation of Christ*, ed. Gardiner, 4. 4. 221.

[91] Erasmus, *Manner and Form of Confession*, [D₆–D₆ᵛ].

a vital part of Erasmus' program of reform because it gave direction to the penitent's quest for Christ.

In drawing a conclusion to the section on the beneficial nature of confession, Erasmus reasoned that "though we do grant that the confession, which is made unto a man is not utterly necessary . . . the contumacy and disobedience against the tradition of the church does both offend and displease God and also does hurt the tranquillity and quietness of the Christian commonwealth. . . . By confession in due form made unto a priest is increased much light and much grace, which lucre and winning no man who is in very deed virtuous and Godly will despise and make light of."[92] Confession was efficacious because it preserved the tranquillity of the mystical body of Christ and promoted virtue. With Luther in mind, Erasmus directed the following comment at Protestant reaction to the sacramental nature of confession: "I see and perceive that the contempt and setting at nought of confession is a special and principal step . . . unto . . . heathen manner of living, whereunto we do see many men nowadays . . . fall again under the false title and name of evangelical liberty."[93] Though Erasmus agreed with Luther that external rites were not essential for salvation, he disagreed with him on the doctrine of free will and predestination. With regard to the latter, Roland H. Bainton has insisted that "Erasmus would rather give up God's absolute power than to make Him no longer amenable to the canons of human reason and the moral sense."[94]

The second part of his treatise on confession identified nine harmful effects of confession, which critics have much discussed, followed by Erasmus' defense of the sacrament itself. The objections to confession may be easily summarized below: (1) the discussing of sin corrupted innocent children; (2) men who were less sinful than others took comfort from their sins; (3) confession caused many priests to become proud and highminded because of the power that had been given to them; (4) evil priests made disciples out of their penitents; (5) confession could jeopardize the reputation of the penitent; (6) the disclosing of sin seemed to teach unshamefacedness; (7) the confession of secret crimes and offenses brought weak persons into desperation; and, at the same time, (8) failed to change their living habits so as to avoid future occasions of

---

[92] Ibid., [E$_3^v$–E$_4$].
[93] Ibid., [E$_5$].
[94] Bainton, *Erasmus of Christendom*, 187–88, 190.

sin; and (9) confession encouraged some to hypocrisy. Despite these many objections to confession, Erasmus restated his defense of the sacrament and promoted its use by every Christian.

As for the qualifications of the confessor, Erasmus wanted a man who was virtuous, learned, mature, and close of tongue: "It was therefore the part and duty of the bishops or else also of the head officers and rulers to choose out such persons as are meet to take this office upon them, both in age, in living, in learning, in trustiness, in wisdom, in mildness. . . ."[95] It is clear from this section of the treatise that Erasmus did not believe that every priest should be authorized to hear confessions, especially inexperienced ones.

Erasmus' view of what constitutes a true confession is worth repeating. He insisted that a superficial confession was no confession at all; that unless a penitent hated all his sins out of "free love toward God," he was wasting his time and that of the priest. The power to overcome sins comes not from the penitent but from God alone in the form of grace. Furthermore, man must learn how to avoid sin in the future by changing his habits, with God's help, in the present.

Having a practical bent, Erasmus advised the businessman, who might be busy, to examine his conscience at least once a week (rather than once a day), followed closely by confession to an authorized priest, one approved by a bishop or pope. For the priest who is obliged to fast before saying Mass, he proposed common sense. He looked upon the taking of medicine, for example, as a means to fight illness rather than as an infraction of the midnight fast.

Erasmus also insisted that the form of confession should be as simple as possible. Brevity should characterize all confessions. At the same time he cautioned: "And yet venial sins are not to be made light of, especially in the examining and amending of our life. For they, if they be neglected and not taken heed of, do bring men unto greater and more weighty offenses."[96]

Erasmus was especially critical of persons who memorized a confessional formula, thereby accusing themselves of sins of which they were not guilty. Confession must be looked upon as a remedy for sinners, as a specific remedy for the particular sins of the individual, and as a bridge between God and man. Too many people, Erasmus feared, offered too

---

[95] Erasmus, *Manner and Form of Confession*, [G_4^v–G_5].
[96] Ibid., [H_7].

many prayers to the Virgin Mary instead of praying directly to Christ. What began as a simple evening anthem had mushroomed into Mariolatry. Instead of concentrating so heavily on prayers to Mary, Erasmus advised the curate to teach his flock knowledge of the Creed and the commandments of God. This could be reinforced by a prayerbook composed in the vernacular.

Erasmus also instructed his reader on how to increase faith, which he defined as the belief in Scriptures. Faith, for Erasmus, could be "quickened with . . . exercises," such as the study of Scripture, communication with good and virtuous men, holy and devout meditations and thoughts. In the end Erasmus noted that faith and charity were the two rules by which all acts were to be tried and examined.[97]

Erasmus concluded his treatise on confession by recommending various forms of penance for the individual transgressor. Instead of rote prayers, he urged the confessor to prescribe the reading of works by such Church Fathers as Origen, Tertullian, Cyprian, and Chrysostom. For those of tender age he recommended fastings, watchings, or other physical labors. For the wealthy he suggested acts that would succor and relieve the needs of his less fortunate neighbors. At the same time, Erasmus insisted that those penances which involved pain must be coupled with ones that involved charity. As Thomas N. Tentler has pointed out: ". . . the purpose of confession for Erasmus is clear: if it is to be worthwhile it must increase virtue."

In order to increase the piety of a community of Benedictine nuns at Cologne, Erasmus wrote the *Comparison of a Virgin and a Martyr* in 1523. It was offered as a response to gifts of sweets that the nuns had sent him on previous occasions. The nuns had been made aware of Erasmus' reputation for holiness and asked for his advice on how to serve God more faithfully. Erasmus applauded their desire for spiritual reading but described himself as an unsatisfactory source. His image of himself was at odds with the view of these religious women.[98]

---

[97] Ibid., [I₇]

[98] Erasmus' own modesty is reflected in his works: "For it is certain, and many things go to prove it, that they [the Dutch] are not wanting in intellectual power, though I myself have it only in a modest degree, not to say scanty—like the rest of my endowments." Erasmus, "Auris Batava" (1508) in Margaret Mann Phillips, *The Adages of Erasmus: A Study with Translations* (Cambridge: University Press, 1964), 211. *The Imitation of Christ* also stressed the importance of humility: "How much ought I, in my heart, despise myself,

The main theme of the *Comparison of a Virgin and a Martyr* was that the life of a martyr and a virgin was pleasing to Christ, who was himself both martyr and virgin. Comparing the two, Erasmus placed the life of a virgin above that of a martyr because virgins "daily conduct a constant warfare of the spirit against worldly enticements." Indeed, Erasmus argued that with Christ's help, the dedicated virgin exceeded human power and assumed a dignity comparable to that of angels.

One is tempted at this point to suggest that Erasmus believed that his own life of virginity was a gift of God and that he took deliberate steps to maintain it throughout his many years as a priest. In advising the nuns at Cologne how to become closer to God, he drew from his own experiences as a religious living in the world. He enjoined the nuns to commit themselves totally to Christ, to be chaste in mind as well as deed, to avoid ornate and costly apparel. Religious virgins must reject the things of this world and seek a life of prayer, fasting, spiritual reading, and pious works, such as helping the poor and needy.

But Erasmus was ever the realist. He drew numerous excerpts from the Bible to emphasize the joy that one will find in following Christ and contrasted them with examples of suffering and humiliation that were also to be found in the life of a true disciple of Christ.

Erasmus ceased to be a member of the Augustinian Canons Regular, who were resident at Steyn, when he received a dispensation from Leo X in 1517, but he was never granted dispensation from the rule or obligations of the order itself. As such, Erasmus spent his entire priestly life as a member of the Canons Regular of St. Augustine. He lived outside the houses of the order and wore a modified habit, but he was in deed as well as in spirit a canon regular.[99]

In offering the nuns at Cologne a blueprint of holiness, Erasmus was keenly aware of the path that his own religious life had taken since his ordination in 1492. Just as he advised these Benedictine nuns to reject riches, honors, pleasures, and a long life, so he himself had rejected such worldly attractions. He went as far as to identify virginity with the true

---

even though I am considered ever so holy and good in the sight of the world. . . ." Kempis, *Imitation of Christ*, ed. Gardiner, 3. 14. 125.

[99] For a discussion of Erasmus' commitment to the Canons Regular, see R. L. DeMolen, "Erasmus' Commitment to the Canons Regular of St. Augustine," *Renaissance Quarterly*, 26 (1973): 437–43.

Catholic faith: "Whosoever swerves from the true Faith Catholic, his virginity is defiled."[100]

But Erasmus advised the nuns at Cologne to go farther than just the rejection of earthly pleasures and urged them to "mortify and flee the flesh." He believed that the religious life required such positive action as physical mortification of the body. The lean, gaunt figure of Erasmus in the paintings of Dürer, Holbein, and Metsys reflects this attitude toward mortification. Is it any wonder that Erasmus would exclaim: "I say gladly depart out of this wretched body."[101]

Having rejected the ornate habit of the Canons Regular of St. Augustine, Erasmus chose the simple dress of a parish priest. He continually insisted that "He [Christ] loves a pure spirit, a clean soul, and a well painted mind" rather than the richly arrayed.[102] In his contrast of the apparel of a woman of the world with that of a bride of Christ, there is a hint in it of his own former dress as a canon regular and his concern for virtue:

> For precious stones she is ornated and decked with virtues; instead of purple she has charity; for gold, wisdom; for feigned colors simpleness of mind; for silks chastity and shamefacedness; for brooches and jewels, soberness and temperance in all her words and deeds. The fair beauty of chastity cannot be defiled with sluttish garments.[103]

Writing to Thomas Linacre in the summer of 1506, Erasmus shared with the London physician the widespread rumor that he had succumbed to the plague. He noted: "I now have a foretaste, while I am still alive, of what those who survive me will say about me when I am dead!"[104] Since thirty years of his life had not yet gone by when these prophetic lines were written, Erasmus knew only a small share of the criticism that would be his later on in life. Yet there was enough of the sting in the air by 1506 to cause Erasmus more than a little discomfort. Bruce E. Mansfield has concluded that "one doubts if in the historiography of the Reformation, not lacking in uncharitable and perverse notions, any

---

[100] Erasmus, *Comparison of a Virgin and a Martyr*, trans. Thomas Paynell (London, 1537); reprinted. Gainesville, Fla.: Scholars' Facsimiles & Reprints, 1970, 29. The English translation has been modernized by this writer both here and elsewhere in the essay.
[101] Ibid., 55.
[102] Ibid., 60.
[103] Ibid., 60–61.
[104] Erasmus to Thomas Linacre (ca. 12 June 1506), *CWE*, 2:117.

figure has suffered more from unsubtle and anachronistic historical thinking, from priggish and 'holier-than-thou' attitudes, from the malice of his enemies and the naïveté of his friends."[105]

Beatus Rhenanus, the first biographer of Erasmus and his personal friend, summed up the last days of the Dutch savant's life with the observation that illness "brought his death with the greatest calm and acceptance as he implored Christ's mercy in his final, oft repeated words."[106] Whether or not Erasmus of Rotterdam actually received the last sacraments on his deathbed remains uncertain. What was important to Erasmus throughout his life and would have been of even greater importance to him in his final hour was that he had lived the life of a Christian to the best of his ability. Having committed himself to Christ after a spiritual awakening at Steyn in 1489, Erasmus took comfort from his lifelong imitation of Christ and from his spiritual link with all Christians in the mystical body of Christ. Surely one can recognize the figure of Erasmus in this passage from the *Imitatio Christi*:

> It is good that we sometimes have griefs and adversities, for they drive a man to behold himself and to see that he is here but as in exile, and to learn thereby that he ought not put his trust in any worldly thing. It also is good that we sometimes suffer contradiction, and that we be thought of by others as evil and wretched and sinful, though we do well and intend well; such things help us to humility, and mightily defend us from vainglory and pride. We take God better to be our judge and witness when we are outwardly despised in the world and the world does not judge well of us. Therefore, a man ought to establish himself so fully in God that, whatever adversity befall him, we will not need to seek any outward comfort.[107]

No more accurate a portrait of Erasmus exists anywhere than this description of a good man by Thomas à Kempis. Erasmus of Rotterdam died on July 12, 1536, misunderstood or despised by Catholics and Protestants alike. True to his commitment to Christ, he had rejected the plaudits of this world so that he could preserve his interior spirituality, and in this way he truly imitated his Master. It was because of his reputation for holiness among a handful of his admirers that a 1537

---

[105] Bruce E. Mansfield, "Erasmus and the Mediating School," *Journal of Religious History*, 4 (1967): 302.

[106] Beatus Rhenanus, "The Life of Erasmus" (1540), in Olin, *Christian Humanism and the Reformation*, 52.

[107] Kempis, *Imitation of Christ*, ed. Gardiner, 1. 12. 43–44.

primer, printed in England, included in script the name of Erasmus for July 12 in its calendar of saints.[108] One can only hope that one day the sanctity of Erasmus of Rotterdam will be acknowledged by the whole Christian church.[109]

---

[108] James K. McConica, *English Humanists and Reformation Politics under Henry VIII and Edward VI* (Oxford, 1965; rev. ed. 1968), 159–60.

[109] For a recent examination of Erasmus' spirituality, see M. A. Screech, *Ecstasy and the Praise of Folly* (London: Duckworth, 1980) and my review of the same in *The Sixteenth Century Journal,* 13 (1982): 113–14.

CHAPTER FOUR

Opera Omnia Desiderii Erasmi: Rungs on the Ladder to the *Philosophia Christi*

Please explain to her [Lady Anna van Borssele] how much greater is the glory she can acquire from me, by my literary works, than from the other theologians in her patronage. They merely deliver humdrum sermons; I am writing books that may last for ever. Their uneducated nonsense finds an audience in perhaps a couple of churches; my books will be read all over the world, in the Latin west and in the Greek east and by every nation.[1]

Erasmus to Jacob Batt, December 1500

THE title Prince of Humanists had not yet been earned by the young Austin canon who penned this letter, and yet the very same priest was abundantly aware of his own intellectual gifts and the power of the printed word.[2] During his lifetime, Erasmus published about one hundred works (if one groups together his various *apologiae* and declamations). His attitude toward these publications was very different from that of Martin Luther, who wished to see his treatises buried after his death. In a letter to a theologian at Louvain, Maarten van Dorp, dated May 1515, Erasmus explained that he wrote his books and treatises in order to serve "some useful purpose": "What I have aimed at in publishing all of my books was to serve some useful purpose through my

---

[1] *The Correspondence of Erasmus,* trans. R. A. B. Mynors and D. F. S. Thomson (Toronto, 1974), 1:301–02. Hereafter cited as *CWE.*

[2] There are a number of good biographies of Erasmus. For three of the best, see Roland H. Bainton, *Erasmus of Christendom* (New York, 1969); Johan Huizinga, *Erasmus and the Age of Reformation,* trans. F. Hopman (New York, 1924, etc.); and Margaret Mann Phillips, *Erasmus and the Northern Renaissance* (London, 1949, and New York, 1950, etc.). The reader should also consult two recent collections of interpretive essays: *Erasmus,* ed. T. A. Dorey (London, 1970), and *Erasmus of Rotterdam: A Quincentennial Symposium,* ed. R. L. DeMolen (New York, 1971). For an edited collection of Erasmus' writings and letters, see my volume in the Documents of Modern History series, entitled *Erasmus* (London and New York, 1973).

efforts, and, if I fell short of this, at least to avoid doing any harm to anyone. . . ." He was anxious, above all, that his works contribute to the development of religious perfection. To insure this, he deliberately disavowed anything he had written up to May 1515 that might inhibit piety: "I would not want anything I wrote in jest to be in any way detrimental to Christian piety. Just give me a reader who understands what I wrote, who is fair and honest, who is eager for knowledge, and not bent on criticism."[3]

Erasmus also believed that learning supports piety, arguing that true piety must be based on genuine learning and must lead to moral action. Toward the end of his life, when he was living in Freiburg, Erasmus penned a letter (February 1530) to some Franciscan friars in which he continued to emphasize his double-edged goal: "Let them read the list of his works and they will see how much this decrepit old man has contributed to learning and to true piety."[4] It will be the purpose of this chapter to substantiate Erasmus' declaration that he offered the reading public only works that served to enhance learning and Christian piety.[5] Early in his career he wrote to Richard Foxe, the bishop of Winchester (January 1, 1506), and defined piety in terms of his conception of Christianity as "that true and perfect kind of friendship which consists in dying with Christ, living in Christ, and forming one body and one soul with Christ."[6]

Erasmus perceived the direction that his writing program would take before he left the monastery of the Canons Regular of Saint Augustine at Steyn. In 1489 or about that date, he identified a thoroughly religious

---

[3] Erasmus to Martin Dorp, May 1515, trans. John C. Olin, *Desiderius Erasmus: Christian Humanism and the Reformation* (New York, 1965), pp. 57, 78.

[4] Erasmus, *Opus Epistolarum,* ed. P. S. Allen et al. (Oxford, 1906–58), vol. 8, Ep. 2275, p. 365, 11. 68–69. Henceforth cited as *Allen*.

[5] I am obviously not the first person to arrive at such a conclusion. E. W. Kohls and R. R. Post et al. have sought to determine the origins of the *philosophy of Christ* in Erasmus' earliest writings, notably the *De contemptu mundi*. See Kohls, *Die Theologie des Erasmus,* 2 vols. (Basel, 1966) and Post, *The Modern Devotion* (Leiden, 1968), pp. 658–80. For a useful discussion of the twin themes of *pia doctrina* and *docta pietas* in Erasmus' letter to Paul Volz (August 14, 1518) and his *Ratio verae theologiae* (1518), see chapter 2 of Georges Chantraine's *'Mystère' et 'Philosophie du Christ' selon Erasme* (Namur-Gembloux, 1971). Moreover, Sister Geraldine Thompson has demonstrated in her study of Erasmus' satirical writings that he wrote in order "to alert a great new reading public to a richer understanding of truth and goodness." See her *Under Pretext of Praise: Satiric Mode in Erasmus' Fiction* (Toronto, 1973).

[6] *CWE,* 2:103.

program of studies to Cornelis Gerard, a fellow canon at a nearby Augustinian monastery, and attributed his change of direction to this friend: "since you kindly remind me of this, I have decided for the future to write nothing which does not breathe of the atmosphere either of praise of holy men or of holiness itself."[7] Erasmus' decision, however, did not mean that he was going to abandon the study of the classics which he had enjoyed from his boyhood, for these works served his purpose by "showing up men's vices" and, at the same time, by emphasizing the pursuit of virtues by other members of society. Erasmus reasoned as follows: those men who object to the study of the classics "fail to perceive how much moral goodness exists in Terence's plays, how much implicit exhortation to shape one's life" is to be found in the literature of the ancients.[8] He believed that the study of the classics was a useful adjunct for those who wished to attain moral perfection. He grew tired of those monks and theologians who railed against the classics under the pretext that they undermined Christian doctrine by promoting paganism. In a letter to a Hebrew scholar at Basel, Wolfgang Faber Capito, dated February 26, 1517, Erasmus urged the continuing study of the three major classical languages as an aid to uncovering the meaning of Christ's teachings:

> I could wish that those dreary quibblings could be either done away with or at least cease to be the sole activity of theologians, and that the simplicity and purity of Christ could penetrate deeply into the minds of men; and this I think can best be brought to pass if with the help provided by the three languages we exercise our minds in the actual sources.[9]

The example of Christ was held up both to aged scholar and young child. Writing to Adolph of Burgundy in 1499, Erasmus reminded the ten-year-old boy that he must follow Christ: "Finally, I shall add something I would wish you to lay very closely to heart: let it be one of your firmest convictions that nothing so well becomes the noble and well born as religious devotion. This is no idle advice, for I know by experience that royal courts contain those who neither hesitate to believe, nor blush to say, that Christ's teaching is no matter that need concern

---

[7] Ibid., 1:51.
[8] Ibid., p. 59.
[9] Translated by Barbara Flower in Johan Huizinga's *Erasmus and the Age of Reformation* (New York, 1957), p. 221.

noblemen but should be left to priests and monks. Stop your ears to their deadly siren-song, and follow where your mother and Batt are beckoning."[10] Erasmus called his program of reform to the attention of the whole world.

In response to repeated requests for a bibliography of his writings, Erasmus drew up a catalogue and sent it to Johann von Botzheim, a canon at Constance, in letter form under date of January 30, 1523. He also sent the very same catalogue of his lucubrations to Hector Boece on March 15, 1530.[11] These catalogues divide Erasmus' writings into the following nine major "orders" or divisions: The first category consisted of works which dealt with instruction on classical letters (*ad institutionem literarum*). Under this classification he listed twenty-one titles (with eighteen subtitles under Lucian and the "Dialogues"), including *On Copia of Words and Things*, the *Colloquies*, *On Civility of Manners for Boys*, the *Dialogue on the Ciceronian*, and *On the Instruction of Boys*. The second division consisted exclusively of the *Adages*, which Erasmus described in a letter to Servatius Roger, prior of the monastery at Steyn (July 8, 1514), as "a profane work, of course, but most helpful for the whole business of education";[12] the third division contained only his *Epistles*. Though Erasmus identified the first three divisions separately, they are related, since all of the individual works in these divisions contribute in some way to improving the writing of classical letters. Erasmus regarded these works as preliminary to his writings on morality and piety. (We see an expression of this idea in the letter to Servatius, referred to above, where Erasmus characterized *On Copia of Words and Things* as "a useful handbook for future preachers.") Erasmus' fourth division consisted of works on morality. It included thirteen titles (with eight subdivisions under the name of Plutarch), among them the *Praise of Folly*, the *Instruction of a Christian Prince*, and the *Complaint of Peace*. The fifth and largest division represented works on piety and included the *Handbook of the Christian Soldier*, the *Method of True Theology*, and *On Preaching*. Concerning the *Handbook*, Erasmus observed in his letter to Servatius (July 8, 1514) that "many people testify that it has fired them with religious enthusiasm." The sixth, seventh, eighth, and ninth categories

---

[10] *CWE*, 1:185.

[11] Erasmus to John Botzheim, Jan. 30, 1523, in *Allen*, vol. 1, Ep. 1, pp. 38–42, and Erasmus to Hector Boece, March 15, 1530, in ibid., vol. 8, Ep. 2283, pp. 373–77.

[12] *CWE*, 2:299–300.

were related to works on piety but enjoyed a separate classification in Erasmus' scheme. The sixth division consisted of only two titles, the New Testament and the *Paraphrases of the New Testament*. The seventh and ninth divisions represented the Church Fathers: the seventh included works by the Greek Fathers, Saint John Chrysostom, Saint Athanasius, Origen, and Saint Basil (with eight subdivisions under the names of Chrysostom and Athanasius); the ninth consisted of nine separate titles and represented the works of the following Latin Fathers: Saint Jerome, Saint Cyprian, Saint Hilary, Saint Irenaeus, Saint Ambrose, Lactantius, Saint Augustine, and Alger of Liège. The eighth division contained twenty-two separate titles, among them various *Apologiae,* including *The Antibarbarians* and *A Discourse on the Freedom of the Will.*

By the middle of the second decade of the sixteenth century, Erasmus had been lauded for his wisdom and received many letters of praise for his dedication to learning. Dean John Colet of St. Paul's Cathedral observed in one of these letters, dated June 20, 1516:

> Indeed, Erasmus, I am surprised at the fertility of your mind, which conceives so many projects, and brings such important works to birth, day after day, in such perfection, especially when you have no fixed abode, and are not assisted by any great or certain emoluments.[13]

Erasmus' devotion to his studies greatly exceeded his desire for material comforts and represents a further indication of his personal devotion to Christ and of his trust in Divine Providence. Many of his correspondents were also impressed by Erasmus' virtue, which is the best indication of all that the prince of humanists was adhering to his belief in the importance of imitating Christ. Writing to Erasmus in August of 1516, John Watson, a fellow of Peterhouse, Cambridge, marveled at the combination of brilliance and virtuousness that he saw in Erasmus:

> I am constantly more and more impressed, when I see Erasmus growing greater as he advances in years, and showing himself every day in a new and more exalted character. You are celebrated everywhere in Italy, especially among the learned of the highest note. It is incredible how favourably your *Copia* is everywhere received; and your *Moria* regarded as the highest wisdom. . . . Your fame is spread throughout all the Christian world; but as others enlarge on the riches of your varied learning or extraordinary eloquence, nothing strikes me so much as the modesty with which you are ready to take the lowest place, while

---

[13] Francis M. Nichols, trans., *The Epistles of Erasmus,* 3 vols. (London, 1901–17), 2:287.

the general suffrage sets you in the highest. The kind of literary skill which you enjoy is apt to inflate the possessor of it, and as it puts him in a peculiar class, to separate him from familiarity with his kind; but you are all generosity in communicating yourself to others; and having for your object the welfare of all, you do not despise the friendship of any. Therefore wherever you are, you so live as to seem present everywhere in Christendom, and will continue to live by the immortality of your fame and the noble monuments you will leave behind you.[14]

And there were others who praised him as well. Capito underscored Watson's observation in a letter to Erasmus, dated September 2, 1516: "You have left behind you here a sort of odour of your kindness and consummate literature, with which you attach to yourself Princes and Nobles, Prelates and People."[15] Erasmus succeeded in attracting such a diverse following because he consciously strove to do so. In pursuing his goal of teaching piety to all, he appealed to members of every class and distinction.

But it would be misleading to suggest that every reader of Erasmus' works found only good things to report about them. Such was not the case. Guillaume Budé, the eminent French humanist, was only one of his unfavorable critics. Budé found fault with Erasmus' efforts to reach the minds of the uneducated masses and suggested that he was damaging his reputation by composing works for boys. In response, Erasmus defended his actions and reiterated his major goal in a letter to Budé, dated October 28, 1516:

As for the risk you point out, of my name being obscured by so many trifling books, this in very truth does not give me the slightest uneasiness. Whatever celebrity, rather than glory, my lucubrations have earned for me, I would willingly and most cheerfully set it aside, if I am allowed to do so. Different people find pleasure in different studies. Some are capable of one thing, some of another. All have not the same genius. It is my fancy to devote my thoughts to such commonplace matters, in which, however, I find less frivolity and more profit than in some subjects which their authors think so magnificent. Finally, he whose single aim it is, not to exhibit himself, but to do some good to others, is not concerned so much with the splendour of the matters in which he is engaged, as with their utility; and I shall not refuse any task even more despised than that despised little *Cato*, if I see that it will conduce to the promotion of honest study.

[14] Ibid., 2: 334–35.
[15] Ibid., p. 379.

Such things are written, not for a Persius or a Laelius, but for boys and blockheads.[16]

Utility was the driving purpose behind the writing program on holiness that Erasmus first conceived while yet a student preparing for ordination at Steyn. It remained so throughout his long career as a scholar and theologian. One should not be surprised, therefore, to find Erasmus laying aside his works on theology and the Church Fathers in the late 1520s in order to instruct boys in good manners and the elements of writing Latin prose. Boys and blockheads were just as important to his *philosophia Christi* as nobles and princes. To quote Craig R. Thompson: "His witty, vivid presentation of men and manners, his literary and educational writings, urbane and tolerant spirit, and conception of Christian piety made him memorable."[17] In his own work on the *Instruction of a Christian Prince,* Erasmus summarized his definition of a Christian by posing a question and offering a reply:

> Who is truly Christian? Not he who is baptized or anointed, or who attends church. It is rather the man who has embraced Christ in his innermost feelings of his heart, and who emulates Him by his pious deeds.[18]

In taking up twenty of Erasmus' works one by one, I shall discuss where and why Erasmus pursued his goal to teach all men how to be truly Christian.

EPISTLES (ca. 1484–)

The letters of Erasmus are a remarkable inheritance because they reveal rather clearly the mind and personality of their author. Between 1514 and his death in 1536 about twenty editions of Erasmus' letters appeared in print.[19] Erasmus was conscious of his epistolary talents as an adolescent and, more importantly, was aware of the significance of his letters when

---

[16] Ibid., p. 415.

[17] Craig R. Thompson, ed., *The Colloquies of Erasmus* (Chicago and London, 1965), p. xiii.

[18] Erasmus, *The Education of a Christian Prince,* trans. Lester K. Born (New York, 1936), p. 153.

[19] Nichols, *Epistles,* 1:xxi–xxxvii, provides us with an informative survey of the various editions of Erasmus' letters. The reader should compare Nichols' findings with those of P. S. Allen in vol. 1, appendix 7, pp. 593–602. Neither author accounts for all of the editions of the correspondence that have survived until now.

he reached full manhood. Writing to Beatus Rhenanus in 1520, Erasmus recalled his earliest efforts: "although when I was a young man . . . I wrote very many letters, yet I hardly wrote any for publication . . . indeed, I did nothing more than amuse myself, as it were, expecting nothing less than that my friends should copy out and preserve such trifles."[20] As early as 1505, Erasmus conceived the idea of publishing his letters. In that year he addressed a letter to Franciscus Theodoricus, prior of the monastery at Hemsdonck, instructing him to "help in collecting, as far as possible, the letters which I have written to various persons with more than usual care—as I have an idea of publishing one book of Epistles."[21]

Having achieved greatness in the second decade of the sixteenth century, Erasmus decided to edit his correspondence in order to stop, or at least impede, the publication of his letters by unauthorized editors. He even went so far as to destroy some of his correspondence: "I myself, having come into possession of many of my letters by chance, burned them, for I realized that they were being preserved by very many people."[22] Nevertheless, unauthorized collections of Erasmus' letters appeared regularly after 1516. Johann Froben introduced the scheme at Basel as early as August of 1515 by printing a modest collection of four letters (*Damiana elegeia*). He was followed by Peter Gillis, secretary of the city of Antwerp, who edited two larger editions of the correspondence that were printed by Thierry Martens at Louvain in October of 1516 (*Epistolae aliquot* . . .) and in April of 1517 (*Aliquot epistolae sane quam elegantes* . . .). Froben reprinted the latter edition in January of 1518.

It seems almost certain that Erasmus had a hand in many of these early editions. Concerning the October 1516 edition, Erasmus admitted that "I was myself rather a conniving than a consenting party."[23] Finally, in August of 1518, Beatus Rhenanus, scholar and afterward biographer of Erasmus at Basel, edited "without authorization" a collection of the correspondence (*Auctarium* . . . , Basel: Froben). Others were to follow. Like all its predecessors, the August 1518 edition only served to irritate

---

[20] This letter served as the preface to Erasmus' *Epistolae ad diversos* (Basel, 1521). For a partial translation, see J. W. Binns' interesting essay, "The Letters of Erasmus," in *Erasmus*, ed T. A. Dorey (London, 1970), pp. 57–58.

[21] Nichols, 1:390.

[22] Erasmus, *Catalogus Lucubrationum* (1523, 1524), trans. J. W. Binns, in *Erasmus*, ed. T. A. Dorey, p. 56.

[23] Erasmus to Guillaume Budé, October 20, 1516, in Nichols, *Epistles*, 1:xxix.

and agitate the republic of belles lettres. Many of his correspondents objected to having their views aired publicly and others felt slighted because their letters were not included. Writing to Rhenanus in 1520, Erasmus observed: "For you know how unhappy was the issue of those epistles, of which you first undertook the editing."[24]

Rhenanus' edition was followed by a second effort in October of 1519 (*Farrago nova epistolarum* . . . , *Basel: Froben*). Erasmus' reaction can be found in his prefatory letter to Rhenanus in the January 1522 edition (*Epistolae . . . ad diversos et aliquot*).[25] It is hardly complimentary: in order to prevent the publication of unauthorized letters, "I sent you a medley (*farraginem*), giving you authority to select, and even to make corrections, in case there should be anything that seemed likely to injure my own reputation, or seriously to embitter anybody's feelings. . . . And yet even in that collection enough was found to excite in some breasts animosities of quite a tragic sort."[26] Shortly after the appearance of the *Farrago*, Adriaan Baerland edited still another edition, entitled *Epistolae aliquot selectae ex Erasmicis,* which was printed by Thierry Martens in December of 1520.[27] Throughout the remaining years of Erasmus' life publishers printed a new edition of his letters nearly every year.

Beginning with the 1522 collection of letters (*Epistolae . . . ad diversos et aliquot*), Erasmus henceforth supervised the editing of his own correspondence. He set forth his reasons for doing so in his prefatory letter to Rhenanus:

I, therefore, permitted some to be published, first, in order that people, having their appetite satisfied, might cease from demanding more, or at any rate abstain from any intention of publication, when they saw that I had myself set my hand to the business; next, that the letters might be issued with some selection and in a more correct form than as they existed in several copies; and, finally, that they might contain less of the bitter ingredient. With this design I have revised the Farrago, cleared up some points which had been unfairly construed, expunged

---

[24] Erasmus to Beatus Rhenanus, May 27, 1520, in Nichols, 1:lxxvii. This letter was later published as a prefatory epistle to Erasmus' *Epistolae ad diversos* (Basel, 1521).

[25] Allen, 1:600, gives the date of this edition as August 31, 1521, taking it from the title page, but this date is incorrect, seeing that one of the letters in the volume has the date November 21, 1521.

[26] Erasmus to Beatus Rhenanus, May 27, 1520, Nichols, 1:lxxvii.

[27] This edition was missed by Nichols and not recorded by Allen until volume 3 of his edition (appendix 12, pp. 627–29). See Alöis Gerlo, ed., *Erasme et la Belgique* (Brussels, 1969), p. 9.

some passages by which the too tender and irritable minds of some people had been offended, and softened others.[28]

Furthermore, Erasmus supervised other succeeding editions of his correspondence. I shall refer only to those of August 1529 (*Opus epistolarum* . . . , Basel: Froben), September 1531 (*Epistolae Floridae* . . . Basel: Herwagen), and February 1536 (*Opus epistolarum* . . . , Basel: Herwagen). In the prefatory epistles to these editions, Erasmus expressed his views on the nature of the epistolary genre and his methodology as editor.

To begin with, Erasmus insisted that letters should represent reality and feeling: "letters of that genuine kind, which represent, as in a picture, the character, fortune, and feelings of the writer, and, at the same time, the public and private condition of the time."[29] Genuine letters were not merely literary exercises.[30] Speaking from experience, however, he discouraged others from publishing nonliterary letters during their own lifetimes: "Therefore if anything of this sort is to be published, I would not advise anyone to bring it out in his lifetime, but rather commit it to some secretary to edit after your death."[31] His reasons for restricting the publication of personal correspondence were well founded: (1) both friends and foes will take offense and (2) one's reputation will suffer on account of the unevenness and inconsistency in the letters: "Whence it happens that with inexperienced persons we fall under the suspicion of inconstancy, when the variation they observe is to be ascribed to a difference of age and of feeling, a change of persons and circumstances."[32]

Having suffered from the fact that many of his letters were misinterpreted and read out of context, Erasmus advised the reader, in his 1529 prefatory epistle, "that there are none of my lucubrations for which I care less than my Epistles." And yet we might ask why, then, did he spend

---

[28] Nichols, 1:1xxviii–1xxix.

[29] Erasmus to Beatus Rhenanus, May 27, 1520, Nichols, 1:1xxxi.

[30] D. F. S. Thomson maintains that the earliest letters of Erasmus to Servatius Roger were literary exercises. See Thomson, "Erasmus as a Poet in the Context of Northern Humanism," *The Guden Passer,* 47 (1969): 187–210. Erasmus, however, would not have regarded such exercises as letters. See his definition of a letter in epistle to Beatus Rhenanus, May 27, 1520, Nichols, 1:1xxxi.

[31] Erasmus to Beatus Rhenanus, May 27, 1520, Nichols, 1:1xxxi.

[32] Ibid., 1:1xxxii.

so much effort collecting, discarding, and editing his letters? How could he justify his labors on the 1529 edition, in which he "divided the whole work into Books, so that the reader may find more readily what he seeks," in which he "added the day and year at the foot of each letter," and printed an "Index with the names of the persons and the numbers of the Books and Epistles" in order to "show who writes to whom, and how many letters"? If his correspondence was really of no consequence, why did he bother to take "the greatest pains that passages likely to produce much irritation should be either omitted or at any rate softened"?[33] I think that the answer to these questions is obvious: Erasmus took seriously the editing of his correspondence because he wanted his letters to serve his cause. Some four months before his death in July of 1536, Erasmus penned an epistolary preface to the 1536 edition of his correspondence in which he emphasized the importance of his reputation and the part his correspondence played in achieving his goal:

> Within the last few days, I determined to look over some confused heaps of papers, partly for the sake of one or two letters which I wished to be published, and partly in order to destroy some documents which others might, perhaps, publish after my death, or even during my life . . . . I have not for some years taken any pains to preserve any copies of my own [letters], partly because I had not clerks enough to write them all out and partly because in answering so many correspondents I am forced to write some and to dictate others, without preparation. I was also a little ashamed of the former publications . . . . I have brought these matters to your notice, candid readers, that you may not too lightly believe everything to be mine above which my name is written; and also that you may not think Erasmus has no one to take his part but a few gossips . . . .[34]

Since Erasmus saw some of his letters as divisive, he wanted to destroy them and to publish only those letters that would serve his underlying purpose.

THE BOOK OF THE ANTIBARBARIANS (1494/95; 1520)

One of the earliest treatises of Erasmus was written in part while he was living in the monastery of the Austin Canons at Steyn: The

---

[33] Erasmus to the Reader, *Opus epistolarum* (Basel, 1529), Nichols, 1:1xxxiii.
[34] Erasmus to Friendly Readers, February 20, 1536, in *Opus epistolarum* (Basel, 1536), trans. Nichols, *Epistles,* 1:1xxxvii, xc, xci.

Antibarbarorum liber was begun about 1489 ("before he attained his twentieth year").[35] Erasmus completed it about 1494/95, when he was in the employment of Hendrik van Bergen, the bishop of Cambrai. It finally appeared in print in May of 1520 and was reprinted in September, November, and December of the same year. Moreover, it was published about a dozen times during the author's lifetime.[36] Begun as an oration, the *Book of the Antibarbarians* was written in its final form as a dialogue. When it was conceived, it was to have consisted of four books, of which only two were completed and only part one survives. Book One offered a vigorous defense of classical letters. Book Two, no longer extant, sketched the practice of rhetoric and presented the major arguments of its critics. Books Three and Four defended rhetoric and poetry, respectively.[37]

The two completed books were revised by Erasmus at Bologna (about 1506) and, together with the materials for the remaining chapters, were given to Richard Pace at Ferrara in 1521, but were lost sometime thereafter. Erasmus refers to this incident in his correspondence. He seems to have believed that his work still existed somewhere, in the hands of a conspirator who would eventually publish it posthumously. In 1551, Roger Ascham wrote from Augsburg to Jerome Froben, claiming that he had received a manuscript copy of the work in 1549; but he was not sure whether he had the complete text or some abridgment, or whether it was the same as the section that had been published but was now out of print.[38] Book One, in its older form, existed in several copies; and since it was too well known to be suppressed, Erasmus revised it again and printed it at Basel in 1520. In the dialogue so published, the scene of the colloquy was laid at a country house in the neighborhood of Bergen, a market town and port in Brabant. As the book appears to have been shown to Robert Gaguin, the leading French humanist, in this form (about August 1495), it may be conjectured that the plan of so arranging

---

[35] See *Allen*, 4, Ep. 1110, p. 279. The letter to Johannes Witz, ca. June 1520, served as the preface to Book 1 of the *Antibarbari*.

[36] For a discussion of this and other matters, see Kazimierz Kumaniecki's introduction to his critical edition of the *Antibarbarorum liber*, in *Opera Omnia Desiderii Erasmi Roterodami* (Amsterdam, 1969), vol. 1, pt. 1, pp. 7–32.

[37] See Nichols' edition of *The Epistles of Erasmus*, 1:100–02, and Albert Hyma's *The Youth of Erasmus* (New York, 1968), pp. 182–204.

[38] Roger Ascham to Jerome Froben, June 10, 1551, in *The Whole Works of Roger Ascham*, ed. J. A. Giles, 3 vols. (London, 1864–65), vol. 1, pt. 2, pp. 288–90.

it was adopted at Bergen during Erasmus' first residence there with the bishop of Cambrai.[39]

The purpose of the *Book of the Antibarbarians* was to launch an attack against the enemies of classical literature—those sixteenth-century schoolmen, whether lay or cleric, who preferred the crude conventions of medieval Latin to classical letters. The theme of the various conversations centered, therefore, on the reasons for the decline in the *optimae artes* of the sixteenth century and the utility of classical learning. The function of scholarship, according to Erasmus, was to elucidate revelation. Direct revelation, by which the apostles were guided, had long ago ceased to be operative. In defending the classics against ignorant schoolmasters, magistrates, monks, and theologians, Erasmus cautioned the reader against an uncritical reading of them. Pure poetry was not necessarily a vehicle for impure and godless thought; nor, on the other hand, was bad Latin a guarantee of true piety. Indeed, one could praise God and, at the same time, aspire to a classical purity of form.

For Erasmus and his contemporaries, the purity and elegance of Latin and the forms of prose and poetry were burning issues of the day, the essence of the new culture, and the subject of conflict between the old and the new. Writing to Johannes Witz, a teacher of Latin, in the prefatory letter to the *Antibarbari*, Erasmus recalled: "In my childhood, polite letters were wholly banished from our schools of learning. Not only was assistance from books and teachers lacking, but there was no reward to stimulate my ability. Moreover, the whole world tried to frighten me away from the study of polite letters and to push me in the other direction. . . . I began to hate all those who I knew were insensible to the humanities; I fell in love with those who delighted in them."[40] For Erasmus, as well as the ancients, revelation was not so much a deposit as a quest, never ending, never amenable to definitive formulation. The *studia humanitatis* (including Latin and Greek literature, rhetoric, history, and moral philosophy) furnished standards of taste and permanent models of excellence. Erasmus' defense of the classics rested on his belief that there was no such thing as "Christian" erudition; there was only a secular erudition. By means of "true" erudition man was ennobled. Speaking through the character of Batt, Erasmus reflected:

> The man whose life is pure has done nobly. But in doing nobly he serves

---

[39] *Allen*, 1, appendix 5, pp. 587–90.
[40] Hyma, *Youth of Erasmus*, p. 185.

merely his own interests, or at the most his influence is exerted on only the few individuals with whom he lives. But if to his upright character erudition is allied, how much more beautifully and widely will his virtue flourish, as if a torch had been lighted? If one is a member of that group who are able to commit to letters the finest reflections of the mind, that is, if he is not only learned but eloquent, necessarily the influence of such a man is most widely spread, not merely to his intimate friends, not only to his contemporaries and to his neighbors, but also to foreigners, to posterity, to the most distant inhabitants of the earth. Untaught virtue dies with its author unless it is handed down to posterity in writings. Not the lands, nor the seas, nor the long succession of ages prevent trained erudition from reaching all humanity in its flight. I do not wish to raise here the invidious comparison whether the blood of the martyrs or the pen of scholars did more to advance the cause of our religion. I do not disparage the glory of the martyrs which no one can reach even by the greatest eloquence. But so far as our advantage is concerned, we owe almost more to some heretics than to our martyrs themselves. And while there have been a great number of martyrs, scholars have been few. The martyrs in dying diminished the number of Christians; the learned writers by their persuasiveness have increased it.[41]

Thus the *Book of the Antibarbarians* addressed itself directly to Erasmus' major goal. Through learning and eloquence the virtuous man can advance the cause of his religion. Christianity will be enriched by "the pen of scholars."

ADAGES (1500–)

As a collection of popular sayings, epigrams, proverbs, and anecdotes, the *Adagia* is a silent tribute to the immense reading of its author. It was reprinted some forty times during his lifetime and was constantly enlarged as edition succeeded edition.[42] The work brought both fame and fortune. Beginning as a collection of 818 adages in 1500 (*Adagiórum collectanea. . .*, Paris: J. Philippi) gathered from Latin and Greek literature, it ended as a collection of 4,151 adages in 1536 (Adagiorum chiliades . . . , Basel: J. Froben and N. Episcopius).[43] In the later editions, the adages were arranged in groups of 1,000 (per book) and subdivided into hundreds: each adage was followed by a commentary that sought to

---

[41] Ibid., pp. 200–01.

[42] Ferdinand van der Haeghen and Marie-Thérèse Lenger, *Bibliotheca Belgica* (Brussels, 1964), 2:382–86.

[43] Margaret M. Phillips gives the number of adages in the 1536 edition as 4,251. See her edition, *The 'Adages' of Erasmus* (Cambridge, 1964), p. 3.

clarify its meaning or its origin. Ostensibly Erasmus published these adages in an effort to aid the reader in improving his style of writing Latin. The fact that his *Adagiorum collectanea* and *Adagiorum chiliades* enjoyed so many editions during the author's lifetime attests to their popular appeal. In his 1500 dedicatory letter to Lord Mountjoy, Erasmus emphasized their utility:

> So I put aside my nightly labours over a more serious work and strolled through diverse gardens of the classics, occupied in this lighter kind of study, and so plucked, and as it were arranged in garlands, like flowerets of every hue, all the most ancient and famous of the adages. . . . I foresaw that while this labour of mine might bring no credit to its author, nevertheless it was likely to bring some profit and pleasure to its prospective readers: those, I mean, who dislike the current jargon and are searching for greater elegance and a more refined style. . . . I felt sure that though they might not admire it as a work of great artistry, at least they would be glad to welcome it on the ground of extreme usefulness. . . . You may draw upon it for all purposes; to find something that will charm by means of a clever and apposite metaphor, or bite with incisive wit; give pleasure by pointed brevity, or delight by brief pointedness . . . they do not merely decorate your style; they are equally helpful in giving strength as well.

But there was a deeper motivation too, Erasmus underscored the point that an eloquent style of writing could serve the church:

> . . . When these are found, I repeat (and I need not list them all), does it never occur to you that this manner of expression contains not merely vain display but rather a genuine element of sanctity, appropriate to religious topics? So for many reasons it seemed to me I had undertaken no vain or unprofitable task in attempting to instruct, or at least interest, studious youth, as well as I could, in a method of composition which a great many learned and pious authors have found good reason to pursue.[44]

Moral instruction was at the heart of the *Adages*. Whoever observed the wise sayings of the ancients and the Church Fathers would be led to a virtuous life in imitation of Christ. Writing in the *Dulce bellum inexpertis*, which first appeared in his 1515 edition of the *Adagia*, Erasmus noted that

> The end and aim of the faith of the Gospel is conduct worthy of Christ. Why do we insist on those things which have nothing to do with morality, and neglect the things which are like pillars of the structure—once you take them away, the whole edifice will crumble at once? Finally, who will believe us, when we take

---

[44] *CWE*, 1:257–58.

our device the Cross of Christ in the name of the Gospel, if our whole life obviously speaks of nothing but the world?[45]

The youthful Christian was here enjoined to follow the message of the Gospel by renouncing the temptations of the world, the devil, and the flesh. Morality alone supports the weight of the Cross.

In a letter to Guillaume Budé, dated June 19, 1516, Erasmus spoke of the philosophical and theological content of the adages. He admitted that "in the *Adages,* a fragmentary work, how often do I roam into the fields of Philosophy and Theology, forgetting, as it may seem, the immediate subject, and take a higher flight than the occasion demands."[46]

THE HANDBOOK OF THE CHRISTIAN SOLDIER (1503)

With conviction and grace, Erasmus drafted the first complete expression of his *philosophia Christi* in the *Enchiridion militis christiani* (i.e. Christian Soldier's Dagger or Handbook) in 1501 and published it two years later. His formula was undogmatic, and yet it was nothing less than "a method of morals," as he himself put it.[47] In preparation for life's inevitable encounters with the world and the devil, Erasmus urged the Christian knight to fortify himself with virtue and knowledge of the classics and the works of the Church Fathers. He was speaking to all men, whatever their age and station in life, when he wrote:

> If you are inflamed by lust, acknowledge your weakness and deny yourself somewhat more, even of lawful pleasures; assign yourself an additional number of chaste and moral duties. If you are enticed by greed or avarice, increase your charitable donations. If you are attracted by empty fame, humble yourself that much more in every respect.[48]

One of Erasmus' most popular works, the *Enchiridion,* according to the *Bibliotheca Belgica* (1964), enjoyed some fifty-one Latin editions (in addition to translations into German, English—there were ten editions between 1533 and 1576—, French, Dutch, and Spanish) during the lifetime of the author.[49] It was conceived as a handbook that could be

---

[45] See Phillips' translation in *The 'Adages' of Erasmus,* p. 346.
[46] Nichols, 2:282.
[47] *CWE,* 2:87.
[48] *The Enchiridion of Erasmus,* trans. Raymond Himelick (Bloomington, Ind., 1963), p. 166.
[49] Van der Haeghen and Lenger, *Bibliotheca Belgica* (1964), 2:838–42.

carried about and was composed specifically at the request of a woman who had asked Erasmus to instruct her wayward husband, Johann Poppenruyter, in virtue. Writing to Johann Botzheim in January of 1523, Erasmus described these circumstances:

> The *Enchiridion militis christiani* was begun by me nearly thirty years ago when staying in the castle of Tournehem, to which we were driven by the plague which depopulated Paris. The work arose out of the following incident. A common friend of mine and of Batt was in the castle—a man whose wife was a lady of singular piety. The husband was no one's enemy so much as his own, a man of dissolute life, but in other respects an agreeable companion. He had no regard for any clergyman except me; and his wife, who was much concerned about her husband's salvation, applied to me through Batt to set down some . . . sense of religion, without his perceiving that it was done at the insistence of his wife. For even with her it was a word and a blow, in soldier's fashion. I consented to the request and put down some observations suitable to the occasion. These having met the approval even of learned persons, and especially of Jean Vitrier [the warden of a Franciscan community at Saint-Omer], a Franciscan friar of great authority in those parts, I finished the work at leisure, after the plague (then raging everywhere) had routed me out of Paris and driven me to Louvain.[50]

Throughout the treatise Erasmus calls the reader to the *divinae scripturae fontes*. He wished to create a world that was inhabited by men, who preferred the example of Christ to that of Judas Iscariot. Erasmus' formula was both Christocentric and universal in its application. Writing to Budé in June of 1516, Erasmus underscored the originality of his theme: "In the *Enchiridion*, I ventured to differ widely from our own age, without being deterred by the authority of anyone."[51]

The *Handbook of a Christian Soldier* is divided into two parts. The first part analyzes the nature of man and his purpose on earth, while part two provides a discussion of twenty-two "rules" for "living a Christian life." It concludes with a section that proposes remedies for such vices as lust, avarice, ambition, pride and haughtiness, and anger and revenge. Erasmus reminded the reader at the very end of the treatise that one should study the classics in order to obtain moral guidance in this life on earth, which he described as "a type of continual warfare." In the

---

[50] Nichols, 1:337–38. The translation has been modified in places.
[51] Ibid., 2:282.

dedicatory letter to his friend Johann Poppenruyter (dated 1501), Erasmus justified his interest in good letters and sacred Scriptures:

> I shall try to cause certain malicious critics, who think it the height of piety to be ignorant of sound learning, to realize that, when in my youth I embraced the finer literature of the ancients and acquired, not without much midnight labour, a reasonable knowledge of the Greek as well as the Latin language, I did not aim at vain glory or childish self-gratification, but had long ago determined to adorn the Lord's temple, badly desecrated as it has been by the ignorance and barbarism of some, with treasures from other realms, as far as in me lay; treasures that could, moreover, inspire even men of superior intellect to love the Scriptures. But, putting aside this vast enterprise for just a few days, I have taken upon myself the task of pointing out to you, as with my finger, a short way to Christ.[52]

And this handbook on piety bore fruit. Writing to Master John, a former tutor to Archduke Philip, on November 2, 1517, Erasmus exclaimed: "The *Enchiridion* is read everywhere; and it is making many people either good, or at any rate—we do hope—better than they were."[53] What more could Erasmus expect?

THE PRAISE OF FOLLY (1511)

This literary triumph was written in the course of a week in late summer of 1509 and revised and published in 1511. Erasmus described it as "a playful booklet too light to become a theologian, too caustic to befit Christian meekness."[54] The *Moriae encomium* enjoyed some forty editions, including French and German translations, during the lifetime of its author, and was certainly one of his best-known works.[55] Erasmus set forth the reasons that motivated him to write it in his dedicatory letter to Sir Thomas More:

> So I beg you to accept this short essay as a souvenir of your comrade, but also to acknowledge and cherish it, inasmuch as it has been dedicated to you and is no longer mine, but yours. For there will perhaps be some wrangling critics who will falsely assert either that these trifles are too airy to be quite suitable to a theologian's pen, or that they are more sarcastic than suits the modesty of a

---

[52] *CWE*, 2:53.
[53] Nichols, 3:116.
[54] *Allen*, 1, Ep. 222, p. 460, ll. 26–27.
[55] See Betty Radice's introduction to her translation of *Moriae encomium*, titled *Praise of Folly* (London, 1974), p. 7.

Christian. They will loudly accuse me of imitating the Old Comedy or some kind of Lucianic satire, and of attacking the whole world with my teeth. Now as for those who find the triviality and humour of the theme offensive, I should like them to reflect that this is no vein of my own invention, but reflects the habitual practice of great writers of the past.... So let them make up stories about me if they wish, alleging that I have sometimes played draughts for recreation, or ridden a hobbyhorse if they would rather; for, considering that every way of living is permitted its appropriate recreation, it would be monstrously unfair to allow no diversion whatever of those who pursue literary studies, especially if nonsense leads to serious matters and absurd themes are treated in such a way that the reader whose senses are not wholly dulled gains somewhat more profit from these than from some men's severe and showy demonstrations.... For, as there is nothing more frivolous than to handle serious topics in a trifling manner, so also there is nothing more agreeable than to handle trifling matters in such a way that what you have done seems anything but trifling. Others will judge me; but unless my vanity altogether deceives me, I have written a Praise of Folly without being altogether foolish.[56]

Through this medium, Erasmus launched an attack on those sycophantic theologians who practiced the letter of the law and ignored its spirit: "Such is the erudition and complexity they all display that I fancy the apostles themselves would need the help of another holy spirit if they were obliged to join issue on these topics with our new breed of theologian."[57] Erasmus was impatient with such scholastic thinkers and insisted on a return to Scripture as a basis for theological discussion:

Yet all the while they are so happy in their self-satisfaction and self-congratulation, and so busy night and day with these enjoyable tomfooleries, that they haven't even a spare moment in which to take a single look at the gospel or the letters of Paul.[58]

In addition to singling out the theologians, Erasmus chose as targets the professional activities of many others, arguing that "We won't go into every kind of life, it would take too long, but will pick out some outstanding examples from which it will be easy to judge the rest."[59] Those who were singled out included the scientist, the schoolmaster, the poet, the grammarian, the orator, the writer, the monk, the monarch,

---

[56] CWE, 2:163–64.
[57] Erasmus, *Praise of Folly*, trans. Radice, p. 81.
[58] Ibid., p. 84.
[59] Ibid., p. 73.

the courtier, the pontiff, the cardinal, the bishop, and the priest. Erasmus poked fun at the foibles and failings of these and others in order to underscore his observation that "all mortals are fools, even the pious." It is indeed because of their foolishness that Christ "by the folly of the cross and through his simple, ignorant apostles, to whom he unfailingly preached folly . . . taught them to shun wisdom, and made his appeal through the example of children, lilies, mustard-seed and humble sparrows, all foolish, senseless things, which live their lives by natural instinct alone, free from care or purpose."[60] This is the reason, according to Folly, why Christ insisted that his disciples learn to depend on him for their sustenance and grace. She was convinced that Christian piety was akin to folly and that there was a closer affinity between Christianity and folly than between Christianity and wisdom.

She also observed that the "biggest fools" appeared to be those who have been "wholly possessed by zeal for Christian piety." These people represented "the very young and the very old, women and simpletons." It is they who "squander their possessions, ignore insults, submit to being cheated, make no distinction between friends and enemies, shun pleasure, sustain themselves on fastings, vigils, tears, toil, and humiliations, scorn life and desire only death."[61] In short, it is these people who pursue the *philosophia Christi* and it is these people whom Erasmus wants all men to emulate. Erasmus also reminded his readers that "Christ seems to have taken special delight in little children, women and fishermen." It is therefore not surprising that Erasmus spent so much of his productive life writing textbooks for the education of children and handbooks on piety for adult laymen. He emphasized the unique qualities of children in this passage from the *Praise of Folly:*

> It's a fact that as soon as the young grow up and develop the sort of mature sense which comes through experience and education, the bloom of youthful beauty begins to fade at once, enthusiasm wanes, gaiety cools down and energy slackens.[62]

Writing to Johannes of Louvain, a Franciscan in Amsterdam, on January 2, 1518, Erasmus noted that his *Moria* had gone through twelve editions and had aroused the ire of monks and theologians. Moreover, he

---

[60] Ibid., pp. 108–09.
[61] Ibid., p. 110.
[62] Ibid., p. 35.

observed with surprise that this work was being read in the classroom by schoolchildren: "though indeed I did take pains to admit nothing in it, that would be corrupting to that age; for as to your fear, that the reading of it might alienate them from all religion, I do not understand what that means. Is there any danger of all religion being disliked, because something is said against those who are superstitiously religious . . . ? Indeed I will say more freely still, I would that priests and people were such true followers of the religion of Christ, that those who are now the only persons called Religious would not appear religious at all."[63] Erasmus insisted here and in the following letter to Maarten van Dorp (May 1515) that his purpose in writing the *Moriae encomium* was "to admonish, not to cause pain; to be of benefit, not to vex; to reform the morals of men, not to oppose them."[64]

ON COPIA OF WORDS AND THINGS (1512)

Erasmus' *De duplici copia verborum ac rerum commentarii duo* was begun in Paris in the mid-1490s as a textbook for boys enrolled in the next to the highest form or class, who were learning how to write elegant Latin. In time it served other purposes as well. Erasmus, in his letter to Servatius Roger, saw it as a "useful handbook for future preachers."[65] The text was not finished, however, until 1511 at the suggestion of Dean Colet, who had only recently established a school at St. Paul's. Erasmus dedicated the work to the dean when it appeared in print in 1512. From then until 1536, some eighty-five editions, periodically revised and enlarged, appeared regularly under various titles.[66]

The work itself was subdivided into two books—hence the "commentarii duo" in the title: Book 1 provided ways of enriching the student's vocabulary by the use of schemes and tropes and through discussions of methods of varying one's writings, in chapters on synonymy, enallage, antonomasia, periphrasis, metaphor, allegory, catachresis, onomatopoeia, metalepsis, metonymy, synecdoche, aequipollentia, comparatives, change of relatives, amplification, hyperbole, etc. Book 2, on the other hand, provided discussions on how to use

[63] Nichols, 3:209.
[64] Olin, trans., *Christian Humanism and the Reformation,* p. 60.
[65] *CWE,* 2:300.
[66] See Herbert D. Rix, "The Editions of Erasmus' *De Copia,*" *Studies in Philology,* 43 (1946): 595–618.

partition, enumeration of antecedents, enumeration of causes, enumeration of effects and consequences, description, digression, epitheton, amplification, extenuation, multiplication of propositions, proof, example, similitude, judicial examination, embellishment, and so forth. Erasmus assumed that the mastery of these skills would enable the fifteen-year-old boy to analyze classical literature on his own: it was merely the means to an end.

In his dedicatory epistle to Dean Colet, dated April 29, 1512, Erasmus emphasized the importance of providing children "with an excellent literary education from their earliest years. For you are profoundly aware both that the hope of the country lies in its youth—the crop in the blade, as it were—and also how important it is for one's whole life that one should be initiated into excellence from the cradle onwards."[67] Since Erasmus saw education as the means to winning young souls to Christ, his *De copia* was an instrument designed to further Colet's lifetime commitment to the conversion of boys into Christian soldiers: "So I have chosen to dedicate to the new school these two new commentaries *De copia,* inasmuch as the work in question is suitable for boys to read and also, unless I am mistaken, not unlikely to prove helpful to them."[68] Erasmus also defended the work against the charges of Guillaume Budé that it was unworthy of its author in a letter dated October 28, 1516: "The *Copia* which we despise (for on this point we are certainly in the same lobby) has been extolled by a great many persons of no ordinary sort, who maintain that no work I have ever written is more clever or equally useful."[69]

Through the use of this treatise, Erasmus hoped to reach child and adult alike and to turn their attention to the powers of persuasive eloquence. The future success of Christianity itself depended upon the ability of mortal men to communicate its gospel message to others.

THE INSTRUCTION OF A CHRISTIAN PRINCE (1516)

Begun in 1515, this treatise was first published in 1516, under the title *Institutio principis christiani,* and reinforced a theme that had appeared in

---

[67] *CWE,* 2:226.
[68] Ibid., p. 227.
[69] Nichols, 2:416.

the adage "Dulce bellum inexpertis" in the previous year. It enjoyed some twenty editions during the lifetime of the author.[70]

Erasmus dedicated the work to the sixteen-year-old Prince Charles (afterward Emperor Charles V) in an attempt to persuade him to pursue a policy of peace in his future role as king and emperor. Returning to an earlier injunction, Erasmus insisted that this young prince must be carefully taught, for "the seeds of morality must be sown in the virgin soil of his spirit so that little by little they may grow and mature through age and experience, to remain firmly implanted throughout the course of life. Nothing remains so deeply and tenaciously rooted as those things learned in the first years."[71] The ethics of Christianity would serve as the foundation for Erasmus' advice to Charles, who was asked to read the *Proverbs* of Solomon, *Ecclesiasticus,* the *Book of Wisdom,* and the Gospels—in that order—together with the *Apophthegmata,* the *Morals* and *Lives* of Plutarch, the works of Seneca, Plato, the *Politics* of Aristotle, the *Offices* of Cicero, and excerpts from Herodotus and Xenophon, Sallust and Livy, providing that the impressionable young mind was protected from any objectional passages that might appear in these latter works.

Erasmus also insisted that a good prince must encourage the education of his subjects: "A prince who is about to assume control of the state must be advised at once that the main hope of a state lies in the proper education of its youth. . . . As a result of this scheme of things, there will be no need for many laws or punishments, for the people will of their own free will follow the course of right."[72] Erasmus advised the prince to know his people and to make judgments only after careful study of the situation. The function of power, he noted, is not to extend the "boundaries of one's realm, but to enrich it." War, above all, is to be avoided, except as a last resort. He bade the prince to remember that Aristotle answered the following question in his *Politics:*

> What does the average man demand in his prince? Is it the figure of Nereus, or the strength of Milo, or the stature of Maximinus, or the wealth of Tantalus? No; it is none of these things. What is the answer then? He must have virtue in its

---

[70] Van der Haeghen and Lenger, *Bibliotheca Belgica* (1964), 2:865–66.

[71] Erasmus, *The Education of a Christian Prince,* trans. Lester K. Born (New York, 1936), p. 140.

[72] Ibid., pp. 212–13.

highest and purest form and he must be content with a golden mean in his private affairs.[73]

Virtue should be the mark of a good prince, just as justice should be his goal. For Erasmus there was only one master of Christian men, He "who alone is in all ways to be imitated."[74] The *Instruction of a Christian Prince* called the attention of the prince to the *philosophia Christi*. With the help of a good prince, honest magistrates and public officials, holy priests, wise schoolmasters, just laws, and good habits, he was certain that his philosophy of Christ would gain public support: all it required was the example of good men. Writing to Capito on February 26, 1517, Erasmus spoke of the future in optimistic terms:

> When I see that the highest sovereigns of Europe, Francis of France, Charles the King Catholic, Henry of England and the Emperor Maximilian, have set all their warlike preparations aside, and established peace upon solid, and, as I trust adamantine foundations, I am led to a confident hope, that not only morality and Christian piety, but also a genuine and purer literature may come to renewed life or greater splendour.[75]

THE APOLOGIES (1515–)

Beginning in 1515, Erasmus answered the charges of his critics by addressing *apologiae* or defenses of his positions to them in the form of epistles or tracts. During the remainder of his life he published some thirty apologies, including those to Maarten van Dorp, a theologian at Louvain, who criticized parts of his *Praise of Folly* and the *Novum Instrumentum* (1515–); Jacques Lefèvre d'Étaples, the Parisian theologian, who accused Erasmus of impiety when he observed that Christ was described in his *Novum Instrumentum* as "a little lower than the angels" in Hebrews 2:7 (1517, 1518, 1520–21); Jacobus Latomus, a theologian at Louvain, who objected to Erasmus' defense of the Hebrew language (1517–19, 1521); those scholars who criticized his work on the Apostolic Epistles (1518); Jan Briaert, the vice-chancellor at Louvain, who pointed out errors in his *Praise of Marriage* (1519, 1521, 1522); those "barbarians" who opposed the study of the classics in the form of the *Book of the Antibarbarians* (1520); Edward Lee, the archbishop of York after 1531, who accused Erasmus of denying Christ's equality with the Father

---

[73] Ibid., p. 189.
[74] Ibid., p. 177.
[75] Nichols, 2:506.

(Arianism) in 1520; those theologians at Louvain who accused him of heresy in 1520; those theologians who found fault with his interpretation of "In principio erat sermo" in St. John's Gospel, in which Erasmus substituted *speech* ("sermo") for *word* ("verbum") in 1520–21; Diego López de Zuñiga (Stunica), a theologian at Alcalá, who also accused Erasmus of Arianism and criticized his notes on the New Testament (1521–25); Nicolaas Baechem, a Dutch Carmelite theologian (Erasmus referred to him as the "camelite"), who objected to Erasmus' interpretation of Paul's Epistle to the Corinthians (1521–22, 1525); Christoph von Utenheim, the bishop of Basel, to whom Erasmus addressed the treatise *On the Prohibition of Eating Meat,* who attacked Erasmus' criticisms of fasting, abstinence, the number of holy days of obligation, and his advocacy of marriage for priests (1522–23, 1532); Sanctius Carranza of Miranda, a theologian at Salamanca, who objected to Erasmus' notes on the New Testament (1522–23); Ulrich von Hutten, a German humanist and nationalist, to whom Erasmus addressed his *Sponge to Wipe Away the Aspersions of Hutten,* who accused Erasmus of cowardliness by not joining forces with Luther (1523); Martin Luther in the form of his *De libero arbitrio diatribe* (1524) and the *Hyperaspistes* (1526–27); Peter Sutor, a theologian at the Sorbonne, who suggested that Erasmus' New Testament undermined the church by calling the Vulgate into question (1525); Josse van Clichtove, who criticized his theological positions (1526); Noel Beda, the syndic of the Faculty at the Sorbonne, who accused Erasmus of heresy and sought to condemn his *Paraphrases,* his edition of the New Testament, and his *Enchiridion* (1526–29); in defense of his seal: *Terminus: concedo nulli* (1528); those Spanish monks who accused him of heresy (1528–29); those Franciscans who opposed his annotations on Saint Paul's Epistle to the Romans (1529); Gerardus Noviomagus (or Geldenhouwer), who accused Erasmus of opposing the Lutheran cause (1529); Albert Pio, the prince of Carpi, who also accused Erasmus of heresy (1529, 1531–32); Louis de Carvajal, a Spanish Franciscan who criticized Erasmus' New Testament (1529–30); those theologians at Strasbourg who called for a return to the primitive church, under the title of *Against the Pseudoevangelicals of Strasbourg* (1530); in defense of his position on piety against Eustace of Sichem (1531); and Peter Cursius (or Corsi) against the charges that he misinterpreted the proverb "Myconius calvus" (1535).

Though Erasmus personally abhorred quarreling and rancor, his patience broke under the strain of being accused of harming religion and of heresy itself. In a letter to Ludwig Baer, rector of the university at Basel (dated March 30, 1529), Erasmus reasoned, "it is a kind of denial of faith not to speak up against a charge of heresy."[76] It should not be surprising that most of his defenses are aimed at those scholastic theologians, labeled as "fools" in his *Praise of Folly* of 1511, who accused him of impiety. Throughout the *apologiae,* Erasmus is concerned with returning to the essential beliefs of Christianity, with stripping away the accumulated pious practices of the institutional church in order to get at the essentials. In drawing a distinction between Christocentric doctrines and manmade customs, he wished to stimulate the growth of the church by promoting Christian living. Nevertheless, at Lewis W. Spitz points out: "Erasmus was perfectly orthodox and 'correct' on all matters of dogma. His long *apologies* are replete with assertions that he had wished only to spread the true faith and that he had always been true to the ecclesiastical teaching office in all submissiveness and obedience. . . . His test was whether a doctrine had been approved by the church, not merely whether it was to be found in the Scriptures or was validated by early tradition."[77]

Erasmus quietly accepted the invectives of those who labeled him as "rude, coarse, stupid, ignorant, a block, a dolt, a fool,"[78] but when it came to charging him with heresy, he shrugged off his reserve and prepared moderate and reasoned defenses of his particular position. For it was no longer merely a matter of inherent flaws in his personality that was of concern but an attack on his belief in Christ. Erasmus set forth the reasons for these attacks in his letter to Baer of March 30, 1529:

> It is not obscure for what frivolous reasons these people first attacked me. To the great advantage of theology I cultivated languages and polite literature, which they now pretend to admire, although more than forty years ago they left no stone unturned to destroy and uproot them when they were just beginning to spring up. And that was the seed of this present tragedy. I exhorted the theologians that, leaving aside their little questions which have more of ostentation than of piety, they should betake themselves to the very sources of the Scriptures and to the ancient Fathers of the Church. Moreover, I did not wish

---

[76] John J. Mangan, trans., *Life . . . of Desiderius Erasmus of Rotterdam,* 2 vols. (New York, 1927), 2:312, and *Allen,* 8, Ep. 2136, p. 120.

[77] Lewis W. Spitz, *The Religious Renaissance of the German Humanists* (Cambridge, Mass., 1963), pp. 226–27.

[78] See Erasmus, *Opera omnia,* ed. Jean Le Clerc (Leiden, 1703–06), 9:317C–D.

that scholastic theology should be abolished, but that it should be purer and more serious. That, unless I am mistaken, is to favour, not to hurt it. I exhorted the monks to be what they said they were, namely, dead to the world, to trust less to external ceremonial, and to embrace rather true piety of soul. Is this wishing well or ill to the monks? . . . Never have I contemned the constitutions and rites of the Church, nor taught that they were to be contemned; but I have given preference to the precepts of God; I have shown the progression from ceremonies to better things; and if by the negligence of man anything foreign to them has crept in, I have indicated how such might be corrected, a thing which the Church has often done.[79]

Earlier, Erasmus had expressed indignation when he learned of the charges made against him by Lefèvre in his commentaries on Saint Paul's Epistles. Writing to Wolfgang Capito on December 6, 1517, he observed: "Within fourteen days after reading Lefèvre's criticism I had finished my Apology: the sole object of which is to repel the charge of impiety and blasphemy, which I know not by whose instigation, he had brought against me."[80] Some two months later he addressed another letter to Guillaume Budé (dated February 22, 1518) in which he emphasized his belief in Christ's divinity and expressed a hope for reconciliation: "To spend your life in the cause of friendship is considered laudable; but for the sake of a friend to admit yourself to be a blasphemer against Christ is not only madness, but impiety. . . . Let him [Lefèvre] change, if he can, the passage in which he lacerates me, and I shall do my best to suppress the Apologias in which I defend myself."[81] Erasmus desired an end to this dispute because it was damaging the cause of Good Letters and was draining away his energies from the pursuit of sacred studies. Cuthbert Tunstall, afterward bishop of London, in a letter dated September 14, 1517, reminded him of this fact:

There is one thing I regret—that, while composing an Apology against this writer [Lefèvre], you have lost the time in which you might have written what would have been more useful to posterity. Do therefore bestow your first attention upon the revision of your Notes on the New Testament, which, in consequence of your promise, is greedily expected by everybody. Having deserved well of profane literature and won immortal fame in its service, you will do well, if you spend the remainder of your life in the illustration of Sacred

---

[79] Mangan, *Life . . . of Desiderius Erasmus,* 2:312–13.
[80] Nichols, 3:179.
[81] Ibid., p. 265.

Letters. Posterity will infer that the studies which concern the salvation of the soul have been dearer to you than those which afford mere amusement, when the latter have most attracted you in youth, but the former, embraced in mature years, have been deemed a worthy occupation for your age.[82]

Erasmus published the first collection of his apologies in October 1521 (part 1) and February 1522 (part 2) at the press of Froben in Basel. He described these works in his subtitle as "vindications" of his position and not as "excuses" ("non satis circumspecte sunt calumniati"). The volume included his *apologiae* against Diego López Zuñiga, Jacobus Latomus, Jan Briaert, those who had objected to his interpretation of "in principio erat sermo," Edward Lee, and Jacques Lefèvre d'Etaples. The border of the title page of this volume betrayed the mood of the author: it consists of humanlike representations of the Seven Deadly Sins.

It is John Olin's opinion that "the letter to Dorp [composed in May 1515 but not published until August in a collection of letters (the *Auctarium*) printed by Froben] is perhaps Erasmus' most important *apologia* and is extremely valuable in understanding *The Praise of Folly* within the context of Erasmus' aims and lifework."[83] In this letter to Dorp, Erasmus refers once again to his major purpose in writing books:

> For reasons such as this I have persuaded myself to guard my writings from any harmdoing or vengeance and to avoid contaminating them with so much as a mention of evil. Nor did I have any intentions in the *Folly* different from those in my other works, although the method may have differed. In the *Enchiridion* I simply set down a design for Christian living. In the pamphlet *The Education of a Prince* I publicly advised in what subjects a prince ought to be instructed. . . . So for the *Folly*; the same thing was done there under the semblance of a jest as was done in the *Enchiridion*. I wanted to admonish, not to cause pain; to be of benefit, not to vex; to reform the morals of men, not to oppose them.[84]

Here, in 1515, Erasmus identified the common theme that pervaded all of his treatises.

THE NEW TESTAMENT (1516)

As early as 1505, Erasmus began work on a text of the New Testament that was to be based in part on the surviving Greek manuscripts. He wrote to Dean Colet of his intentions late in 1504:

---

[82] Ibid., p. 62.
[83] Olin, *Christian Humanism and the Reformation*, p. 56.
[84] Ibid., pp. 59–60.

I am now eager, dear Colet, to approach sacred literature full sail, full gallop; I have an extreme distaste for anything that distracts me from it, or even delays me. But the ill will of fortune, which has ever regarded me with steadfast hostility, is the reason why I have not been able to free myself from these vexations. . . . Three years ago, indeed, I ventured to do something on Paul's Epistles to the Romans, and at one rush, as it were, finished four volumes; and would have gone on, but for certain distractions, of which the most important was that I needed the Greek at every point. Therefore for nearly the past three years I have been wholly absorbed by Greek. . . . I have gone through a good part of Origen's work; under his guidance I think I have achieved worthwhile results, for he reveals some of the wellsprings, as it were, and demonstrates some of the basic principles of the science of theology.[85]

Erasmus' earlier efforts at preparing annotations on Saint Paul's Epistle to the Romans failed because he lacked expertise in Greek. He realized as early as 1501 that he would need to perfect his knowledge of that language if he wanted to understand the writings of the Church Fathers on the New Testament and to get closer to the actual words of Christ. However, progress was slow. In his July 8, 1514, letter to Servatius Roger, Erasmus assured the prior at Steyn that he was "resolved to live and die in the study of the Scriptures. I made these my work and my leisure."[86]

Erasmus' New Testament was finally published in Basel by Froben in March of 1516 under the title *Novum Instrumentum*. He dedicated this *New Instrument* to Pope Leo X. Erasmus was justified in renaming his New Testament, for it included an impressive number of innovations: a preface to the annotations, an exhortation ("Paraclesis") to the readers, an *apologia* for the Greek text, a Latin translation that differed somewhat from Saint Jerome's Vulgate text, and an explanation of his methodology. Erasmus also added a preface before each one of the Gospels and Epistles and provided over 1,000 notes both to help explain given passages and to call the reader's attention to the way of Christ. Throughout the annotations, Erasmus condemned superstition, ignorance, and false piety. In a letter to Dorp (May 1515) he explained his methodology: "I have translated the entire New Testament according to

---

[85] *CWE*, 2:86–87. For a useful discussion of Erasmus' exegesis, see John B. Payne, "Toward the Hermeneutics of Erasmus," in *Scrinium Erasmianum*, ed. J. Coppens (Leiden, 1969), 2:13–49.

[86] Translated by Flower in Huizinga, *Erasmus and the Age of Reformation*, p. 216.

the Greek original, with the Greek appended directly to allow for quicker comparison. I added notes separately in which, partly by proofs and partly by the authority of early theologians, I show that what I emended was not changed rashly, lest my corrections should lack credence or my emendations be easily altered."[87]

Erasmus' *Paraclesis* was an exhortation to the reader to follow the *philosophia Christi* as well as an eloquent plea for the vernacular translation of Scripture. It was obvious to him that he could achieve a following among Christians only if they understood the words of Christ; and the best way to achieve such understanding was by urging the translation of the New Testament into vernacular languages:

Indeed, I disagree very much with those who are unwilling that Holy Scripture, translated into the vulgar tongue, be read by the uneducated, as if Christ taught such intricate doctrines that they would scarcely be understood by very few theologians, or as if the strength of the Christian religion consisted in men's ignorance of it. The mysteries of kings, perhaps, are better concealed, but Christ wishes his mysteries published as openly as possible. I would that even the lowliest women read the Gospels and the Pauline Epistles. And I would that they were translated into all languages so that they could be read and understood not only by Scots and Irish but also by Turks and Saracens. Surely the first step is to understand in one way or another.[88]

Further on in the *Paraclesis,* Erasmus defined his *philosophia Christi:* "what else is the philosophy of Christ, which He himself calls a rebirth, than the restoration of human nature originally well formed? . . . if we seek a model for life, why does another example take precedence for us over that of Christ himself?"[89]

In preparing the first edition of his New Testament, Erasmus, according to his prefatory letter, collated ten Greek manuscripts, one dating back to the tenth century. However, we now know that most of these manuscripts were incomplete and of fairly recent origin; hence they were of little value. As a result of these limited sources and a careless job of proofreading, there were a small number of serious errors and a larger number of typographical errors in the 1516 edition. Even so, the demand for the *Novum Instrumentum* was so great that it was quickly sold out. Erasmus was applauded for his labors by many of the leading scholars of

---

[87] Olin, *Christian Humanism and the Reformation,* p. 90.
[88] Ibid., pp. 96–97.
[89] Ibid., pp. 100, 102.

his day, including Johann Oecolampadius, Bishop Richard Foxe, Sir Thomas More, Henry Bullock, and John Watson. In replying to Watson on January 13, 1517, Erasmus declined to talk about the merits of his edition but did emphasize his purpose in publishing it, "that we have striven our utmost by our humble industry to commend the philosophy of Christ to virtuous minds."[90]

Erasmus sought to allay criticism of his work by dedicating his New Testament to the pope. His dedicatory letter of August 8, 1516, tried to emphasize the conservative nature of the text and his reliance on the Church Fathers:

For by this labour, we do not intend to tear up the old and commonly accepted edition, but to emend it in some places where it is corrupt, and to make it clear where it is obscure; and this not by the dreams of my own mind, nor, as they say, with unwashed hands, but partly by the evidence of the earliest manuscripts, and partly by the opinion of those, whose learning and sanctity have been confirmed of the authority of the Church—I mean Jerome, Hilary, Ambrose, Augustine, Chrysostom, and Cyril. Meantime we are always prepared either to give our reasons, without presumption, for anything which we have rightly taught, or to correct, without grudging, any passage where as men we have unwittingly fallen into error.[91]

This letter to Leo X shows clearly that Erasmus was ready to retract any statement or translation of his that was based on erroneous evidence. All he asked for was a fair reading. Before actually publishing his text, he submitted it to the bishop of Basel, in whose jurisdiction he was living. The bishop accepted it without question. After it had appeared in print, Erasmus also submitted it to William Warham, archbishop of Canterbury; two doctors of theology, Ludwig Baer of Paris and Wolfgang Capito of Basel; Gregor Reisch, the prior of the Carthusians at Freiburg; Bishop John Fisher; Domenico Cardinal Grimani; Raffaele Cardinal Riario—all of whom praised it; and finally to Pope Leo X, who, according to Erasmus, sent him two letters of approbation.

With so much praise, Erasmus felt confident that he had satisfied all of the requirements that had been laid down by the Lateran Council (1512–17) on this matter. But his critics thought otherwise. Before the end of 1517, Erasmus was angrily criticized for issuing a new translation of Scripture without the express authority of a general church council.

[90] Nichols, 2:454
[91] Ibid., p. 316.

Erasmus answered the charge by asking his adversaries if they knew whether or not Saint Jerome had been required to submit his Vulgate to a church council before it had been completed. In a letter to Bullock dated August 1516, Erasmus observed: "I believe it was written first, and approved afterwards; and the same may take place with respect to my edition, though that is a thing I neither solicit nor expect."[92]

No sooner was the first edition out when Erasmus decided to correct it and to publish a second edition. He hoped in this way to satisfy his wrangling critics. Writing to Marcus Laurinus, the dean of St. Donatian at Bruges, on April 5, 1518, Erasmus spoke openly of his intentions: "But these wrangling critics, naturally stupid and rendered doubly blind by the malady of evil-speaking, believe, I fancy, that it has been my intention to supersede entirely the translation [of Saint Jerome] which we have in use, and which in several places, I myself prefer to the reading of the Greek copies; whereas all that I have done is to translate the text which I found in the Greek manuscripts, pointing out in the notes which reading I approve or disapprove. . . . I show by manifest proofs, that in a multitude of passages our version is depraved, but not so far as to endanger the Faith; and I point out how Cyprian, Jerome, and Ambrose agree with the Greek manuscripts."[93]

Erasmus fought an almost uphill battle when he attempted to improve the accuracy of the Vulgate. So entrenched had that Latin version of the Scriptures become by the sixteenth century that Erasmus decided to retain the text of Saint Jerome when he issued his third edition in 1522. Erasmus was, nevertheless, disappointed that a number of his readers had missed the whole purpose of his labors. His letter to Cardinal Wolsey of May 18, 1517, reiterates his lifelong commitment to piety and the instruction of children that lày at the base of his scriptural studies:

At any rate I have taken every precaution, that nothing should proceed from me, which would either corrupt the young by obscenity, or in any way hinder piety, give rise to sedition, or draw a black line across any one's character. Whatever exertions I have hitherto made, have been made for the assistance of honourable studies and the advancement of the Christian religion; and all persons on every side are thankful for what has been done, except a few theologians and monks, who have no wish to be wiser or better than they are. May I lose the favour of

---

[92] Ibid., p. 325.
[93] Ibid., 3:325–26.

Christ, if I do not desire that whatever I have of talent or of eloquence should be wholly dedicated to His glory, to the Catholic Church, and to sacred studies.[94]

This was an eloquent statement by Erasmus of his orthodox religious position some six months before Martin Luther drew the attention of Christendom to his Ninety-five Theses. Who could have been more catholic in his concern for the church than Erasmus, who preferred peace and harmony to revolt or sedition?

The second edition of the New Testament required a change in title, and Erasmus decided to name it the *Novum Testamentum*. His new edition appeared in 1519 (a third edition in 1522, a fourth in 1527, and a fifth in 1535) and included a justification for each book and an expanded discussion of his methodology (known as the *Ratio verae theologiae,* which was first published in 1518) and enlarged annotations. Ignoring the criticisms of his foes, Erasmus also published an entirely new translation of the Greek text which differed considerably from that of the Vulgate. Erasmus explained to Antonio Pucci, an ecclesiastical official, on August 26, 1518, the plan of his second edition of the New Testament:

Having first collated several copies made by Greek scribes, we followed that which appeared to be the most genuine; and having translated this into Latin, we placed our translation by the side of the Greek text, so that the reader might readily compare the two, the translation being so made, that it was our first study to preserve, as far as was permissible, the integrity of the Latin tongue without injury to the simplicity of the Apostolic language.

Our next care was to provide that any sentences, which had before given trouble to the reader, either by ambiguity or obscurity of language, or by faulty or unsuitable expressions, should be explained and made clear with as little deviation as possible from the words of the original, and none from the sense; as to which we do not depend upon any dreams of our own, but seek out the writings of Origen, Basil, Chrysostom, Cyril, Jerome, Cyprian, Ambrose, or Augustine. Some annotations were added (which have now been extended), where we inform the Reader, upon whose authority this or that matter rests, relying always upon the judgment of the old authors.[95]

It was Erasmus' intention to clarify the meaning of Scripture by determining its actual words. This could only be done by returning to the original Greek language in which it was first written and then by comparing it with later Latin translations. The study of theology itself

---

[94] Ibid., pp. 385–86.
[95] Ibid., pp. 430–32.

depended on this kind of clarity. Erasmus underscored his interest in reforming theology in the same letter to Pucci referred to above: to "theology, which is almost too prevalent in the Schools, is to be added a knowledge of the original sources; it is to this result that our work especially leads."[96] Clarity of meaning would lead theologians to the actual teachings of Christ and put more emphasis on what he defined as necessary doctrine than on what later scholastic theologians have tended to emphasize. But in promoting such a program Erasmus only succeeded in antagonizing these very same theologians. They were outraged that he was suggesting to all of Christendom that theology might be harboring false ideas by giving undue emphasis to certain matters of faith and morals.

THE CHURCH FATHERS (1516–)

To support his textual studies of Scripture, Erasmus turned to the writings of the Church Fathers. He relied heavily on their learning and judgments. He discovered in their writings a keen appreciation for the study of Scripture and for its application to the lives of individuals. Erasmus succeeded in publishing the *opera* of the following Church Fathers: the letters of Saint Jerome (in four volumes) appeared in July of 1516, the works of Saint Cyprian in 1520, Arnobius in 1522, Saint Hilary in 1523, Saint Irenaeus in 1526, Saint Ambrose and Saint Athanasius in 1527, Saint Augustine in 1528–29, Lactantius (a single work) in 1529, Saint John Chrysostom and Alger in 1530, Saint Gregory Nazianzen in 1531, Saint Basil in 1532, and Origen posthumously in 1536.

Jerome and Origen were the two most important influences on Erasmus, and he valued their writings above all the others. He expressed his great admiration for both men by composing biographies of them, which he attached to his critical editions and in which he acknowledged their rational syntheses of classical and Christian learning. Throughout Erasmus' writings it is evident that he preferred the ancient Church Fathers to such medieval scholastic theologians as Saints Thomas Aquinas and Bonaventure, and the reason should not be surprising: the ancient Church Fathers, with their knowledge of ancient languages and history, were closer to the sources of Christianity and emphasized in their own writings the importance of imitating Christ. In a letter to Pope

---

[96] Ibid., p. 431.

Leo X, dated April 29, 1515, Erasmus detailed his admiration for Saint Jerome:

> I saw that St. Jerome was so completely the first among Latin theologians, that we might almost call him the one person worthy of that name. What a fund in him of Roman eloquence, what skill in languages, what a knowledge of antiquity and of all history, what a retentive memory, what a perfect familiarity with mystic literature, above all, what zeal, what a wonderful inspiration of the divine breath! He is the one person who at the same time delights by his eloquence, teaches by his erudition, and ravishes by his holiness.[97]

Erasmus wanted to edit the works of Saint Jerome in order to promote Christian piety. Later on in the above letter he concludes: "I do not myself expect any other outcome of my exertions, but that Christian piety may obtain some aid from the memorials of Jerome. He, for whose sake I undergo this labour, will abundantly recompense me for it."[98] Christ was never far from his thoughts. Erasmus had begun work on the letters of Saint Jerome even before he started his study of the New Testament. He delayed it only because he saw the letters as an adjunct to Scripture. Erasmus' edition of Saint Jerome was judicious. It retained both Greek and Hebrew spellings and made a concerted effort to designate those letters that he regarded as spurious or doubtful. His notes display both erudition and restraint: a delicate balance.

Erasmus used the format of the preface to his critical editions to emphasize his Christocentric perceptions. Two examples will suffice. The first is taken from Erasmus' edition of Saint Hilary (1523). The prefatory letter (dated January 5, 1523) was addressed to Jean de Carondelet, the archbishop of Palermo:

> When life leaves us, when faith is in the mouth rather than the heart, when we lack knowledge of the Sacred Scriptures, we drive men to believe what they do not believe, to love what they do not love, to understand what they do not understand. What is coerced cannot be sincere, and what is not voluntary cannot please Christ.[99]

The second example is taken from Erasmus' dedicatory letter to King John III of Portugal, dated March 24, 1527, in the *Chrysostomi lucubrationes* (Basel, 1527), which had also been scheduled to be inserted

---

[97] Ibid., 2:201.
[98] Ibid., p. 203.
[99] Hans J. Hillerbrand, ed., *Erasmus and His Age* (New York, 1970), p. 169.

in his 1530 edition of Saint John Chrysostom; but when the king declined to acknowledge it, Erasmus withdrew the letter. The dedicatory letter urges the preacher to inspire Christian piety by promoting the study of Scripture:

A preacher will readily find a means of winning over his audience if he succeeds in getting people to know and love what they are learning. One can find in the Scriptures an abundance of material for charming and captivating pious hearts, without searching for bait in witty phrases from poets and mimes. If the teacher is on fire, he will easily set others aflame. If he deeply enjoys the things he preaches, he will easily inspire his listeners with that same feeling. This heart, this golden tongue [of Chrysostom] which was aimed at the secular forum was diverted by Christ to the preaching of the gospel.[100]

Erasmus' efforts won the plaudits of many men of learning. François Deloynes, a French humanist, described his reaction to the edition of Saint Jerome's letters in an epistle to Erasmus dated November, 1516: "and the works of Jerome are in hand, a laborious task, which was reserved for the strength of a Hercules, that is, of an Erasmus; in which I seem to see Jerome himself by your care and diligence come back to light, and anticipate the promised day of Resurrection."[101] But Erasmus was also aware of the fact that his work sometimes aroused the ire of readers. In an effort to pacify his critics, he promised restraint. Erasmus referred to this subject in a letter to Ludwig Baer, dated January 1, 1517, where he also emphasized his didactic purpose:

I only endeavour by my small exertions to promote the general instruction. It has been thought that I express myself in some places with too much heat; but those who think so do not take into account the want of due respect with which sacred literature and the writings of the Fathers are received. While I was pushing on through my work, although my indignation was repeatedly curbed by reason, I could not in every case hide my feelings. But I was afterwards forced to be more restrained by the extreme scrupulosity of some of my friends. For indeed, if it can be done, I should wish to assist study in such a way as not to offend any mortal being. If I do not always succeed in this; I am comforted by the consciousness of rectitude, and by the consideration that up to this time I have the approval of the most approved persons; and we may well hope that what now satisfies the candid will in time satisfy all. At any rate I trust that I

[100] Ibid., p. 197.
[101] Nichols, 2:440–41.

shall never be pleased with anything that is false in learning or religion, even in my own books.[102]

Erasmus pledged to Baer and to his other friends that henceforth he would pursue his scholarship with regard for the eyes of the beholder as well as for truth itself. Since truth required impartiality, he weighed the merits and shortcomings of the writings of the Church Fathers. In a letter to Johann Botzheim (August 19, 1529) Erasmus justified his dissensions from the Church Fathers by observing that these mortal men "sometimes fall into heretical error." For example, he noted that "Jerome translated and interpreted the Prophets and yet he often admitted that he could not understand their meaning."[103] Erasmus' power of discrimination mark him as a man of great strength and originality. He bent his full faculties to the task of uncovering the meaning of Scripture, but without offending "any mortal being." It was, to quote Deloynes, a "laborious task, which was reserved for the strength of Hercules."

THE COMPLAINT OF PEACE (1517)

Querela pacis was written in 1516 at the request of Jean Le Sauvage, chancellor of Brabant, and dedicated to the bishop of Utrecht, Philip of Burgundy. It appeared in print in December of 1517. Some thirty-four editions, including German and Dutch translations, were published before 1536.[104] In raising objections to war, Erasmus naturally turned to the Old and New Testaments, where he freely quoted from the Psalms, Isaiah, Saints Paul, Matthew, John, and Luke. Erasmus not only condemned wars between nations but hostilities that took place between members of a family or among scholars, particularly theologians and monks. He especially abhorred warfare among Christians, and, in turn, was repelled by the fact that the very instruments of war, namely guns, were frequently blessed by the clergy before the start of a battle, and not infrequently named after an apostle or decorated with the images of saints.

The Complaint of Peace called true Christians back to Christ. It held up the image of the Prince of Peace in order to promote concord; after all, "truly Christ doth no other thing, commanding them to learn one certain

---

[102] Ibid., pp. 451–52.
[103] *Allen*, 8, Ep. 2206, p. 260.
[104] Van der Haeghen and Lenger, *Bibliotheca Belgica* (1964), 2:1017.

thing of Him: to be meek of mind and not fierce."[105] But Erasmus was not content with merely condemning wars and those who participated in them, he sought to find a way to permanent peace. He thought he saw a solution to this crisis in the second decade of the sixteenth century when three young rulers sat on three of the leading thrones of Europe: Francis I of France, Charles I of Spain, and Henry VIII of England. Through his friendship with each of them and through the persuasive power of the written and printed word, he hoped to convince these rulers to seek only peaceful solutions to any of their future difficulties:

> I pray thee, O thou Christian prince, if thou be truly a Christian, behold the image of thy Prince. Observe and mark how He entered into His Kingdom, how He proceeded, how He departed hence; and thou shalt easily understand how He would have thee to rule . . . that peace and concord might be the sum and conclusion of all thy care and rule.[106]

Erasmus went so far as to ask these princes to sue for peace at any price: "Sometimes peace must be bought. And if thou calculate what war shall consume and waste, and that thou shalt keep thy citizens from destruction, it shall seem, although thou didst buy it full dearly, to be bought for little. And when a great deal more besides the blood of thy citizens should have been spent in war, thou shalt reckon how great and manifold evils thou eschewdest and how much goodness thou defendedst; so shalt thou not repent thee of thy expenses and charges."[107] Human life was obviously of greater value than money or material goods.

Erasmus also directed other petitions to the papacy and to Christian men in general. On May 21, 1515, he wrote to Pope Leo X, pleading with him not to resort to war even for the purpose of repelling the Turks and recovering the Holy Land:

> . . . those savage beasts, will not withstand the roar of our Leo, and truculent though they be, they shall feel, yes, they shall feel the unconquerable strength of our gentle Leo, and they will be impotent before a Pontiff armed more with piety than with might of numbers, and who bears into battle the immortal assistance of the Heavenly Power.[108]

It was far better to subdue the Turks by setting a good example before

---

[105] Erasmus, *The Complaint of Peace*, trans. William H. Hirten (New York, 1946), p. 24.
[106] Ibid., p. 20.
[107] Ibid., p. 44.
[108] Mangan, *Life . . . of Desiderius Erasmus*, 1:395.

them than by force of arms. Prior to this letter, he addressed one to Antonius van Bergen under date of March 14, 1514, in which he promoted peace among all men, but especially among Christians:

> I often wonder what it is that drives the whole human race, not merely Christians, to such a pitch of frenzy that they will undergo such effort, expense, and danger for the sake of mutual destruction. . . . For us, who boast of naming ourselves 'Christians' after Christ who preached and practised naught save gentleness, who are members of one body, one flesh, quickened by the same spirit, nurtured upon the same sacraments, joined in union to a single head, called to the same eternal life, hoping for that supreme communion whereby, even as Christ is one with the Father, so we too may be one with him—how can anything in this world be so important as to impel us to war, a thing so deadly and so grim that even when it is waged with perfect justification no man who is truly good approves it?[109]

Moreover, Erasmus lamented the consequences of man's aggressive nature on the future of Christendom, but saw signs of hope in Divine Providence: "I can see vast disturbances in the making, and what their outcome will be is not clear; may God in his mercy vouchsafe to quiet the storm that now afflicts Christendom."[110] Erasmus placed his faith in man's future in the mercy of God.

PARAPHRASES OF THE NEW TESTAMENT (1517–)

According to Wallace K. Ferguson, Erasmus emphasized the *philosophia Christi* in his studies on Scripture, but he also revolutionized that study: "Erasmus introduced a new note into biblical interpretation by demonstrating the part played by human authorship and error. He insisted on treating the Bible as a human document, to be studied in the light of modern historical and philological knowledge. He said little, it is true, about dogma; but he had much to say about the philosophy of Christ."[111] After the New Testament appeared in 1516, John Colet and other scholars urged Erasmus to prepare paraphrases of the books of the New Testament that would expand upon the meaning of the texts.

The *Paraphrase of St. Paul's Epistle to the Romans* was published at the

---

[109] *CWE*, 2:280.

[110] Ibid., pp. 279–80.

[111] Wallace K. Ferguson, ed., *Erasmi Opuscula: A Supplement to the Opera Omnia* (The Hague, 1933), pp. 225–26.

end of 1517 and was dedicated to Domenico Cardinal Grimani, a patron of letters. It was followed in turn by the paraphrases of Corinthians and Galatians (in 1519); by Ephesians, Timothy, Titus, and Philemon, together with the Epistles of Peter and Jude (in 1520); by Philippians, Colossians, Thessalonians, and the Epistles of John, James, and Saint Paul to the Hebrews (in 1521); by the Gospel of Saint Matthew (in 1522); by the Gospels of Mark, Luke, and John (in 1523); and by the Acts of the Apostles (in 1524).[112] Moreover, collected editions of these paraphrases appeared in 1524, 1532, and 1534, and certain paraphrases (for example, the Gospel of Saint Matthew and Saint Paul's Epistle to the Corinthians) were translated into German as early as 1521. So popular did this work become that during the reign of King Edward VI (1547–53), the Paraphrases in English were ordered to be placed alongside the Bible in every parish church in England: John Byddell had earlier printed Leonard Cox's translation, titled *The Paraphrase of Erasmus . . . upon ye Epistle of . . . Paule unto . . . Titus* (about 1535), and Nicholas Udall, Thomas Caius, and John Old et al. translated a two-volume edition of the Paraphrases in 1548–49 that was used by the Church of England. These paraphrases, unlike Erasmus' edition of the New Testament and his annotations, provided a single interpretation of the text that reflected the considerable erudition and good judgment of its author.

Erasmus set forth the circumstances surrounding his writing of the *Paraphrases* in a letter to an unknown recipient, dated November 1517:

> I send, meantime, our Paraphrase upon the Epistle of Paul to the Romans, which is our latest offspring; for, being now employed in the most troublesome of all literary labours, I mean, in the revision of the text of the New Testament I am wont to refresh my mind with such relaxation, when tempted by satiety to steal away from work. They thus serve as my ball or my die, sending me back with fresh vigour to my task. . . . Perhaps I may deal with the other Epistles in the same way, if I find this first taste is not displeasing to the palates of my readers. For it is wonderful how much hazard there is, even in these matters; so that it often happens that where you expect the most appropriation, you carry away a poor return; and on the other hand, where you expect no favour at all, you come in for a great amount of praise.[113]

---

[112] Ferdinand van der Haeghen, *Bibliotheca Erasmiana* (Ghent, 1893), cites 1520 editions of the Paraphrase of the Gosepl of Saint Matthew and the Paraphrase of the Epistles of Saint James. See pp. 149 and 143 of his *Bibliotheca Erasmiana*.

[113] Nichols, 3:163–64.

In an earlier letter of October 31, 1517, Erasmus wrote to Pierre Barbier, an official at the court of King Charles I of Spain, expressing pleasure at the wonderful reception that was given to his *Paraphrase on St. Paul's Epistle to the Romans* by men of learning. He regarded this epistle as "the principal and most excellent part of the New Testament." Taking advantage of the opportunity, Erasmus employed the prologue to this edition to urge the reader to "commit himself wholly unto Christ."[114] Moreover, in a dedicatory letter to Archduke Ferdinand of Austria which accompanied his edition of the Gospel of Saint John, he advised even princes to imitate the message of the Gospel: "A prince does not preach and teach the Gospel, but he does observe, practice, and fulfill it."[115]

THE COLLOQUIES (1518–)

The *Colloquia* originated as exercises for the teaching of Latin to boys during the time when Erasmus was supporting himself and pursuing theological studies at the University of Paris (1495 to 1499). They were never meant to be published, and when they did appear in an unauthorized edition, edited by Beatus Rhenanus and printed by Johann Froben in November of 1518, Erasmus was distinctly annoyed. Under pressure, he finally approved their publication in 1519. The text of the *Colloquies* is of an intensely personal nature. Erasmus chose the names of his own pupils to identify the various speakers. He did so deliberately in an effort to make the study of Latin more attractive to his youthful readers. It is clear from the design of this book that Erasmus had mastered the arts of teaching before he had published his first book! So popular did this work become that within a year of its appearance it was reprinted in Paris, Antwerp, Louvain, London, and again in Basel by Froben himself. It has been estimated that eighty-seven reprints appeared before Erasmus' death.[116]

The *Colloquies* enjoyed such great success because it was an immensely useful book: both grammar-school boys and style-conscious adults benefited from its novel approach to writing. But it was also much more than a book on rhetoric. According to Craig R. Thompson: "The result was a book of unusual variety: debates on moral and religious questions:

---

[114] Erasmus, *Opera Omnia*, ed. Jean Le Clerc (Leiden, 1703–06), 7:771–72.
[115] Ibid., pp. 493–94.
[116] Thompson, *The Colloquies of Erasmus*, p. xxv.

lively arguments on war, government, and other social problems; advice on how to train husbands, wives, and children; discourses on innkeepers, beggars, pets, horse thieves; on methods of study or of sleep or of burial; on diet and on sermons—all this and much more."[117] As usual, uppermost in Erasmus' mind was his *philosophia Christi*. He was anxious to persuade everyone, from the tender-aged child to the aging adult, that the best means to heaven was through the imitation of Christ in the Gospels. In his *De utilitate colloquiorum* (1526), Erasmus reminded his readers that even though "Socrates brought philosophy down from heaven to earth; I have brought it even into games, informal conversations, and drinking parties. For the very amusements of Christians ought to have a philosophical flavor."[118]

Even earlier though, in his 1522 colloquy entitled *The Godly Feast*, which was "in some ways the most typical and has always been one of the most popular" of the colloquies,[119] Erasmus stressed the importance of "obeying the commandments of the Gospel." Speaking through the characters Eusebius and Timothy, he observed:

> *Eusebius:* Does he [i.e. the doorkeeper in the form of a statue of Saint Peter] seem to you an uncivil porter who at one and the same time warns us to avoid sin and turn to the pursuit of godliness; next, warns us that we do not attain to the true Christian life by works of the Mosaic law but through gospel faith; finally, that the way to life eternal is by obeying the commandments of the Gospel?
>
> *Timothy:* And look: the path on the right shows us presently an exquisite little chapel. On the altar Jesus Christ gazes heavenward, whence his Father and the Holy Spirit look out, and he points to heaven with his right hand while with his left he seems to beckon and invite the passerby.
>
> *Eusebius:* Nor does he receive us in silence: you see in Latin, "I am the way, and the truth, and the life"; in Greek, "I am Alpha and Omega"; in Hebrew, "Come, ye children, hearken unto me; I will teach you the fear of the Lord."[120]

Christ commanded the faithful to imitate his example.

Erasmus revised and added to his *Colloquies* regularly. In 1519, for

---

[117] Ibid., p. xxvi.
[118] Ibid., p. 630.
[119] Ibid., p. 47.
[120] Ibid., p. 50.

example, he added an appendix to them in which he addressed himself to the Protestant cause:

"I clearly bore witness to my thorough opposition to the Lutheran teaching. At that time I warned Luther privately—he had written to me first—to act with sincerity and with that moderation which befits one who professes the Gospel."[121] Erasmus found fault specifically with Luther's cause because Luther and his followers failed to imitate the example of Christ in the Gospel. Yet, in spite of his opposition to Lutheranism, portions of the *Colloquies* were held to be heretical by the Sorbonne as early as May of 1526. In an attempt to satisfy these critics and others, Erasmus wrote a defense of them (*De utilitate colloquiorum*, dated May 21, 1526) which he appended to his edition of June 1526. Erasmus emphasized the pedagogical purpose of his work: "Now if someone protests that it is undignified for an old man to play in this childish fashion, my answer is: 'I don't care how childish, if only it's useful.' And if graybeard grammar masters are commended for coaxing youngsters with bits of cake into wanting to learn the rudiments, I don't think I should be reproached for attracting youth with like zeal to refinement of Latin speech and to godliness. . . . But to implant from the start a taste for excellence in young minds *is* urgent. Moreover, I'm not sure anything is learned better than what is learned as a game."[122]

Thoroughly practical in his approach to learning and pedagogy, Erasmus never forgot that the real object of education was Christian piety. He willingly played the part of "a fool" in order to entice young minds to learn of Christ and to imitate his way of life: "And this little book, if taught to ingenuous youth, will lead them to many more useful studies: to poetry, rhetoric, physics, ethics, and finally to matters of Christian piety. I have played the part of a fool in making myself eulogist of my own writings, but I was forced to it, partly because of the villainy of slanderers, partly because of service to Christian youth, for whom we must do all we can."[123]

Erasmus took the trouble to answer his critics because he wanted to promote goodwill and to uproot blind judgment. He implored his adversaries to end their bitterness and dissension, and to advance "the

---

[121] Erasmus to Duke George of Saxony, December 12, 1524, ed. Hillerbrand, *Erasmus and His Age*, p. 179.

[122] Thompson, *Colloquies*, p. 625.

[123] Ibid., p. 633.

fellowship of the heavenly Jerusalem."[124] Erasmus also perceived that the way of Christ was something other than "a dismal mode of life." Christ was not a pessimist: he loved life and urged his followers to enjoy it. Erasmus, speaking through the character Hedonius, describes his own conception of Christ: "Completely mistaken, therefore, are those who talk in the foolish fashion about Christ's having been sad and gloomy in character and calling upon us to follow a dismal mode of life. On the contrary, he alone shows the most enjoyable life of all and the one most full of true pleasure."[125] Erasmus added a new perspective to Christian life, one that combined piety and joy and was rooted firmly in the image of Christ himself.

THE METHOD OF TRUE THEOLOGY (1518)

The *Ratio verae theologiae* was first written as prefatory material for the 1516 edition of the New Testament. It was later expanded and printed separately at Louvain in November of 1518 under the title: *Ratio seu methodus compendio perveniendi ad veram theologiam*. Eighteen editions appeared during the lifetime of the author.[126] In fashioning this theological treatise, Erasmus drew upon Scripture and such Church Fathers as Origen, and Saints Basil, Gregory Nazianzen, Athanasius, Cyril, John Chrysostom, Jerome, Ambrose, Hilary, and Augustine.

In this handbook for students of theology, Erasmus impressed upon his readers the importance of attaining a virtuous life before embarking on the study of theology. He also insisted on the learning of Hebrew, Greek, and Latin and the mastery of the *studia humanitatis* (including dialectic, rhetoric, arithmetic, music, poetry, and history) as preliminary skills to the study of theology. The theological curriculum itself consisted of the following subjects: exegesis, especially the study of the Church Fathers, church history, civil and ecclesiastical law, and ethics. Finally, Erasmus devoted attention to the methodology for interpreting figurative language. He encouraged allegorical interpretation of both classical and Christian texts in order to teach morality. Writing to Johann von Botzheim on August 19, 1529, he justified his own interpretations of certain figures of speech or tropes in the New Testament by arguing that

---

[124] Ibid., p. 637.
[125] Ibid., p. 549.
[126] Van der Haeghen and Lenger, *Bibliotheca Belgica* (1964), 2:1040.

Saint Jerome had removed "all the Hebrew tropes [from the Old Testament] despite Augustine's vain protests." For Erasmus, Scripture was more than "a merely human product" since "the essence of Scripture lies in its meaning not in its words."[127]

The Method of True Theology was soon attacked by theological adversaries; among them was Jacobus Latomus of Louvain, who criticized Erasmus for his emphasis on piety in the formation of the theologian. Indirectly, Erasmus responded to this charge by underscoring the importance of virtue in the life of a theologian, in his letter to Bishop Fisher, dated April 2, 1519:

> I had said in my *Method* that piety and edification are theology's good side. Latomus attacks this view and demonstrates at length that to be a theologian is not equivalent to being pious. But I fear, in the future, if they carry on, some may say that to be a theologian is not equivalent to being a wise man. . . . The folly of it all: while we are wasting our labours and the peace of others in such wrangling, we count ourselves as saints, as theologians and as Christians: But, meanwhile, where is Christian peacefulness, where is simplicity, and where are our happy blithesome games in the fields of Scriptures?[128]

Erasmus insisted that theologians as spokesmen for the Church should assume responsibility, paying particular attention to the encouragement of concord and order. In his dedicatory letter of June 1, 1523 (*Allen*, 5, Ep. 1365) to Archbishop Albert of Brandenburg (which appeared in a new edition of the *Ratio*), Erasmus discussed the religious strife that was then consuming the world and his own efforts toward securing peace:

> It is part of my unhappy fate that my old age has fallen on these evil times. We must implore the Lord Jesus that He, who alone has the power to do so by his spirit, will turn the hearts of the Christian people to the love of peace and concord. . . . And yet what is our religion if peace be gone? The world would be no darker if you were to extinguish the sun. For my part I would rather be a grocer in the possession of Christian tranquillity, and rejoicing in evangelical simple-mindedness, than the greatest and most renowned theologian in the world, and be involved in these dissensions. I, at any rate, for my own part, am devoting all my strength to eliminating this poison from the inmost fibres of my heart, recovering the simplicity and peace of the Gospel spirit, and composing myself to that habit of mind in which I may appear with all confidence before the

---

[127] Erasmus to John Botzheim, August 19, 1529, in *Allen*, 8, Ep. 2206, p. 260.

[128] Jean Rouschausse, trans., *Erasmus and Fisher: Their Correspondence* (Paris, 1968), pp. 67–69.

judgment seat of Christ, to which perhaps tomorrow or any day I may be summoned.[129]

Erasmus was staunchly committed to securing Christian tranquillity, and he devoted his energies to achieving it in the spirit of the Gospel. Lewis W. Spitz has identified and summarized Erasmus' pursuit of the Gospel message in terms of his *philosophia Christi:* "Erasmus constantly stressed the imitation of Christ, the exemplar of virtue and wisdom, an imitation which involved the mystic and spiritual indwelling of Christ in the human heart, not merely the outward mimicking of his actions—as one would copy the charity of a saint, for example."[130]

THE OUR FATHER (1523)

In works of biography, it has been customary to suggest that Erasmus of Rotterdam[131] was more concerned with exegesis and the classics than with Christian meditation and prayer.[132] As the Prince of Humanists, he was supposedly caught up in the scholarly pursuits of the age and, therefore, had little time for religious devotion. Notwithstanding his humanistic orientation, certain biographers would also argue that Erasmus developed a philosophy of Christ—a way of life which chose Christ as its model but selectively deemphasized acts of Christian piety.[133] Somehow, Erasmus was able to equate humanism and Christianity but not Christianity and piety. It is of interest, therefore, to examine a treatise such as the *Precatio Dominica,* which was written at the very peak of Erasmus' career, and to judge his religious disposition and interior life in terms of its content. Those biographers who maintain the second of the above positions would expect to find a secularly oriented mind, a kind of text which reflected the vanities of a scholar, who had been laden with academic and courtly honors. But such is not the case. For Erasmus was a more devoted disciple of Christ than he was of human

---

[129] Robert B. Drummond, trans., *Erasmus: His Life and Character* (London, 1873), 2:187–88.

[130] L. W. Spitz, *The Religious Renaissance of the German Humanists,* p. 225.

[131] Erasmus, *Precatio Dominica* (Basel: Johann Froben, 1523).

[132] Johan Huizinga, *Erasmus of Rotterdam,* trans. by F. Hopman (London: Phaidon Press, 1952), p. 113; Albert Hyma, *The Youth of Erasmus.* Second ed. (New York: Russell & Russell, 1969), p. 142; and P. S. Allen, *Erasmus: Lectures and Wayfaring Sketches* (Oxford: Clarendon Press, 1934), pp. 96–97.

[133] Hyma, *The Youth of Erasmus,* p. 142.

vice and folly. Highly reflective, the *Precatio Dominica* emphasizes a deeply devout, and often neglected, side of Erasmus' nature. Like the Brethren of the Common Life, who instructed him during his youth, Erasmus was a master of the art of Christian meditation. Taking leave of mundane preoccupations, he soared heavenward in search of a comforting and loving father. Indeed, only an exceptionally pious practitioner could have observed:

> As often soeuer as for thy loue we despice and sette nought by the realme of this worlde/ and with full trust hange vpon the heuenly kyngdome/ that thou hast promysed vs: as often also/ as we forsake and leaue honourynge of erthely richesse/ and onely worshyp and embrace the precious and gostly lernyng of the gospel/ as often as we refuse those thynges/ . . . So often father thou warrest in vs/ and ouercomest the realme of the deuyll/ and openyst the myght and power of thy realme.[134]

Yet, at the same time, the work also reveals one of Erasmus' principal faults: a form of religious anti-Semitism, rather than racial, which was shared by many contemporary humanists. With unkind disparity, he lashes out at the Jews of his own day in these words:

> The iewes also neuer cesse in their sinagoges and resorte of people/ from dispitefull and abominable bacbytinge of thy onely sonne/ wherby in the meanetyme they sclaundre the/ sithe it can nat be chosen whan thy sonne is misfamed (whiche is the very clerenesse of thy glorie) but that infamy also must redounde in the.[135]

But, then, was not this the real Erasmus? Like other men of his time, was he not a composite of virtue and vice; both a lover of Christ, whom he had never seen, and a hater of certain men's beliefs with whom he was in daily contact? Even so, his anti-Semitism appears all the more jarring in the face of the syncretism of more enlightened humanists. In the last analysis, we are especially fortunate to have record of this anomaly and to have had it expressed so poignantly in the garb of the *Precatio Dominica*.

Erasmus first published his *Precatio Dominica* at the press of Johann Froben in 1523. Before the year was out, the work itself proved to be

---

[134] Erasmus, *A devout treatise vpon the Pater noster*, trans. by Margaret More Roper and ed. by R. L. DeMolen in *Erasmus of Rotterdam: A Quincentennial Symposium* (New York: Twayne Publishers, 1971), p. 112.

[135] Ibid., p. 107.

immensely popular and appeared in three Latin editions. By 1524, six Latin editions and two translations, one in English and the other in German, were circulating in Europe. Eventually, according to the *Bibliotheca Erasmiana,* twenty-seven separate editions of the *Precatio Dominica* were variously published between 1523 and 1861. In addition, ten more editions of this work have survived for which there are no dates of publication.[136]

A DISCOURSE ON THE FREEDOM OF THE WILL (1524)

De libero arbitrio diatribe seu collatio (*A Diatribe or Discourse on the Freedom of the Will*) was published in September 1524 at presses in Basel, Antwerp, and Strasbourg, and appeared in some seven editions during the author's lifetime.[137] Erasmus described the work as follows in a letter to John, the elector of Saxony (March 2, 1526): "I gave the book a very modest title, calling it a discussion or conference. I do not assume the role of a judge, but of one who is questioning and discussing, meanwhile laying aside all authority except that of Holy Scripture."[138] Throughout the treatise Erasmus insisted that salvation without freedom of choice was a non sequitur. He argued that the belief in man's free will rests on Scripture, the Church Fathers, ancient philosophers, and human reason itself. He concluded that "the will is not powerless though it cannot attain its end without grace."[139] Erasmus based this conclusion on the following reasoning:

> I ask what merit can a man arrogate to himself if whatever, as a man, he is able to achieve by his natural intelligence and free choice, all this he owes to the one from whom he receives these powers? And yet God himself imputes this to our merit, thus we do not turn our soul away from his grace, and that we apply our natural powers to simple obedience. And this surely goes to show that it is not wrong to say that man does something and yet attributes the sum of all that he does to God as its author, from whom it has come about that he was able to ally his own effort, with the grace of God. . . . Here there is nothing that a man

---

[136] For a discussion of the various editions, see E. J. Devereux, "Some Lost English Translations of Erasmus," *Transactions of the Bibliographical Society,* Fifth series, 17 (1962), pp. 255–59.

[137] Van der Haeghen, *Bibliotheca Erasmiana* (1893), p. 20.

[138] Hillerbrand, *Erasmus and His Age,* p. 191.

[139] Erasmus, *De Libero Arbitrio,* trans. E. Gordon Rupp et al. under the title *Luther and Erasmus: Free Will and Salvation* (Philadelphia, 1969), p. 79.

can arrogate to his own strength and yet, with sure confidence, he may hope for the reward of eternal life from God, not because he has merited it with his good deeds, but because it seemed in accordance with God's goodness to promise it to those who trust in Him.

According to Erasmus, God required man to cooperate freely with His saving grace:

> It is man's part to pray without ceasing that God will impart and increase in us his Spirit, giving thanks if anything is done well by us, that we may marvel at his power in all things, everywhere wondering at his wisdom, everywhere loving such goodness. This way of viewing the matter seems to me also completely plausible, for it agrees with Holy Scripture, and answers to the confession of those who, once for all dead to the world, are buried together with Christ in baptism, that the flesh having been mortified, they afterward may live and act in the Spirit of Jesus, in whose body they have been implanted by faith.[140]

Uppermost in Erasmus' mind was the need to "live and act in the Spirit of Jesus," and this could only be accomplished if the individual participated willingly and actively in the imitation of Christ's life.

Luther responded to Erasmus' tract in December of 1525 with his *De servo arbitrio* (*The Bondage of the Will*), in which he flatly rejected Erasmus' argument and accused him of impiety, insisting that man could not effect his salvation without Christ's prior saving grace. Erasmus answered Luther in the *Hyperaspistes* (*The Heavenly Armed Soldier*) which was published in two parts (March 1526 and September 1527). In this work Erasmus accused Luther of being a dogmatist and extremist, who in his enthusiasm for Scripture rejected reason as a second source of truth.

Though Erasmus sympathized with the original purpose of the Protestant Reformation, he refused to join that movement. He recoiled at the thought of a revolutionary band that lacked sincerity and fomented discord. He tried to explain his reasons in the following letter to Martin Bucer, the reformer of Strasbourg, on November 11, 1527:

> However it was the duty of the leaders of the movement, if Christ was their goal, to refrain not only from vice, but even from the appearance of evil; and to offer not the slightest stumbling block to the Gospel, studiously avoiding even practices which, although allowed, are not yet expedient. Above all they should have guarded against all sedition. If they had handled the matter with sincerity and moderation, they would have won the support of the princes and bishops:

---

[140] Rupp et al., *Luther and Erasmus*, pp. 84–85, 86.

for they have not all been given up for lost. And they should not have heedlessly wrecked any thing without having something better, ready to put in its place.... So I could wish that with your good sense you would strive to the end that this movement, however it began, may through firmness and moderation in doctrine and integrity of conduct be brought to a conclusion worthy of the Gospel. To this end I shall help you to the best of my ability. As it is, although the host of monks and certain theologians assail me with all their artifices, nothing will induce me wittingly to cast away my soul.[141]

It was obvious that Erasmus wanted the Church to undergo the reforms these men were advocating, but he was quite unwilling to divorce himself from the institutional Church. He described his undogmatic position and his allegiance to the Church and Holy Scripture in his *Discourse on the Freedom of the Will:* "so far am I from delighting in 'assertions' that I would readily take refuge in the opinion of the Skeptics, wherever this is allowed by the inviolable authority of the Holy Scriptures and by the decrees of the Church, to which I everywhere willingly submit my personal feelings, whether I grasp what it prescribes or not."[142]

Throughout the controversy with Luther, Erasmus preached moderation to Protestants and Catholics alike. He sought to build a church that promoted greater faith but fewer dogmas, one that was based exclusively on Christ's teachings and precepts. He abhorred the thought of a divided Christendom, of two hostile camps that would promote dogmatism and eschew tolerance. Erasmus encouraged the Lutheran cause at the outset because he saw in it the possibility of restoring the "philosophy of Christ." He expressed this idea in a letter, dated December 6, 1520, to Lorenzo Cardinal Campeggi:

So I have favored Luther; I have favored the good points I noticed in him, or which I believed to be there. Actually, I favored not him but the glory of Christ. At the same time, I also noticed things in him which made me feel somewhat uneasy and suspicious. Consequently when he, of his own accord, provoked me with a letter I seized the opportunity at once to give him some careful advice as to what I thought he should avoid. My purpose was that, once his natural qualities were corrected and purified, he might with rich results and also great glory and profit for Christ restore for us the philosophy of the gospel which had almost become cold from neglect.[143]

---

[141] Translated by Flower in Huizinga, *Erasmus and the Age of Reformation*, pp. 245–46.
[142] Rupp et al., *Luther and Erasmus*, p. 37.
[143] Hillerbrand, *Erasmus and His Age*, p. 159.

But when the leaders of Protestantism discarded "the philosophy of the gospel" and adopted revolutionary positions, Erasmus refused to support them. How could he reconcile the actions of Luther with those of his exemplar, the Prince of Peace?

DIALOGUE ON THE CICERONIAN (1528)

The *Dialogus Ciceronianus* appeared in print for the first time in 1528. There were eight editions during the author's lifetime.[144] Erasmus dedicated the work to Johann von Vlatten, a humanist-statesman in the service of the duke of Cleves, on February 14, 1528. The *Ciceronian* was presented in the form of a dialogue between the two anti-Ciceronians (Bulephorus and Hypologus) and one Ciceronian (Nosoponus). Most of the discussion takes place in the latter's study. Bulephorus begins the assault by pointing out some of Cicero's imperfections as a stylist: (1) he lacked a sense of humor; (2) he was too verbose; (3) he was not always reliable; (4) he lacked skills in certain literary genres; and (5), most serious of all, Cicero's writing was irrelevant to the moral issues of the day. Since Ciceronian writers used only words that had been found in Cicero's writings, it was virtually impossible for them to express Christian concepts in a language that had never dealt with such ideas.

Erasmus also argued that he perceived "neopagan" ideas in contemporary Ciceronian writings, masked behind certain stylistic conventions. In turn, Ciceronian writers accused Erasmus of being a fraud and dubbed him "Er-rasmus" in an effort to discredit his works. As the coup de grace, Erasmus concluded his treatise by observing that some of the major Latin writers in the period after Cicero. who were admired by all Ciceronians, were totally un-Ciceronian in style. In the end, Bulephorus and Hypologus (with Erasmus incognito) persuade Nosoponus that he is suffering from a malady and that the only remedy lies in abandoning his allegiance to Ciceronianism.

Despite the satirical quality of this work, Erasmus stressed the point in his dedicatory letter to Von Vlatten that he wrote this dialogue not to ridicule Ciceronians per se but to warn his readers against the neopagan ideas that were imbedded in Ciceronian texts and to lead them to a greater appreciation of Christian piety. Speaking through the character Bulephorus, Erasmus noted in the last few pages of the *Ciceronian* that

---

[144] Van der Haeghen, *Bibliotheca Erasmiana (1893)*, p. 75.

"The liberal arts, philosophy, and oratory are learned to the end that we may know Christ, that we may celebrate the glory of Christ."[145]

ON THE INSTRUCTION OF BOYS (1529)

The *Declamatio de pueris statim ac liberaliter instituendis* (*Declamation on the Immediate and Kindly Instruction of Boys*) drew the readers' attention to two key words in its title, *immediate* and *kindly*. Erasmus advocated instruction in the *studia humanitatis* that was to begin early in the life of a child and was to be accompanied by kindness. According to W. H. Woodward, Erasmus' *On the Instruction of Boys* is the "ripest of his educational tracts."[146] In it, one finds the often quoted phrase of Erasmus that "Men are not born, they are made." This maxim serves as the theme of his treatise.

In his preface, Erasmus indicated that he composed this work during his stay in Italy between 1506 and 1509. Moreover, he viewed it as a complement to his *De copia*. It was not published, however, until September of 1529 in Basel by Froben. At least four other editions appeared in the same year in Cologne, Antwerp, Strasbourg, and Paris. Some ten editions appeared in Erasmus' lifetime.[147] The work was dedicated to the young duke William of Cleves (1516–92), who sent Erasmus a silver cup in appreciation of the honor.

The treatise is a synthesis of classical and contemporary ideas and methods. Erasmus drew from Greek and Latin sources, especially from the Old and New Testaments, Plutarch, and Quintilian, but he also borrowed from Marsilio Ficino, Pico della Mirandola, Robert Gaguin, John Colet, and others. In turn, Erasmus influenced such educational theorists as Thomas Elyot, Juan Luis Vives, and Johann Amos Comenius. Erasmus summarized his methodology as follows:

My principles of method then are briefly these. First do not hurry, for learning comes easily when the proper stage is reached. Second avoid a difficulty which can be safely ignored or at least postponed. Third, when the difficulty

---

[145] Erasmus, *Dialogue Ciceronianus*, trans. Izora Scott under the title *Controversies over the Imitation of Cicero* (New York, 1910), p. 129.

[146] William H. Woodward, *Desiderius Erasmus: Concerning the Aim and Method of Education* (Cambridge, 1904, and New York, 1964), p. 27.

[147] Jean-Claude Margolin, ed., *Declamatio de pueris statim ac liberaliter instituendis: Etude critique, traduction et commentaire* (Geneva, 1966), p. 127.

must be handled, make the boy's approach to it as gradual and as interesting as you can.[148]

Boys were to be lured to learning by making it as interesting as possible. Erasmus also insisted that the progress of the individual child depended on these three conditions: (1) innate capacity, (2) the skilled application of instruction and guidance, and (3) proficiency through practice. In addition to making learning interesting and keeping the individuality of the child in mind, Erasmus stressed the importance of employing a qualified and sympathetic schoolmaster. Indeed, the success of education depended largely on the skill of the teacher:

> Seeing, then, that children in the earliest stage must be beguiled and not driven to learning, the first requisite in the Master is a gently sympathetic manner, the second a knowledge of wise and attractive methods. Possessing these two important qualifications he will be able to win the pupil to find pleasure in his task.[149]

Erasmus valued education because it taught children how to be virtuous and how to be of service to the state and to their God:

> For I hesitate not to affirm that those things which men covet for their sons—health, riches, and repute—are more surely secured by virtue and learning—the gifts of education—than by any other means. True, the highest gifts of all no man can give to another, even to his child, but we can store his mind with that sound wisdom and learning whereby he may attain to the best. . . . Your children are betgotten not to yourself, but to your country; not to your country alone, but to God.[150]

ON CIVILITY OF MANNERS FOR BOYS (1530)

De civilitate morum puerilium was first printed in Basel by Froben in 1530. Erasmus dedicated it to an eleven-year-old boy, Henry of Burgundy, Lord of Veere. Two other editions appeared in the same year (one in Cologne, the other in Paris). It has been estimated that some thirty editions appeared during the lifetime of the author, including translations in German (1531) and English (1532).[151] Moreover, throughout the seventeenth, eighteenth, nineteenth, and twentieth centuries, translations of the work appeared in German, Dutch, French, and Spanish.

---

[148] Woodward, trans., *Concerning the Aim and Method of Education,* p. 217.
[149] Ibid., p. 203.
[150] Ibid., pp. 185, 187.
[151] Van der Haeghen, *Bibliotheca Erasmiana* (1893), pp. 29–30.

Erasmus wrote this work on etiquette for children. He did so by maintaining a simple and clear Latin style which could be easily understood by school-age readers. He offered them advice on how to behave in church, at play, in the school dormitory, how to dress and walk correctly. In addition to imitating good manners, Erasmus also insisted in his introduction to the work that children should pursue the liberal arts and be trained as responsible members of society. Moreover, they should be instructed in piety as early as possible. Writing to John and Stanislaus Boner, sons of Severin Boner, a Polish nobleman, on December 12, 1532, Erasmus emphasized the importance of cultivating piety in young children:

> There is nothing better for man than devotion to God, and its seeds must be implanted in small children bit by bit right along with their mother's milk. . . . And yet, there is nothing more natural for us than virtue and learning, and if you took these away from man he would cease to be a man.[152]

In addition, Erasmus made the point that education placed an obligation on the recipient that called him to a life of public service: "he is not educating you for himself but for Christ and the good of your country."[153] In an earlier letter to Severin Boner, Erasmus stressed the importance of early education in the sound formation of young minds: "For you appreciated the fact that we understand most thoroughly and remember most accurately the things we imbibe in those early years when we are still impressionable and . . . adaptable to any habit."[154] More important still was the character of the nurse or tutor who first instructed the child in the elements of piety and learning. In his letter to John and Stanislaus Boner, Erasmus described the young child as "free from any defects and, like soft wax, is plastic and readily copies any and every habit found in his model."[155] Genuine piety in the nurse and first teacher begets piety in the young.

ON PREACHING (1535)

Ecclesiastes, sive de ratione concionandi (*Ecclesiastes: On the Art of Preaching*), divided into four books, was begun by Erasmus about 1523 but was

---

[152] Hillerbrand, *Erasmus and His Age,* pp. 256–57.
[153] Ibid., p. 257.
[154] Ibid., p. 253.
[155] Ibid., p. 257.

not completed and printed until 1535. There were four editions before Erasmus' death in 1536.[156] Throughout the work, Erasmus urges the preacher to base his sermons on Scripture in an effort to reform society along Christian lines. He provided the preacher with a battery of illustrations and examples to support his efforts. Erasmus dedicated the treatise to Christoph von Stadion, the bishop of Augsburg, only after he had learned of the senseless execution of his friend Bishop Fisher, at whose request he had undertaken the composition of the work.

Part 1 deals with those qualities, whether natural or acquired, that ought to be cultivated in a good preacher. Erasmus specifically condemned those preachers who preferred to pursue wealth and fame rather than to serve Jesus Christ. In relating a story about a Franciscan preacher named Robert de la Lice, who epitomized greed, Erasmus, speaking through the mouth of a conventional Franciscan, commented on his qualities:

> It was not your eloquence that drew those tears, but the compassion which I then felt for you, and a concern that one of such happy talents should choose rather to serve the world than Jesus Christ.[157]

Just as Erasmus saw man in terms of flesh and spirit, so he interpreted the Bible in terms of its literal and spiritual meanings. The spiritual meaning of Scripture referred to its allegorical or tropological (i.e. moral) sense. It was the allegorical sense that Erasmus found the hardest to explain because it was not self-evident. Though he was willing to set aside the literal or historical meaning of a scriptural passage when it conflicted with Christ's teachings or with morality itself, Erasmus maintained the importance of using historical and allegorical interpretations in combination with one another, since the allegorical and tropological senses of Scripture ultimately depend on their historical foundation. Above all, however, Erasmus was concerned with identifying the meaning of Scripture so that it could be made applicable to human conduct. Moral action lay at the heart of his exegesis.

Nevertheless, Erasmus was aware of man's limited knowledge and his inability to comprehend every passage in Scripture. In his *Discourse on the Freedom of the Will*, for example, Erasmus had acknowledged that man's mind is unable to freely understand all the mysteries of Scripture:

---

[156] Van der Haeghen, *Bibliotheca Erasmiana* (1893), p. 78.
[157] John Jortin, trans., *The Life of Erasmus*, 3 vols. (London, 1808), 2:215.

For there are some secret places in the Holy Scriptures into which God has not wished us to penetrate more deeply and, if we try to do so, then the deeper we go, the darker and darker it becomes, by which means we are led to acknowledge the unsearchable majesty of the divine wisdom, and the weakness of the human mind.[158]

Shortly after the appearance of *Ecclesiastes,* Erasmus expressed chagrin at the tumultuous conditions in which Christendom found itself, but he also took time to reiterate the lifelong goal of his writing program. The following excerpt is from a letter composed at Basel and was addressed to Damião de Goes, a humanist-statesman in the service of King John III of Portugal, on August 18, 1535:

If the Lord would only take me to his rest and away from the mad world: so far am I from desiring the long life you are invoking for me. If my writings have helped anyone to attain pure piety I am glad. I am not concerned about fame and wish that I were not burdened with it.[159]

These touching words from the Prince of Humanists, within a year of his death, should serve as a reminder to us all that Erasmus of Rotterdam died convinced that he had not only preached the philosophy of Christ but had lived it as well. In an earlier letter to Jean Morin (November 30, 1531), Erasmus confessed that "I would have had a mitre too, except that I have preferred to serve Christ rather than men."[160] The glory of his life was in the living of it. In serving Christ he exposed the vanities of mortals and the follies of organized society with the grace and charm of his engaging personality. And yet, no doubt, greater glory awaited this man of peace and compassion when he reached his Maker and laid bare his immortal soul that had been purified by a lifetime's commitment to "the glory of Christ" and to Christian piety. Throughout his life and his works, Erasmus sought to bridge learning and piety: "from the body to the spirit, from the visible world to the invisible, from letter to mystery . . . as if by the rungs of Jacob's ladder."[161]

---

[158] Rupp et al., *Luther and Erasmus,* p. 38.

[159] *Allen,* 11, Ep. 3043, p. 207.

[160] Hillerbrand, *Erasmus and His Age,* p. 256.

[161] Erasmus, *The Handbook of a Christian Soldier,* trans. Margaret E. Aston in "The Northern Renaissance," *The Meaning of the Renaissance and Reformation,* ed. R. L. De Molen (Boston and London, 1974), p. 90.

CHAPTER FIVE

FIRST FRUITS: *The Place of* Antibarbarorum Liber *and* De Contemptu Mundi *in the Formulation of Erasmus'* Philosophia Christi

I

PROMINENT in the *oeuvre* of Erasmus are the two treatises that were begun when he was a professed religious at the monastery of the Canons Regular of St. Augustine at Steyn and were completed before the end of the fifteenth century. Both the *Antibarbari*, which is the older of the two works, having been begun before he was twenty, and *De Contemptu Mundi*, composed just after he turned twenty, inform us of the principal concerns that occupied the mind of Erasmus during the period of his religious formation.[1]

About 1489, while in residence at Steyn, Erasmus encouraged by Cornelis Gerard, "decided for the future to write nothing which does not breathe the atmosphere either of praise of holy men or of holiness itself."[2] Cornelis belonged to the reformed Canons Regular of the Windesheim congregation in the district of Lopsen near Leiden—a monastery that owed its origin to Gerard Groote, the founder of the Brethren of the Common Life.[3] Writing to Cornelis in an apologetic vein for his poetical offerings, Erasmus concluded:

---

[1] For critical editions of *Antibarbarorum Liber* and *De Contemptu Mundi*, see *Opera Omnia Desiderii Erasmi Roterodami*, I-1, ed. by Kazimierz Kumaniecki (Amsterdam: North-Holland Publishing Co., 1969), pp. 35–138, and *ibid.*, V-1, ed. by Sem Dresden (Amsterdam: North-Holland Publishing Co., 1971), pp. 40–109; hereafter cited as *ASD*.

[2] *The Correspondence of Erasmus (1484 to 1500)*, trans by R. A. B. Mynors and D. F. S. Thomson and ed. by Wallace K. Ferguson (Toronto: University of Toronto Press, 1974), 1, p. 51; hereafter cited as *CWE*.

[3] For the most detailed examination of Erasmus at Steyn, see Albert Hyma, *The Youth of Erasmus*, second ed. (New York: Russell and Russell, 1968), pp. 145–219. Hyma insists that Erasmus approved the monastic life while at Steyn but later on condemned it. R. R. Post maintains that "apart from Erasmus' stay in 's-Hertogenbosch," the Brethren of the Common Life had no influence on Erasmus. See Post, *The Modern Devotion* (Leiden: E. J. Brill, 1968), pp. 11–12.

Yet if any of the poems I am sending to you seems more self-indulgent than is proper you will readily forgive this in consideration of the time of life at which I wrote them; for, apart from the lyric ode which I was writing when your letter arrived, and the funeral speech [for Berta de Hegen] which as a new production I thought I ought to send you in order that you may have evidence of my capacities in prose also, and that one solitary satire, all the rest of the poems were written by me when I was a youth [*adolescens*] and virtually still a layman.[4]

1489 serves as a watershed in the life of Erasmus. He rejected the idle pursuit of intellectual pleasures and committed himself to a life of holiness, choosing for his spiritual mentor a follower of the *Devotio Moderna*. He would lay aside the emotional attachment which had figured so prominently in his relationship with Servatius Roger and devote his energies to a spiritual reformation. Poetry was for the praise of the Muses; prose would promote his *philosophia Christi*. In a letter to Hector Boece, dated 8 November [1495], Erasmus emphasized his change of pursuits:

Please consider how unfair it is of you to insist upon having something which I do not even own myself. I swear to you most solemnly that for a long time now I have not been engaged in the pursuit of poetry and if I wrote trivial verse as a boy, I left it in my native land. I did not even venture to import my barbarous Muses, with their uncouth foreign accent, into this famous university of Paris, for I was aware that it contained a great many persons who were exquisitely gifted in every branch of letters.[5]

Although not published until the 1520's, the *Antibarbari* and *De Contemptu Mundi* were circulating as manuscripts in one form or another since 1489, much to the displeasure of Erasmus, who wished to regulate the circulation and supervise the publication of his works. In his prefatory epistles Erasmus recognized these works as stemming from his residence at Steyn and felt somewhat embarrassed by their lack of sophistication. When they were published in 1520 and 1521 respectively, Erasmus was recognized as a world figure whereas in the 1490's his reputation was confined to his immediate surroundings.

[4] *CWE*, 1, pp. 51–52.
[5] *Ibid.*, p. 94. See Cornelis Reedijk, *The Poems of Desiderius Erasmus* (Leiden: E. J. Brill, 1956), pp. 120 and 172.

II

Erasmus' surviving correspondence before 1489 reveals the anguish of a tormented soul, intensified by the recent death of his parents, the separation from his older brother, Pieter, who had entered the house of the Canons Regular of St. Augustine at Sion near Delft; and rejection by two of his companions at Steyn, Servatius Roger and Franciscus Theodoricus.[6] The earliest letters of Erasmus to Elisabeth, Pieter Gerard, Servatius Roger, Franciscus Theodoricus, and an otherwise unidentified correspondent named Sasbout were composed while Erasmus was a resident of the monastery at Steyn; and with the exception of two of them, none of the letters from Steyn was published during Erasmus' own lifetime.[7] Erasmus, who so carefully selected those letters that he wished to have printed, may have been embarrassed by their emotional fervor.[8] Writing about 1487, Erasmus expressed in torrid language his ardor for Servatius Roger: "But I beg you earnestly, O 'half of my soul,' by that extraordinary love I bear to you, not to cast me again down into the pit of sorrows."[9] It is clear from a letter such as this one that Erasmus had not as yet committed himself to "the praise of holy men."

The letters to Servatius Roger and Franciscus Theodoricus were written after Erasmus had entered the novitiate and displayed his unhappiness with the monastic practice of maintaining silence except during periods of recreation. Erasmus had assumed the role of mentor, striving to turn his two confreres into Latinists when neither of them had his innate gifts. When the style of Servatius failed to show sufficient improvement Erasmus accused him of laziness:

> But as things stand, since there is nothing that does not encourage you to apply yourself to study, neither the subject nor the setting nor the very season, it seems

---

[6] For a discussion of Erasmus at Steyn that differs from Albert Hyma (see note 3 above), read my "Erasmus as Adolescent," *Bibliothèque d'Humanisme et Renaissance*, 38 (1976), pp. 7 25.

[7] *Opus Epistolarum Desiderius Erasmi Roterodami*, ed. P. S. Allen (Oxford: Oxford University Press, 1906), I, letters 26 and 29; hereafter cited as *Allen*.

[8] See Léon-E. Halkin's *Erasmus ex Erasmo: Érasme Éditeur de sa Correspondance* (Aubel: P. M. Gason, 1983), which elaborates on this idea.

[9] *CWE*, 1, p. 14. The rule of St. Augustine condemned secret correspondence. See *The Rule of Saint Augustine: Masculine and Feminine Versions*, ed. by Tarsicius J. van Bavel, O.S.A. (London: Darton, Longman, & Todd, 1984), p. 18.

to me that you have incentives enough to cultivate letters. See that you shake off all the remnants of laziness and languor that have plagued you hitherto.[10]

It seems obvious from the earliest correspondence that Erasmus turned the novitiate into a classroom and diverted the unhappiness that characterized his personal life into a passionate pursuit of good letters. Erasmus attempted to improve the education of the canons by promoting the study of the classics among them. The monastery itself offered two incentives: a good library and learned scholars. Although Erasmus praised the monastery at Steyn on this occasion, he does not inform us of the nature of the formal education that he received before his ordination to the priesthood on April 25, 1492. It is clear, however, that he had not earned any degrees in theology before his admission to the College of Montaigu (Paris) in 1495. Steyn offered Erasmus the opportunity to effect a reformation in the curriculum pursued by the canons, but few of them were equal to it. Directing his displeasure at Servatius, Erasmus asked with indignity: "And with what pretext, pray, will you cover idleness in a place where there are so many books and such a company of learned scholars at hand and eager, indeed, to encourage you? What grounds for excusing yourself can you offer?"[11]

Having failed to persuade Servatius to join him in literary pursuits, Erasmus turned to Cornelis Gerard, who proved to be more amenable. Erasmus found a kindred spirit in Cornelis and praised him for his assistance even though he was criticized by other canons: "In conclusion let me say that you cannot possibly be held guilty in the eyes of the envious, inasmuch as you have driven a friend to self-improvement by means of your praises. . . ."[12]

Supported by Cornelis, Erasmus defended his study of good letters because it promoted piety. In 1489 his chief challengers were the members of his own order and Erasmus referred to them in his letter to Cornelis:

But does it follow that we shall have to censure for indecency everything that is wittily expressed or poetic? You at least, accustomed as you are to reading the poets' works, are clearly aware how much the honeyed flow of poetry abounds not only in elegance of style but in gravity of thought and in knowledge of all

---

[10] *CWE*, 1, p. 18.
[11] *Ibid.*, p. 20.
[12] *Ibid.*, p. 34.

things. Where there are so many shining virtues, am I to be offended by a few flaws? But those worthies are only drawing a cloak over their own lack of culture, with the result that they seem to despise what they despair of achieving. If they looked carefully at Jerome's letters, they would see at least that lack of culture is not holiness, nor cleverness impiety.[13]

Using the authority of St. Jerome, who was regarded throughout the Middle Ages as the ideal monk, Erasmus hoped to convince his fellow canons that classical learning enhanced piety and added centuries of erudition to the cause of the gospel message. His reference to "drawing a cloak over their own lack of culture" brings to mind the external mark of Canons Regular of St. Augustine: the black cloak that distinguished them from the white canons or Premonstratensians. Erasmus won supporters for his cause both in and outside the monastery at Steyn, but he would eventually fail in his efforts at promoting classical studies among all the Canons Regular. He would have to be content with only a handful of admirers.

Cornelis returned Erasmus' compliments with adulation of his own:

Your lavish kindness, dear Erasmus, reveals itself on all hands, and it has placed me under strong obligation to you by a service that will not be forgotten. For you have consented to what I long ago requested and shall always continue eagerly to demand—such is your unequalled good will and innate amiability. You did it of your own free will too, and even did more than I requested. You say in your letter—and I cannot believe that you wrote without meaning it—that nothing has given you more pleasure than the fact that you and I are joined in our studies and compensate for our separation by frequent correspondence.[14]

By the middle of 1489 the two Canons Regular had joined forces to begin what Erasmus would later call his *philosophia Christi,* a program of reform that combined good letters and personal piety. Later on, Erasmus chose St. Augustine's *Enchiridion* as the title of his treatise on piety. Erasmus compared his friendship with Cornelis to that of St. Jerome and St. Augustine, the model monk, on the one hand, and the author of the rule of the Canons Regular, on the other:

One can find no more pleasant or familiar kind of intercourse, among those who are separated, than an exchange of letters in which the correspondents draw a picture of themselves for each other, while each of them places at least his mind

---

[13] *Ibid.,* p. 35
[14] *Ibid.,* p. 41.

and feelings, if not his physical presence, at the other's disposal. It was by such means that the two famous Fathers of the church, Jerome and Augustine, prevented as they were by enormous temporal and spatial distances from being together and enjoying each other's embrace as they would have wished, still managed never to lack each other's presence; and each was ever aware of the other's feelings of good will. Let us accordingly, my sweet Cornelis, be careful to ensure that frequently something of yours is on the wing to me or something of mine to you.[15]

Erasmus' 1514 letter to Servatius Roger, then prior of Steyn, and the 1516 letter to Lambertus Grunnius, a fictitious papal official, provide us with a persuasive picture of the circumstances that surrounded his entry into the monastery in 1487.[16] The letters also reveal his dislike for ceremonies, fasting, and the self-indulgences which he found at Steyn. Erasmus frequently complained of insomnia and dietary restrictions. But, no doubt, Erasmus' inability to convince Servatius to pursue literary studies in the 1480's was the ultimate reason why he refused to return to Steyn in 1514. Even so, Erasmus declined to identify by name the individual members of his monastery who were guilty of the offenses he described. Writing to Grunnius, Erasmus observed:

But for this, that gifted nature would have mouldered away among lazy, lascivious men and drinking-parties. Not that he casts aspersions on his society, but for his nature it was quite unsuitable; it often happens that what is life to one man is death to another. But such is his modesty and bashfulness that he never speaks of his old community in any hostile spirit. . . .[17]

In these letters to Servatius and Grunnius, Erasmus never denied that he had a vocation to the priesthood. Rather, he insisted that he did not have a vocation to the religious life of the canons. His bodily constitution and mental state reacted against such ceremonial obligations as the chanting of the divine office in choir. He also shared with Willem Hermans, a fellow member of the monastery, an aversion for the prior of Steyn in the 1490's who opposed his literary studies. Hermans wrote to Erasmus just after the latter had become the secretary to the bishop of Cambrai. In the course of extending his congratulations he described his own feelings about their superior:

---

[15] *Ibid.*, p. 36.
[16] See *Allen*, letter 296, dated 8 July 1514, and *Allen*, letter 447, dated [August 1516].
[17] *CWE*, 4, pp. 21–22.

Indeed, after I received your messenger I began to urge, beg, and finally pray the prior to allow me to go, and after the messenger's departure and his refusal, I upbraided him bitterly for his great unkindness. But what can one do? That is the way he is. It would be intolerable, were it not that it was rather a kind of fear, awkward and ungenerous indeed, that underlay the action, rather than any ill-will. Still, I find very tedious the sort of person who is anxious where there is no need for anxiety, and where there is has no trace of any misgiving.[18]

Neither Willem Hermans, who had replaced Cornelis Gerard as promoter of Erasmus' studies, nor Erasmus could abide what Hermans described as the "difficulties you escaped from." Erasmus found in Hendrik van Bergen, the bishop of Cambrai, a powerful and sympathetic ally, even though he proved to be penurious. It was in the bishop's country residence at Halsteren, near Bergen, that Erasmus revised the *Antibarbari*, to which we shall now turn.

III

Erasmus began the *Antibarbari* before he was twenty (ca. 1488–89); revised it in 1495 and again about 1501/02; and published it in May of 1520 (Basel: Froben) for the first time. In a letter from Steyn about 1489, Erasmus refers to the *Antibarbari* which he had written in the form of an oration at the request of Cornelis Gerard: ". . . I have resumed this occupation for your sake and have finished, as diligently as I could, that oration of yours for which you had asked me."[19] It was rewritten in the form of a dialogue. Writing to Cornelis in 1494, Erasmus informed his friend of its present state:

If you ask me what I am up to, I have in hand at present a work on literature which I have been threatening for a very long time to write and have been attending to during my retreat in the country, though I do not very well know how it is going. I intend, at any rate, to finish this work in two books. The first book will be almost entirely concerned with refuting the absurdities perpetrated by the barbarians, while in the second I am going to depict you talking about the glory of letters with some scholarly friends of your own sort.[20]

---

[18] *CWE*, 1, p. 63.

[19] *Ibid.*, pp. 55–56. Silvano Calvazza, "La Cronologia degli 'Antibarbari' e le Origini del Pensiero Religioso di Erasmo," *Rinascimento*, 25 (1975), 141–79, argues that the Gouda manuscript of the *Antibarbari* must be dated circa 1501/02 and not 1494/95.

[20] *Ibid.*, pp. 71–72.

Because Erasmus never fulfilled his plan to publish the second volume of the *Antibarbari,* we are deprived of the effect this work would have had on his generation. Nevertheless he made it clear in his letter to Cornelis that he intended to make him, who was a Canon Regular of St. Augustine, the centerpiece of the book, surrounded by other scholars who shared his appreciation for good letters. This is in contrast to volume one in which the two Canons Regular, Erasmus and Willem Hermans, play only minor roles. In characteristic fashion Erasmus used individuals whom he knew as persona in his works. On the one hand, the Canons Regular became promoters of good letters, while the mendicant friars on the other, would oppose them.

In his dedicatory epistle to Johann Witz, schoolmaster in Sélestat, which appeared in the 1520 *Antibarbari,* Erasmus singled out "men who credit themselves with every virtue" as responsible for a decline in classical studies. It was a veiled reference to the mendicant friars whom he attacked vigorously throughout the book:

> In any case it is a shameful story, the stupidity with which some men reject what is far the most excellent province of knowledge, dismissing as 'poetry' all that belongs to an ancient and more civilized culture. These were the men who, when I was a boy, spitefully enough put obstacles in my path and kept me away from my first love; and I had planned to take my revenge with pen and ink, with this one proviso, that I would attack no man by name.[21]

One of the purposes of the *Antibarbari* was to take revenge against those adults who had attempted to thwart Erasmus' study of the classics during his childhood. We can only assume that he was speaking of certain members of religious orders who had directed his studies, following the death of his parents, and who had no regard for Erasmus' proclivities.

Even though the publication of the *Antibarbari* would satisfy his desire for revenge, Erasmus regretted its appearance in print. He observed: "I myself revised the book and sent it to the printers, though in other respects I would rather it had been suppressed entirely.... But I thought it had better face the world with such revision as I could give it than in the form taken by the manuscript copies, which were badly corrupted."[22]

---

[21] Erasmus of Rotterdam to his Friend Johann Witz in *CWE,* 23, p. 16, trans. by Margaret Mann Phillips.

[22] *Ibid.,* p. 17.

The chief barbarians whom Erasmus attacked in his treatise were the members of the major religious orders of mendicants: the Carmelites, Dominicans, and Franciscans. Many of the members of these orders believed in apostolic rusticity, that is, the notion that clerics do not need to be well educated since Christ selected a group of unlettered fishermen as his disciples. They also maintained that the Holy Spirit would guide their judgments when they were counseling or administering the sacraments to the faithful. Blind faith was far more important to these friars than commitment based on erudition.

It is worth noting that Erasmus as a member of the Canons Regular of St. Augustine was neither a monk nor a mendicant friar nor a secular priest. The canons were officially authorized by the Lateran Synod of 1059 and appear midway between the orders of monks (e.g., Benedictines, Carthusians, and Cistercians), who originated in the sixth century, and the mendicant friars of the thirteenth century. As such the canons were often the rivals of the orders of monks and friars. It is not surprising, therefore, that Erasmus never singled out Austin Canons for criticism in the fifteenth century but chose instead members of the various orders of monks and friars, who competed with the canons for religious vocations as well as temporal power within the church structure. Even so, it should be kept in mind that Erasmus had close relations with a number of professed members of these two groups (Jean Vitrier, Paul Volz, and Antoon van Bergen come readily to mind).

Erasmus wrote the *Antibarbari* neither as a merely literary work nor as an educational treatise nor as a defense of classical studies per se, but, as Erasmus himself categorized it, as an *apologia* for the learned Christian who employed the erudition of the ancients to strengthen his faith in Christ. He wanted to attack the notion, current in 1495 as well as in 1520, that piety was incompatible with erudition; that a knowledge of the classics would corrupt the unsuspecting Christian.[23]

The setting for the *Antibarbari* was a country estate, located near the town of Bergen-op-Zoom. Of the five participants in the dialogue, two

---

[23] For recent assessments of the *Antibarbari*, see the introduction to *ASD*, I-1, by Kazimierz Kumaniecki, pp. 7–32, and the introduction to *CWE*, 23, by Margaret Mann Phillips, pp. 2–15. Erasmus listed it among his *apologia* in letters to Johann von Botzheim (30 January 1523) and Hector Boece (15 March 1530). See *Allen*, 1, pp. 38–42, and 8, pp. 373–77. See also James D. Tracy's "Against the 'Barbarians': The Young Erasmus and His Humanist Contemporaries," *The Sixteenth Century Journal*, 11 (1980), 3–22.

were visitors to Bergen and three were town officials (although Batt spoke from the perspective of an enlightened schoolmaster). At the same time all were trained humanists who were familiar with the *optimae artes*. The characters were friends of Erasmus and represented prototypes of some leaders of society: Willem Hermans, a former resident of Steyn, was a poet and theologian; Jacob Batt, who had studied at the University of Paris and had taught briefly at Bergen, where he had attempted to introduce humanist studies in the town school, was the town secretary of Bergen; Willem Conrad was the burgomaster and leading citizen of Bergen; and Jodocus was the local physician. Erasmus served as the host and referee.

The leading characters were all laymen. The role played by Erasmus and his fellow canon was advisory at best. The chief defender of the humanities was Jacob Batt, and much of the dialogue centered around his opinions and the criticisms of them. As a layman he represented a group of reformers who wished to persuade the opponents of classical studies to abandon their position and to support good letters. He was especially critical of friars and monks, and devoted much of his argument to a refutation of their ideas. Though Erasmus remained on the sideline during most of the dialogue one can detect his position in the words that fell from Batt's lips. Batt's part in the dialogue was pivotal. The other speakers were ancillary to the message that Batt offered. The burgomaster served as his foil, the defender of the position maintained by the friars.

It is not surprising, therefore, that the *Antibarbari* was critical of the educational attainments of the orders of mendicant friars. Through the mouth of Batt, Erasmus insisted: "You might as well ask a camel's advice on dancing or a donkey's about song. What else are you doing when you consult a Friar Minor, a Dominican, or a Carmelite as if he were an oracle, asking him who should be put in charge of a boy destined for the best education to form his mind...." Erasmus rejected the friars as teachers because "to these idiots Quintilian is a poet, and Pliny, and Aulus Gellius, and Livy—in short everyone who wrote in good Latin." He accused them of being "born and bred in unrelieved barbarism."[24] As preachers and confessors these same friars spread their ignorance among the uneducated. In the presence of two Austin Canons, who were themselves scholar-poets, Batt directed his criticism to representatives of those religious orders who condemned classical learning. Even in the face

---

[24] *CWE*, 23, p. 33.

of the efficacy of good letters, these friars stubbornly refused to concede. As Batt acknowledged: "For religion, while it is the best of all things, is also, the famous historian [Livy?] tells us, the most convenient cloak for any vice you like to name, because if anyone tries to draw attention to the vices themselves he appears to many people to be attacking religion, by which they are masked. . . ."[25]

In a 1520 insertion, Erasmus underscored the hostile attitude of the friars toward other religious orders as well as toward the secular clergy:

> When they bawl about the vices of the secular clergy, and preach revolt, and incite the ignorant mob to stone them, they never think of the risk of rousing the anger of Christ, the Founder of *that* order—for he was a priest, but not a Dominican. If anyone dares to divulge any of their secrets and disturb the Augean stable, they announce that he is in danger of destruction from an irate Francis, or Dominic, or Elijah, so help me!

Erasmus exposed the subversive power of the mendicant friars and charged them with keeping concubines, and through the mouth of Batt asked: ". . . what colour would he wish the cross to be for the Dominicans, the Carmelites, and the rest. Would he like the concubines of the Friars Minor to wear grey crosses, those of the Carmelites white, of the Dominicans black?. . . ."[26] Though violators of their vows, the mendicant friars detested the classics because "they say that there is a high reward among the blessed which awaits those who for religion's sake can despise these heathen teachings, invented for ostentation and pride; ignorant piety, they say, is most pleasing to heaven. . . ."[27]

Quoting from St. Augustine, whose rule governed the lives of the Canons Regular, the physician noted: "My opinion is the same as I see expressed by St. Augustine in his dialogues, that is to say, I believe that knowledge can hardly be divorced from virtue. . . ."[28] At the same time the physician recorded the viewpoint of some of his patients: ". . . as you know, my profession leads me to deal with all kinds of people, and I often meet with certain monks who are steadfastly persuaded that there is no way in which what they call secular literature can be combined with Christian piety." Even in the light of the teachings of St. Augustine and St. Jerome, they denied the meritorious nature of good letters. Batt in a

[25] *Ibid.*, p. 48.
[26] *Ibid.*, p. 49.
[27] *Ibid.*, p. 50.
[28] *Ibid.*, p. 74.

sarcastic vein agreed with the physician's assessment: "in their case it can't, because they lack both [i.e., *bonae litterae* and piety], but it can in the case of Jerome, Cyprian, Augustine, and a thousand others; and who would dare to put on the same footing the piety of these men and the sluggishness of the monks?" It is clear that Erasmus believed that some friars rejected the teachings of the Church Fathers in order to maintain their own view. Indeed their lives were antithetical to the followers of Christ. In a prefatory letter to Paul Volz (August 14, 1518), Erasmus observed: "I have no wish to upbraid the Franciscans for being devoted to their own rule and the Benedictines for devotion to theirs; I object that some of them think their rule more important than the Gospel."[29] While expressing reverence for the monastic life, the physician did not exempt monks from all reproach. Instead he noted: "I see some of them getting close to the Epicurean way of life, taking incredible care to escape work, embracing sloth and a sheltered life . . . they think themselves quite religious enough if they never touch anything in the way of literary culture. . . ."[30]

In contrast to the self-serving life of worldly mendicants, Erasmus maintained an interior discipline based on the teachings of Christ. Though he was in the service of the bishop of Cambrai and was no longer a resident of the monastery at Steyn, he was committed to a life of withdrawal. Willem Conrad described the kind of life that Erasmus was leading in 1495:

> I am envious of your delightful life, you happiest of all men alive! While we poor wretches are tossed hither and thither by the raging sea of public affairs, you are strolling about all the time with your Muses, entirely at leisure and unoccupied, now chatting on whatever topic you like with a friend, now holding a conversation with one of the ancient writers, at times beating out the rhythm of some ditty, or at others committing to paper, as to faithful companions, whatever you are turning over in your mind. It does not surprise me at all that, however often we invite you, you can never be dragged away from the woods to go to town.

In case Conrad was misled by the outward appearance of his life, Erasmus offered the following corrective: "If those Sirens of yours—money-making and ambition—would allow you, I have no doubt that

---

[29] *CWE*, 6, p. 86.
[30] *CWE*, 23, p. 75.

you would find it easy to despise that raging sea and all the towns as well. But you are ashamed to appear inadequate as an important citizen, and so you choose the wrong kind of life to lead to happiness."[31] Erasmus believed that the good Christian should reject worldly honors and material comforts in order to communicate more easily with Christ. It is clear from this passage that Erasmus was promoting an internal formation which would be oblivious to the enticements of the external world. In other words, Erasmus believed that a lay person could lead a religious life outside the monastery so long as he forsook the world's temptations.

In a final barb against the friars, Erasmus accused the burgomaster of complicity in the decline of good letters in Bergen-op-Zoom. Speaking through Batt, he insisted:

> You, little as you know it, are the instigator of this evil; the whole blame for it falls on you. To your hands the community has committed all its fortune, its safety, honour, prosperity, and lastly what is dearest to it, its children—and you allow a set of black-guards to dwell in the city—did I say dwell? I mean, unchecked.[32]

In this veiled reference to the Dominicans as "blackguards" Erasmus laid the blame on the teaching friars who suppressed the study of the classics in the schools of Europe.

Though Erasmus revised the *Antibarbari* about 1520, it reflected that period in his life when he was a newly ordained priest in the service of the bishop of Cambrai and still a member of the Canons Regular whose rule he was obliged to obey and whose religious habit he was still obliged to wear. The *Antibarbari* appeared in print one year before *De Contemptu Mundi* and, like it, combined the two themes uppermost in the mind of Erasmus: a defense of good letters and a pious life. Since the first two prose works of Erasmus were written in the fifteenth century, they should be seen as a diptych, mirroring the central concern of Erasmus' program of reform, namely the *philosophia Christi*, before it was fully enunciated in the *Enchiridion* of 1503.

IV

Erasmus wrote *De Contemptu Mundi* about 1488/89 when he was scarcely twenty years of age. Circulating in manuscript form, it un-

---

[31] *Ibid.*, p. 21.
[32] *Ibid.*, p. 28.

doubtedly served as promotional literature to entice prospective candidates to enter the order of Canons Regular of St. Augustine. It was written at the request of Theodoricus of Haarlem, a fellow canon at Steyn, in order to persuade his nephew to join the order.[33] It is obvious that Theodoricus asked Erasmus to write the oration because of his literary skills.[34]

In 1533, twelve years after its publication at Louvain in 1521, Thomas Paynell, a member of the Canons Regular of St. Augustine at Merton priory in Surrey, published an English translation, which, no doubt, was used by the English-speaking houses of the order to foster vocations. Paynell insisted in his dedicatory letter that Erasmus openly declared "the hygh goodnes" of the religious life.[35] Being the most famous member of the order, Erasmus' endorsement of the religious life of the canons carried considerable authority.

If, as some have suggested, Erasmus had thoroughly rewritten *De Contemptu Mundi* or even added an entire chapter (twelve) to the treatise in 1521, why would he have been so apologetic in his prefatory letter to the reader? Here Erasmus protested that *De Contemptu Mundi* was one of "suche trifils as I wrote whan I was yong to exercise my style, nat thinkynge that they shulde spred abrode. . . ."[36] He also expressed disappointment that this work was printed in the 1520's, many years after its composition, and complained that it was not representative of his present literary skills and was written "*alieno stomacho*." There is no evidence in the prefatory letter that Erasmus wrote the first eleven chapters long before he wrote chapter twelve. Instead he insisted that the whole work was composed before he was instructed "in redynge of good auctours" and that he only "changed a fewe wordes."[37]

---

[33] *Allen*, 4, p. 457. The title page of the 1521 Louvain edition of *De Contemptu Mundi* has: "conscripsit adolescens in gratiam ac nomine Theodorici Harlemei, canonici ordinis diui Augustini."

[34] For recent assessments of *De Contemptu Mundi*, see the introductions to *ASD*, V-1, by Sem Dresden, pp. 7–36; the facsimile reproduction of the Berthelet edition of 1533 by William James Hirten (Gainseville, Florida, 1967), pp. v–xliv; and the forthcoming *CWE*, 65, by Erika Rummel. I want to thank Dr. Rummel for sharing her introduction and translation with me. See also *Allen*, 4, p. 457, and *Hyma*, pp. 173 and 179.

[35] Erasmus, *De Contemptu Mundi*, trans by Paynell; ed. by Hirten (Gainesville, Florida: Scholars' Facsimiles & Reprints, 1967), p. 6.

[36] *Ibid.*, p. 7. See Post, *The Modern Devotion*, pp. 669–670.

[37] *Ibid.*, p. 9. Marcel Haverals discovered an early manuscript version of *De Contemptu*

In defending the religious life Erasmus quoted from St. Augustine, whose rule he followed, St. Ambrose (author of a treatise on virginity), St. Bernard of Clairvaux (a Cistercian abbot and reformer), and St. Cyprian (the champion of sacerdotalism). This array of authorities was gathered in the fifteenth century to underscore his belief that the religious life was a holy one and should be pursued by those capable of benefiting from it.

Chapter twelve, on the other hand, is not a denunciation of monastic life. It is a necessary outgrowth of the first eleven chapters and a fitting conclusion to a letter of advice by an uncle for his nephew. Theodoricus concluded: "Let it not disturb your mind that you are not one of the Dominican or Carmelite community, if only you are truly a member of the Christian community."[38] As a twenty-four year old canon, Theodoricus wanted to persuade his nephew, who was of similar age, to enter the religious life, but at the same time, he wanted him to know that if he chose not to follow him, he could still remain in the world and be saved, provided that he be "of the flocke of true Christen people."[39] Erasmus believed that one could live in the world as long as one was not worldly. Theodoricus' advice to his nephew is not a new theme in *De Contemptu Mundi*. Earlier, in chapter two, Theodoricus maintained a similar position:

... Will monks alone be saved? And all the rest go to their doom? Not at all. I do not deny that there, too, are men whose names are marked in the Book of Life. Nor do I say that by entering a monastery a man has immediately arranged his affairs so securely that he can live quite without concern. The difference between the two kinds of lives is as great as the difference between the man who is already sailing within the harbour though his ship is not yet moored and the man who is still borne along on the high seas. ... The man who remains in this world is not doomed, but he is in greater danger.[40]

Mundi (written between 1502 and 1513) that lacks chapter twelve. The existence of this manuscript version, however, does not prove that Erasmus wrote chapter twelve in the sixteenth century. Erasmus complained of the large number of imperfect manuscript versions that were then in circulation in his prefatory letter of 1521. See Haverals, "Une première Rédaction du *De Contemptu Mundi* d'Erasme dans un Manuscrit de Zwolle," *Humanistica Lovaniensia*, 30 (1981), pp. 40–54.

[38] *Ibid.*, p. 176. This translation is taken from the text of Erika Rummel which will appear in *CWE*, 65.

[39] Erasmus, *De Contemptu Mundi*, trans. by Paynell; ed. by Hirten, p. 176.

[40] *Ibid.*, pp. 24–25; translation is taken from the forthcoming *CWE*, 65.

Salvation is available to all, but the monk is protected by the vows of poverty, chastity, and obedience.

De Contemptu Mundi is divided into three parts: Chapters one through seven focus on the evils of this world; chapters eight through eleven on the pleasures of the religious life; and chapter twelve on the ultimate choice of this world or the religious state. At the same time, chapters three, four, and nine are written as specific defenses of the monastic vows and underscore the liberty, tranquillity, and pleasure that can be found in religious life:

> Although I think that I have said quite enough, I would not want you to jump up and run away from the world in alarm, but rather to fly here happily and willingly, that is, not so much disgusted with the evils of the world as eager for our sweet life.[41]

It is obvious from Erasmus' letters to Servatius Roger and Lambertus Grunnius that Erasmus recognized his own unsuitability for the religious life and through the mouth of Theodoricus wished to emphasize the voluntary nature of a religious vocation, which should not be regarded as an escape from the world but as an acceptance of the responsibilities that form the everyday life of a canon.

Two years before the publication of *De Conemptu Mundi* Erasmus defended the religious orders and at the same time clearly distinguished between good and bad friars. Writing to Justus Jonas in 1519, Erasmus cautioned:

> Nor should one be severe at random against whole orders of men; it is better to protest against those who by their faults bring otherwise admirable orders into disrepute. It will be found more profitable to demonstrate how far from true religion are those who profess the rule of Benedict or Francis or Augustine and yet live for their bellies, for gluttony, lust, ambition, or avarice, than to attack the regular religious life itself.[42]

Erasmus penned this defense of the religious life long after he had received papal dispensations from Julius II (1506) and Leo X (1517) which freed him from the obligations of obedience to his superiors and from

---

[41] *Ibid.*, p. 85; *CWE*, 65. See Erika Rummel, "Quoting Poetry Instead of Scripture: Erasmus and Eucherius on *Contemptus Mundi*," *Bibliothèque d'Humanisme et Renaissance*, 40 (1983), pp. 503–09.

[42] *CWE*, 6, p. 376.

residence in the monastery at Steyn.⁴³ He had nothing to gain from this *apologia* or from later ones in 1529 and 1533.⁴⁴ Writing to Jan of Heemstede, a Carthusian, on February 28, 1533, Erasmus insisted: "Therefore, what sort of perversity is it that some display who despise a man because he is a monk? When you mention the name monk you are speaking of one who is the sum of all the heroic virtues, one who merits benevolence and favor from the good, and wrests it from the wicked."⁴⁵ Erasmus' defense of the monastic life is simply a reflection of an opinion that originated during his residence at Steyn. In a funeral oration for Berta de Hegen of Gouda (about 1489), Erasmus expressed the very ideas that are inherent in chapter twelve of *De Contemptu Mundi*: "Berta was beautiful and rich and devout. Why didn't she enter a convent? It would have been more prudent, I admit, but in my opinion it is far more meritorious to lead a pure and innocent life amidst the seductions of vice, to pass her existence in tranquillity in the midst of the turmoil of the world."⁴⁶ Erasmus believed that holiness can be found in or outside the religious life. He defended the religious life for those who are attracted to it because he felt it was a safer route to achieve piety, having been sanctioned by the two great Church Fathers, St. Augustine and St. Jerome.

v

The *Antibarbari* and *De Contemptu Mundi* function as a two-way mirror, illustrating twin themes of *bonae litterae* and Christian piety against the background of the author's personal life in the fifteenth century. Erasmus was very much a member of the Canons Regular in 1489 and 1494/95 and it was only natural that he would write from a perspective that included the events of his present circumstances. Although Erasmus did not draft the first complete expression of his *philosophia Christi* until 1501, and did not publish it until 1503 under the title of *Enchiridion Militis Christiani* (Antwerp: Martens), he had envi-

---

⁴³ See *Allen*, 3, p. xxix, and letter 517.

⁴⁴ See *Allen*, 8, letter 2136 (to Ludwig Baer, 30 March 1529) and *Allen*, 10, letter 2771 (to Jan of Heemstede, 28 February 1533).

⁴⁵ Translated by John J. Mangan in *Life, Character, and Influence of Desiderius Erasmus* (New York: The Macmillan Co., 1927), 2, p. 346.

⁴⁶ *Desiderii Erasmi Roterodami Opera Omnia*, ed. Jean Le Clerc (Leiden, 1703–06), 8, cols. 551–60.

sioned his program of reform in the preceding century.[47] Writing to Johann von Botzheim in January of 1523, Erasmus described the origins of the work when he was a student in Paris: "The *Enchiridion militis christiani* was begun by me nearly thirty years ago [that is, about 1495] when staying in the castle of Tournehem, to which we were driven by the plague which depopulated Paris."[48] In his conclusion to the *Enchiridion,* Erasmus repeats both themes. He noted: "There are certain detractors who think that true religion has nothing to do with good literature. Let me say that I have been studying the classics since my youth. . . . I did not undertake this merely for the sake of empty fame, or for the childish pleasures of the mind. My sole purpose was that, knowing these writings, I might the better adorn the Lord's temple with literary richness."[49] At the same time he cautioned his readers against assuming that piety is confined to the religious life. Erasmus observed: "Monasticism is not holiness, but a kind of life that can be useful or useless depending on a person's temperament and disposition. I neither recommend it nor do I condemn it."[50] Completed in the 1490's but not published until the 1520's the *Antibarbari* and *De Contemptu Mundi* bridge the fifteenth and sixteenth centuries and reflect the spirit of the *philosophia Christi,* which Erasmus expressed succinctly in his 1518 letter to Paul Volz:

> The result is therefore that no one should be foolishly self-satisfied because his way of life is not that of other people, nor should he despise or condemn the way of life of others. But in every walk of life let this be the common aim of us all, that to the best of our power we should struggle towards the goal that is set before us all, even Christ, exhorting and even helping one another, with no envy of those who are ahead of us in the race and no scorn for the weak who cannot yet keep up with us.[51]

---

[47] See the introductory essay by John P. Dolan in Erasmus, *Handbook of the Militant Christian,* ed., and trans. by J. P. Dolan (Notre Dame, Indiana: Fides Publishers, 1962), pp. 28–32.
[48] *Allen,* 1, p. 19.
[49] Erasmus, *Enchiridion,* trans. by Dolan, p. 158.
[50] *Ibid.,* p. 159.
[51] *CWE,* 6, p. 90.

CHAPTER SIX

Erasmus on Childhood*

"The husband and wife of a household constitute a senate, as it were, children the nobles, servants the common people."[1]

WRITING in 1526, Erasmus outlined in this brief quotation his concept of childhood in the sixteenth century. He turned to Roman models of the past to underscore the role of parents as the lawmaking body within the family and servants as domestic aids. But it was the child who enjoyed a special status—that of a nobleman or patrician. Erasmus insisted that the child was the central figure in the Renaissance household. His physical, mental, and moral development was directed by parents and assisted by servants.

Erasmus' view of childhood is in marked contrast to Philippe Ariès' reading of sixteenth-century records. In a highly original and provocative book which first appeared in 1960, Ariès argued that the concept of childhood was not developed until the seventeenth century.[2] He wrote from the perspective of a demographer and non-Renaissance specialist in order to throw light on the concept of the modern family. At the heart of his thesis is the argument that pre-seventeenth-century Europe considered the child who had reached the age of seven as a miniature

---

* This essay was originally presented at the Folger Shakespeare Library's noontime colloquium on August 13, 1981. I wish to thank Dr. Susan Zimmerman, formerly associate chairman of the Folger Institute, for inviting me to speak.

[1] *Christiani matrimonii institutio, per Des. Erasmvm Roterodamvm*. . .(Basel, 1526), sig. [u¹]: "Domus igitur consummata in has partes distribuitur, in maritum & uxorem, uelut in senatum; in liberos, uelut in ordinem equestrem, in familitium, uelet in plebem. . . ." Leah S. Marcus, *Childhood and Cultural Despair* (Pittsburgh, 1978), insists to the contrary that "in the sixteenth century, children were still placed at the bottom of the social hierarchy and expected to behave with humility and reverence toward parents and other superiors" (p. 29).

[2] Philippe Ariès, *Centuries of Childhood: A Social History of Family Life*, trans. by Robert Baldick (New York, 1965), 129–133.

adult, one who was deprived of any special status and was expected to adhere to adult standards:

> In medieval society the idea of childhood did not exist; this is not to suggest that children were neglected, forsaken or despised. The idea of childhood is not to be confused with affection for children: it corresponds to an awareness of the particular nature of childhood, that particular nature which distinguishes the child from the adult, even the young adult.[3]

The so-called medieval perception of the seven to fourteen year-old child changed supposedly in the seventeenth century when western Europe acknowledged pre-adolescence as a special period of human development: "Henceforth it was recognized that the child was not ready for life, and that he had to be subjected to a special treatment, a sort of quarantine, before he was allowed to join the adults."[4] Pre-adolescent children were now permitted to dress in children's fashions and to mature at their own rate of growth. It is my intention in the following chapter to call this thesis in question and to demonstrate that the sixteenth-century's leading humanist, Erasmus of Rotterdam, not only devoted a large proportion of his writings to the education of children but articulated "an awareness of the particular nature of childhood, that particular nature which distinguishes the child from the adult, even the young adult"[5] in order to teach parents and schoolmasters how to instruct children in virtuous living.

Before looking at Erasmus' views it might be well to identify the place of the child in the Renaissance perception of human development. It was believed that infancy as a distinct phase of human growth lasted from birth to age seven; childhood from seven to fourteen; and adolescence or youth from fourteen to eighteen. In accordance with Greek and Roman models, children in the fifteenth and sixteenth centuries were admitted to elementary school between the ages of six and seven; proceeded to secondary school between the ages of thirteen and fourteen; and were prepared to enter college at the age of seventeen or eighteen.[6] There were physiological as well as intellectual reasons why children advanced to these levels of education at those particular ages. For example, the child

---

[3] *Ibid.*, p. 128.
[4] *Ibid.*, p. 412.
[5] *Ibid.*, p. 128.
[6] For a statistical analysis, based on English schools, see R. L. DeMolen, "Ages of Admission to Educational Institutions in Tudor and Stuart England," *History of Education*, 5 (1976), 207–219.

acquires his first molar at age six and his second molar at twelve and the adolescent receives his third molar between eighteen and twenty.[7] Moreover, between the ages of seven and fourteen, it was believed that children arrived at the age of reason (or discretion); that they were capable of determining right from wrong and were capable of benefiting from a schoolmaster's instruction.[8] Since the schoolmaster was portrayed as a dispenser of rewards (the apple) and punishments (the switch) it was unthinkable to send a child to school before he was responsible for the consequences of his misdeeds. At fourteen (twelve for girls) the child was assumed to be physically mature. It was also believed that when the young adult reached the age of consent (or perfect age) he was capable of choosing a marriage partner or entering a religious order. Finally, at eighteen the student ceased to be a minor and assumed adulthood. The young adult was believed to be physically, intellectually, and emotionally prepared to pursue college-level courses. Under English law, an adolescent became a legal adult only at twenty-one, having attained "full age" or the age of majority.[9]

With regard to the admission of boys to religious orders, canon law stipulated that boys had to be at least fourteen years of age before they could be received as novices[10] (The Council of Trent changed the age of profession to sixteen for both men and women during its deliberations in 1563).[11] But this rule was not always strictly enforced because we have examples of boys being admitted to religious houses at the age of ten or

[7] See A. A. Dahlberg, "Teeth," *Encyclopedia Britannica*, 21 (1967), p. 756. For the earliest work on the subject in the sixteenth century, see Eucharius Rösslin, *Der Swangern Frauwen und Hebammen Roszgarten* (Hagenau, 1513).

[8] See Joseph A. Burroughs, "Age of Reason," *New Catholic Encylopedia* (New York, 1967), 12, p. 118. The author of the ca. 1495 Boy-Bishop sermon noted that "in token herof childerne newely sette to scole, lackynge the use of reason and the habyte of cognycyon, have a recourse to Goddes dyrccyon . . . ." See *Two Sermons Preached by the Boy Bishop at St. Paul's. . . and at Gloucester. . .* , ed. by John G. Nichols (London: Camden Society, 1875), The Camden Miscellany, 7, p. 2.

[9] John Cowell and Thomas Manley, *The Interpreter of Words and Terms, used either in the Common or Statute Laws of the Realm* (London, 1701), sig. c^v.

[10] For the effect of canon law's prohibition on English boys, see Nicholas Orme, *English Schools in the Middle Ages* (London, 1973), p. 228.

[11] "In quacumque religione tam virorum quam mulierum professio non fiat ante decimum sextum annum expletum, nec qui minore tempore quam per annum post susceptum habitum in probatione steterit, ad professionem admittatur." See *Canons and Decrees of the Council of Trent*, ed. H. J. Schroeder (St. Louis, 1941), p. 494.

eleven. They were, no doubt, postulants rather than novices for a number of years, but their very admission to a religious house violated the spirit of canon law.[12]

Between 1514 and 1516 Erasmus challenged the view that adolescents who had reached the age of maturity (i.e., fourteen) were capable of making prudent judgment and, therefore, qualified to enter a novitiate. Erasmus reasoned:

> But someone will say, "What about the year of probation (as they call it) and the age of maturity?" That is ridiculous. As if one should demand that a boy in his seventeenth year, especially educated to literature, should know himself, which is a great thing in an old man; or as if he would learn in one year what many grey-haired men do not yet understand. . . .[13]

> All bodies do not mature at the same age, much less minds. It matters not that perchance puberty has rendered them mature for marriage; they may not be mature enough to enter a religious life; for many indeed have entered therein, men of about thirty years of age otherwise well experienced in the ways of the world, who have withdrawn before their profession, saying "I had not thought."[14]

It is instructive to observe that Erasmus maintained the opinion that a sixteen year-old adolescent was still a boy—that is a *puer* or child. Moreover, in two 1489 letters to Cornelis Gerard, a fellow Austin canon in a nearby monastery, he felt justified in describing himself as a boy, when he would have been about nineteen.[15] Fear based on an inability to

---

[12] J. R. H. Moorman, *The Grey Friars in Cambridge, 1225–1538* (Cambridge, 1952), 106–113.

[13] Erasmus to Servatius Roger, 8 July 1514, *Opus Epistolarum Des. Erasmi Roterodami*, ed. P. S. Allen *et al.*, 12 vols. (Oxford, 1906–58), 1, p. 566 (hereafter cited as *Allen*); trans. by John J. Mangan, *Life . . . of . . . Erasmus* (New York, 1927), 1, p. 362. R. A. B. Mynors and D. F. S. Thomson have incorrectly translated "puer anno decimo septimo" as a "youth of sixteen." See *The Correspondence of Erasmus* (Toronto, 1975), 2, p. 295 (hereafter cited as *CWE*).

[14] Erasmus to Lambertus Grunnius, *Allen*, 2, p. 309; trans. by Mangan, *Life of Erasmus*, 1, pp. 25–26.

[15] Erasmus to Cornelis Gerard, *Allen*, 1, pp. 112–115 and pp. 119–120. Mynors and Thomson translate "scripsit pver" as "written as a boy." See *CWE*, 1, pp. 44 and 53. W. K. Ferguson points out that by 1521, when these words first appeared in the salutation of these letters, Erasmus had either "forgotten how old he was when he wrote the letters, or wished to appear to have been younger" (p. 44), but he gives no evidence, in the absence of which it is better to assume that Erasmus remembered well enough and wrote what he remembered.

support himself in 1486/87 finally forced Erasmus to accept the religious habit of the Austin Canons when he was sixteen years of age, and it was pride under coercion that led him to profess vows a year later. He explained his profession as follows:

> "Now it is too late to retreat," said they. "You have put your hand to the plough; it is wrong to turn back; if you put aside the habit which you assumed before many witnesses, you will always be the common talk of everybody." . . . "Where will you turn?" said they. "You will never be able to come into the presence of good men; you will be execrated by the monks, and hated by common people." Now the youth had a mind which felt dishonor keenly, and feared death less than disgrace. On the other hand, he was urged on by his guardians and friends, some of whom had lessened his property by theft. In a word, they conquered by villainy. The boy, with abhorrence in his soul and reluctance in his words, was compelled to put his head into the halter, just as captives in war stretch forth their hands to the victor to be bound, or as men overcome by protracted torments are wont: they do, not what they wish, but what their conqueror wishes.[16]

Writing in his forty-seventh year, Erasmus was obviously convinced that a seventeen year-old novice was still a boy; that adolescence did not confer maturity; and that childhood extended over a far longer period of time in the sixteenth century than Ariès leads us to believe.

Since the miniature-adult thesis of Ariès rests so heavily on evidence drawn from surviving portraiture and seventeenth-century French sources, he seems unaware that the early church had developed a set of sacraments that were specifically designed for persons who had not yet reached full maturity. Baptism, Penance, the Eucharist, and even Extreme Unction (now referred to as the Anointing of the Sick) were administered to children at various stages in their lives for the purpose of developing their spirituality.[17]

The Christian Church in the first few centuries after Christ administered Baptism, Confirmation, and the Eucharist to infants immediately following birth. The church recognized the spiritual equality of all its

---

[16] Erasmus to Lambertus Grunnius, *Allen*, 2, 303–304; trans. by Mangan, *Life of Erasmus*, 1, p. 20. Mynors and Thomson translate "adolescens" as "young man." See *CWE*, 4, p. 21. These translators thus miss the emphasis that Erasmus had placed on his immaturity.

[17] See R. L. DeMolen's article, "Childhood and the Sacraments in the Sixteenth Century," *Archiv für Reformationsgeschichte*, 66 (1975), 49–71, for an analysis of the significance of the sacraments for children.

members, whether children or adults. The Fourth Lateran Council (1215) rejected this early tradition and forbade infants from receiving the Eucharist until they had reached the age of discretion. Finally, in 1563, the Council of Trent deprived infants of the sacrament of Confirmation, insisting that only children who had attained the age of discretion were entitled to it. Infants who had enjoyed full membership in the church in times past were reduced to catechumen status by the actions of the Lateran Council and the Council of Trent.

After the Lateran Council decree of 1215, the Catholic Church prescribed the following sequence for the reception of the seven sacraments: Baptism, Confirmation, Penance, the Eucharist, Matrimony or Orders, and Extreme Unction. Though Unction has been placed last in this sequence, its reception depended more on circumstance than order. It was administered to any baptized member who had reached the age of discretion and who was seriously ill. The church's sequence for the sacraments seemed fixed by Scripture and tradition. Even the Protestant Reformation of the 1520's did not alter the sequence. Abruptly in 1563, the Council of Trent introduced a reordering of the sacraments. Confirmation no longer had to precede Penance and the Eucharist. The council decreed that it could be postponed until the child reached the age of twelve: "It is to be observed that, after Baptism, the Sacrament of Confirmation may indeed be administered to all. . . . If not, therefore, to be postponed to the age of twelve, it is most proper to defer this sacrament at least to that of seven years."[18] Instead of linking Confirmation to infancy, the council tied it to the indeterminate "age of discretion," which occurred sometime between the ages of seven and fourteen, depending on the individual maturity of the child. Confirmation was no longer deemed suitable for the infant. It became a rite of discretion, a sign of mental as well as spiritual maturity.

Trent decreed further that the father of the child and the parish priest were best suited to determine whether or not a child was ready to receive the Eucharist:

But the age at which children should be admitted to the sacred mysteries, no one can better determine than the father and the priest, for it is their office to

---

[18] *The Catechism of the Council of Trent,* trans. by Theodore A. Buckley (London, 1852), p. 205. Trent issued its original catechism in 1566. See *Catechismus et decreto concilii Tridentini ad Parochos Pii Quinti Pontificis Maximi iussu editus* (Rome, 1566).

examine, and to inquire from the children, whether they have acquired any knowledge of, and experience a relish for, this admirable sacrament.[19]

Trent's conception of Penance also evolved from the decrees of the Fourth Lateran Council. The *Catechism of the Council of Trent* observed: "As there can be no doubt that the law of confession was enacted and established by our Lord himself, it is naturally our duty to ascertain, by whom, at what age, and at what season of the year, it ought to be observed. In the first place, then, from the canon of the Council of Lateran . . . it is clear, that no person is bound by the law of confession, until the age when he arrived at the use of reason, a time, however, that has not been defined by any fixed number of years; but it may be laid down as a general principle, that a child is bound to go to confession, as soon as he is able to discern between good and evil, and as soon as his mind is capable of malice."[20] Though Erasmus suggests that contemporary authorities assumed that "puberty . . . gives the power to discriminate between good and evil," the church legislated that the age of discretion could occur before adolescence, indeed as early as seven years.[21]

Throughout its early history, the Catholic Church did not assign any definite ages as preconditions to the reception of the first four sacraments. Beginning in 1563, however, the Council of Trent determined that twelve was the ideal age for conferring Confirmation, and that no child under the age of seven should be admitted to that sacrament. Trent determined that Confirmation was the kind of sacrament which required discretion for validity. Apparently the only requirements of Trent with regard to sequence were that Baptism must precede Confirmation, that Penance must precede the Eucharist, and that the recipient of the latter three sacraments must have attained the age of discretion.

In effect, the Council of Trent admitted that the order of the sacraments could be altered and that the change reflected its changing attitude toward children. Instead of associating Confirmation with

---

[19] *The Catechism of the Council of Trent*, trans. by Buckley, p. 247.

[20] *Ibid.*, p. 282. The Code of Canon Law (*Codex iuris canonici* [Rome, 1918; repr. Graz, 1955], c. 88) states that a child has attained the age of reason by the completion of his seventh year, though this varies according to the individual child. See Burroughs, "Age of Reason," *New Catholic Encyclopedia*, 12, p. 118.

[21] See *Two Sermons Preached by the Boy Bishop at St. Paul's. . . and at Gloucester*, ed. Nichols, p. 1.

infancy, Trent saw it as the sacrament of discretion—a source of grace for a child in his pre-adolescent years. Candidates for Confirmation were expected to display a measure of *spiritual* maturity. They were asked to profess publicly their own commitment to Christ and his church. Though Trent insisted that children who had reached the age of discretion were obliged to confess their sins and to receive the Eucharist annually, it showed special deference to those under the age of adolescence by deferring ecclesiastical penalties until they reached the age of fourteen.[22]

Unlike most Protestant churches, the Catholic Church promoted the reception of Penance, the Eucharist, and Confirmation before the child reached puberty. For most Protestant reformers, spiritual maturity was equated with physical maturity. Their rites of Confirmation and the Eucharist became in effect twin rites of puberty—a public acknowledgment that the physically mature Christian was also spiritually mature and morally responsible.

The Prince of Humanists did not anticipate Trent's view nor share that of most Protestant reformers concerning the order or age requirements of the sacraments.[23] Erasmus differed most strongly from Protestant theology on the sacrament of Confirmation. Writing in 1533, he asserted that Confirmation "by which the yong christen soldyer is confirmed and strengthed against the temptations of the dyuell [sic] with this sacrament were they wonte to be fenced or armed/ whiche were of age inclynyng and leanynge towardes the ieoperdye and pareyll of synnynge/ that is to wyte after they were seuen yeres olde."[24] Like Trent, Erasmus believed that Confirmation would protect the child from the proclivity to sin, and, at the same time, it would increase his "aptenes vnto vertue . . . that it sholde not be infected with vyces afore that it doth playnly know what vyce is."[25] It should be kept in mind that Erasmus did not believe that a child of seven was capable of sinning, only that he might acquire bad habits from constant exposure to wickedness and eventually learn to commit serious sins. Erasmus maintained that the age of consent must be

---

[22] Minors before puberty were exempt from penalties *latae sententiae.* See J. D. McGuire, "Age (Canon Law)," in the *New Catholic Encyclopedia,* 1, p. 197.

[23] For a scholarly assessment of Erasmus' views on the sacraments in general, see John Payne, *Erasmus: His Theology of the Sacraments* (Richmond, Va., 1970).

[24] Erasmus, *A playne and godly exposytion or declaration of the commune crede [Symbolum Apostolorum],* trans. by William Marshall (London [1534]), sig. 118.

[25] *Ibid.,* sig. 119^v.

associated with puberty.[26] With regard to penitential fasting, Erasmus cautioned children not to observe it until they reached full maturity. Speaking through the lips of Gaspar in the colloquy titled "The Whole Duty of Youth," he insisted: "With fasting I have nothing to do. For Jerome taught me that health should not be weakened by fasts until the body has reached its proper, mature strength; but I haven't yet reached my seventeenth year."[27]

In keeping with Protestant theologians, and in opposition to the Lateran Council, he also insisted that the Eucharist should be associated with adolescence when the "dyuell doth laye all his ordenaunce/ and vse all his engynes agaynst the soldyer of Christe."[28] Erasmus went further than most Protestants, however, by arguing that the Eucharist should be delayed, specifically, until the age of sixteen. For Erasmus, the sacraments of Baptism, Confirmation, Penance, and the Eucharist were divinely instituted for specific purposes and for particular times of life. He associated Baptism with infancy, Confirmation with the age of reason, and Penance and the Eucharist with adolescence (i.e. "after the age of .xvi. yeres").[29] Since each sacrament conferred special graces, which were appropriate to, and effective at, a particular point in one's spiritual and physical development, it was senseless to administer Confirmation and the Eucharist to infants. Children who had not yet reached a certain measure of maturity were simply not capable of benefiting from such sacramental graces:

> In the old tyme/ they gaue the bodye and bloude of the lorde euen vnto yonge infantes/ forthwith after theyr baptyme. That custome is chaunged/ and peraduenture it were expedient/ that also the custome of certayne regions were changed [i.e. Spain and Portugal]/ in which confirmation is gyuen to infantes.

---

[26] "'The age of puberty,' they say, 'brings with it the power to distinguish between good and evil,'" Erasmus to Lambertus Grunnius, *Allen*, 2, 309; trans. by Mynors and Thomson, *CWE*, 4, p. 28. In his *Paraphrase of the Gospel of Saint Luke* (1524), he distinguished between "infancy," "the stature of a young stripling," "the degree of a young man," and "full perfection of manhood," noting that "big laddes and strieplynges growe quite a waie from the purenesse of babehood to boyishe wantonnesse." See *The first tome or volume of the Paraphrase of Erasmus vpon the Newe Testamente* (London, 1548), sig. e₄.

[27] This is not to suggest that children of twelve, for example, could not commit serious wrongs or faults. See "The Whole Duty of Youth," *The Colloquies of Erasmus*, trans. by Craig R. Thompson (Chicago, 1965), p. 38.

[28] Erasmus, *A playne and godly exposytion*, trans. by Marshall, sig. 120.

[29] *Ibid.*, sig. 119ᵛ.

For asmuche as these two sacramentes are not of absolute necessyte/ so as baptyme is. And therefore the mothers doo well to make haste vnto the sacrament of baptyme: but those other two are gyuen more conueniently in theyr mete tyme/ and they are gyuen more profytably: if to the sacrament be added also some lytle admonition or counsayll.[30]

Though Erasmus clearly distinguishes between the absolute necessity of Baptism for salvation, on the one hand, and Confirmation and the Eucharist, on the other, he nevertheless urged the reception of the latter sacraments because of their efficaciousness. Furthermore, he recommended instruction on the meaning of these two sacraments in an effort to stress their inward character.[31]

The Anglican Reformation at the outset followed an Erasmian direction. The *King's Book* (1543) rejected the necessity of infant Confirmation, promising that all baptized children who died in infancy would be saved: "And although men ought not to contemn this sacrament [Confirmation], but should present their children unto the bishop to receive at his hands the sacrament of confirmation, yet it is not to be thought that there is any such necessity of confirmation of infants, but that they being baptized, and dying innocents before they be confirmed, shall be assured to attain everlasting life and salvation by the effect of baptism received."[32] However, the Erasmian influence ends here. The confirmation of *children* ceased to be practiced in England after the appearance of Thomas Cranmer's *Book of Common Prayer* in 1549. Archbishop Cranmer emphasized the point that it was to be administered only to those who had reached the "perfect age" of adolescence.[33] In the Protestant tradition, Confirmation for the English church was the rite of puberty. It would protect adolescents from those temptations to sin which occur most often at that stage of life: ". . . forasmuch as Confirmacion is ministred to theym that be Baptised, that by imposition

---

[30] *Ibid.*, sig. 120–120ᵛ.

[31] John Payne, *Erasmus: His Theology of the Sacraments,* p. 179.

[32] Henry VIII, *A Necessary Doctrine and Erudition for any Christian man* (1543), ed. T. A. Lacey for the Church Historical Society (London, 1932), p. 78.

[33] Cranmer believed that instruction on the Eucharist must "be so plain, that the least child . . . in the town may understand them. . . ." See Peter Brook. *Thomas Cranmer's Doctrine of the Eucharist* (London, 1965). Queen Mary (1554) returned to the tradition of confirming children during her reign. See *Tudor Royal Proclamations,* ed. Paul L. Hughes and James F. Larkin (New Haven, 1968), 2, p. 37: ". . . That children be christened by the priest and confirmed by the bishops, as heretofore hath been accustomed and used."

of handes and prayer, they may receiue strengthe and defence agaynst all temptacions to synne, and the assaultes of the worlde and the Deuill: it is most mete to be ministred when children come to that age, that partely by the frailtye of their awane fleshe, partely by the assaultes of the worlde and the Deuill, thei begyn to be in daunger to fal into sondry kyndes of synne."[34] Erasmus, on the other hand, saw a real need for divine grace when the child reached the age of reason; and he insisted that Confirmation was the sacrament from which young Christian soldiers could benefit most.

By accepting the sacramental concept of children that had been developed by Luther, whereby the sacraments or rites of Confirmation, Penance, and the Eucharist were administered only to adolescents and adults, the Anglican Church rejected early accountability. It refused to believe that an eight-year-old child could distinguish between right and wrong, and hence commit sin. By delaying Confirmation, Penance, and the Eucharist until adolescence, the Anglican Church not only delayed full participation of the child in the church, but it freed him from moral responsibility. In a sense it guaranteed the innocence of every child until the age of physical maturity by recognizing a separate state in life between the ages of seven and fourteen. Children who died before the reception of the adult sacraments were assured of salvation because they were not responsible for their sins.[35] The Anglican concept of childhood protected the child by extending the age of innocence over a longer period of time. In 1593, for example, Elizabeth I acknowledged that children were not required to attend church services until they were sixteen years old: "Be it ordeined and enacted by our Souereigne Lady the Queenes Maiestie. . . that euery person aboue the age of xvi. yeres borne within any the Queenes Maiesties Realmes. . . being a Popish Recusant, and before the end of this Session of Parliament convicted for not repayring to some Church. . . to hear Diuine seruice there, but forbearing the same contrary to the Lawes and statutes heretofore made and prouided in that behalfe. . . ."[36]

---

[34] *The booke of the common prayer* (London, 1549), sig. b$_3$^{r}.

[35] For a useful discussion of the sacrament of Baptism in sixteenth-century England, see G. W. Bromily, *Baptism and the Anglican Reformation* (London, 1953).

[36] See "An Acte for the restreining of Popish Recusants to some certaine places of aboade," in *Anno XXXV. Reginae Elizabethae: At the Parliament begun and holden at Westminister the xix. day of Februarie* . . . [London, 1593], sig. A$_4$^{v}.

Most Protestants and Anglicans viewed children in a manner that differed from the Catholic perspective. Because they did not believe that pre-adolescent children were capable of sin, they refused to admit them to full participation in the church. It was not until a child reached adolescence that he was permitted to receive Communion. Before then, he was expected to imitate Christian conduct as best he could within an environment which encouraged virtue and punished vice. Children were assigned a special status as catechumens, intermediary between the absolute innocence of infants and the spiritual maturity of adult communicants. For the Catholic, on the other hand, the Eucharist was less a sign of spiritual and physical maturity than a mark of intellectual readiness. The Eucharist (as well as Penance) was the beginning of the child's quest for maturity, not its culmination. Childhood was viewed as a battle ground and the devil as the leading opponent. The Catholic child who reached the age of discretion was expected to behave as an adult and was held accountable for his shortcomings by having to confess his sins to a priest. The grace of Penance and the Eucharist might be looked upon as aids or spurs from a Catholic perspective but they could just as well be thought of as strait jackets, requiring the seven to fourteen year-old child to measure up to adult standards or face eternal perdition.

Erasmus as a religious reformer anticipated the Protestant concept of childhood but went even further. Childhood for him was a period of time that extended from late infancy (about the age of four) to eighteen, four years after the beginning of adolescence. In his classic statement on children's education, *De pueris statim ac liberaliter instituendis libellus* (or the argument of Erasmus of Rotterdam that children should straightway from their earliest years be trained in virtue and sound learning) that appeared for the first time in 1529, Erasmus insisted that infancy should be shortened from six years to three years; that is, when a boy reached the age of four he should begin instruction in "the rudiments of learning."[37] Erasmus reasoned: "For if in early childhood a boy acquires

---

[37] Though J.-C. Margolin suggests "environ trois ans" (p. 20), Erasmus made it clear that the first three years of a child's life should be left to the care of the nurse or mother. See Erasmus, *De Pueris Statim ac Liberaliter Instituendis Libellus* (1529), trans. by William H. Woodward (Cambridge, 1904), p. 199: "If figures are to be mentioned at all, we may remember that Chrysippus judges the first three years to be the province of the nurse . . . . And I freely allow that." For a useful analysis of *De Pueris Instituendis*, see J.-C. Margolin's essays in *Erasme, Declamatio De Pueris Statim Ac Liberaliter Instituendis* (Geneva, 1966), pp. 13–122. For the definitive Latin text, see Margolin's edition in *Opera Omnia Desiderii*

such useful elements he will be free to apply his youth to higher knowledge, to the saving of time." But more importantly for Erasmus: "Whilst he is thus occupied in sound learning he will perforce be kept from some of the temptations which befall youth, seeing that nothing engages the whole mind more than studies."[38] Erasmus believed that the four year-old child was capable of storing up knowledge of virtue that could be used to sustain him against the assaults of the devil, the flesh, and the world when he reached sixteen and became morally responsible for his actions.

Erasmus pleaded with fathers not to follow the current practice of delaying instruction until the child was seven years old when "the allurements of indulgence have made application more difficult."[39] Above all, he warned fathers not to listen to the babblings of serving women and weak relations who wished to prolong infancy because they believed that early instruction could cause physical harm to the child. In developing the text of his argument, Erasmus preserves the sixteenth-century concern that mothers showed toward the physical needs of their children both before and after birth:

> Consider, in this regard, the care which a boy's mother will lavish upon his bodily frame, how she will take thought should she but faintly suspect in him a tendency to become wry-necked, cross-eyed, cross-backed or splay-footed, or by any mischance prove ill-formed in proportions of his figure. Think, too, how she is apt to busy herself about his milk, his meat, his bath, his exercise, following herein the wise foresights of Galen. Will she defer this carefulness until the seventh year? No, from the very day of his birth charge is taken lest mischief hap, and wisely, knowing that a weakly manhood may be thus avoided. Nay, even before the child be born, how diligent is the wise mother to see that no harm come to herself for her child's sake. No one blames this as undue or untimely care for the young life.[40]

Erasmus wished to combine this great concern for the health of the child with a recognition of the preeminent importance of the intellectual

---

Erasmi Roterodami (Amsterdam, 1971), I–2, pp. 21–78. Margolin discusses the innovative nature of Erasmus' pedagogy in "The Method of 'Words and Things' in Erasmus' *De Pueris Instituendis* (1529). . . ," in *Essays on the Works of Erasmus*, ed. R. L. DeMolen (New Haven, 1978), pp. 221–238.

[38] Erasmus, *De Pueris Instituendis*, trans. by Woodward, p. 181.
[39] *Ibid.*, p. 182.
[40] *Ibid.*, pp. 182–183.

and spiritual life as well. He strongly condemned parents who exposed their children to material comforts, over-indulgence at the table, and the military arts. Concerning the latter, he wrote "Straight from their mother's arms they are bidden to finger swords and shields, to thrust and strike."[41] How then, Erasmus asks, can parents blame others when their child develops a combative nature?

Since Erasmus believed that a child, like a ball of wax, could be molded and shaped by early instruction, he rejected the notion that children are by nature prone to evil. He insisted that a "child's nature . . . is the primitive endowment with which he is born" and believed that a healthy and virtuous mother can contribute to a healthy and virtuous child. He also described the kind of home environment that is conducive to the proper development of a child:

> The links that bind together mind and body are so close that it cannot be but that the physical nature affects the spiritual. Again, as the child reflects the disposition of its parents, let them observe moderation in appetites and keep strict guard over themselves that they should be temperate, not given to anger; the father sober, the mother, especially during the months preceding the child's birth, of good conscience and free from anxieties. Further, it will be good for the child that it be nursed by the mother; should necessity arise for a foster-mother, she must be strong and of right disposition.

Furthermore, Erasmus underscored the special importance of early childhood as a phase of human growth in the following passage: "Neglect in this respect may have enduring results for harm, physical and moral. For it is at this period that education truly begins; not, as some would have it, at the seventh year—or the seventeenth!"[42] Since Erasmus was conscious of the fact that most children began elementary school at the age of seven and adolescents went off to the university at seventeen, he heartily disapproved of delaying education to conform to these traditional ages of entry.

Even more important than parental influence for the sound development of the boy was the influence of the tutor. The tutor should try to identify at the outset of his instruction the special gifts or talents of the child; and emphasizing these interests, he should develop a course of training. Speaking from experience, Erasmus confidently asserted: "I am

---

[41] *Ibid.*, p. 189.
[42] *Ibid.*, p. 194.

personally of opinion that where the method is sound, where teaching and practice go hand in hand, any discipline may ordinarily be acquired by the flexible intellect of man. What, indeed, should be beyond his power when, as we are told, an elephant has been trained to walk a tightrope?"[43] Erasmus simply re-echoed the prevailing philosophy of Renaissance humanists.

To counter charges that he was proposing an unworkable program of educational reform, the Dutch savant offered evidence that children between the ages of four and seven were presently being "taught manners and conduct." Moreover, because children at those ages were able to acquire appropriate behavioral skills, he insisted that these same children were not too young to acquire instruction in the "rudiments of letters": "Thus it is established that what is poured into our nature, so to say, in our earliest years becomes an integral part of us."[44]

The presence of "an ape-like instinct of imitation" convinced Erasmus that no age is too early to begin instruction.[45] In this respect he was going against some classical prescriptions.[46] The words of Seneca, for example, recommended the opposite position: "No age is too late for learning." Seneca's apparent endorsement of contemporary practice elicited this response from Erasmus:

It is probably, however, that this contention implies no more than this, that the laborious side of studies, such as learning by heart, repetition, long written exercises, should be avoided as far as possible in early education.[47]

---

[43] *Ibid.*, p. 196. Despite this passage, Leah Marcus, *Childhood and Cultural Despair* (Pittsburgh, 1978), maintains that "in the work of the very early humanists, Erasmus and Thomas More, we find a fascinating blend of enthusiasm for classical learning and distrust, inherited from late medieval affective piety, for what the human intellect can hope to accomplish" (p. 25).

[44] Erasmus, *De Pueris Instituendis*, trans. by Woodward, p. 197.

[45] In the colloquy "Courtship" (1523), Erasmus asserts by way of Pamphilus: "Next, we'll see that our children are imbued from birth with sacred teachings and beliefs. What the jar is filled with when new matters most." See *The Colloquies of Erasmus*, trans. Thompson, p. 97.

[46] Quintilian, however, believed in beginning a child's education immediately after birth. See Quintilian, *Institutio Oratoria*, Book I, trans. by H. E. Butler (London, 1921), p. 27: "Those however who hold that a child's mind should not be allowed to lie fallow for a moment are wiser. Chrysippus, for instance, though he gives the nurses a three years' reign, still holds the formation of the child's mind on the best principles to be a part of their duties."

[47] Erasmus, *De Pueris Instituendis*, trans. by Woodward, p. 198.

Erasmus insisted that instruction before the age of seven must be made enjoyable so that every child will want to participate eagerly in it. Subjects must be few, attractively taught, and adapted to the age and tastes of the child: "Such study may hardly be distinguished from play, and is a source of enjoyment to the child."[48] At the same time Erasmus warned that unless the child in his earliest years is exposed to virtue and knowledge he will instinctively imitate what is trivial or follow the allurement of the senses rather than the rule of reason.

Recognizing children as imitators, Erasmus advised the tutor or schoolmaster to present a sympathetic manner and to develop wise and attractive methods. Possessing these two important qualifications he will be able to persuade boys to find pleasure in school. Above all, he warned the tutor not to resort to physical force. Erasmus cautioned even parents that they cannot train their children by using corporal punishment. Instead he argued that "love must be the first influence; followed and completed by a trustful and affectionate respect, which compels obedience far more surely than dread can ever do."[49]

Erasmus also castigated contemporary schoolmasters for their cruelty. He described sixteenth-century schools as torture chambers: "blows and shouts, sobs and howls fill the air."[50] He cites two examples of boys, ages ten and twelve, who were soundly beaten simply for the purpose of impressing upon them the authority of the schoolmaster. Moreover he frowned upon schools run by religious orders, including the Brethren of the Common Life, whom he accused of possessing inferior qualifications, even though they were "often good, kindly men."[51] Of his schooldays he complained: "My own childhood was tortured by logical subtleties which had no reference to anything that was true in fact or sound in expression."[52] Erasmus preferred instruction in a public school or at home. In this connection he regarded the household of Sir Thomas More as the ideal.

Instead of flogging the child who misbehaves, Erasmus recommended the use of "two spurs to industry: shame and desire for praise, shame is

---

[48] *Ibid.*, p. 202.

[49] *Ibid.*, p. 203.

[50] *Ibid.*, p. 204. Erasmus provides a description of classroom discipline in the colloquy "Off to School." See *The Colloquies of Erasmus,* trans. by Thompson, pp. 43–45.

[51] *Ibid.*

[52] *Ibid.*, p. 221.

the fear of just reproach; by praise a boy is quickened to excel in all he does. Let these, then, be the schoolmaster's weapons today."[53] A clever teacher, Erasmus suggested, will also utilize the motive of emulation among children; for this will often be found effective with boys who will not respond to warnings, to encouragement, or the offer of rewards. Finally for those boys who were intellectually unable to benefit from instruction, Erasmus advised the schoolmaster to send them home.

Though he urged the schoolmaster to be gentle, Erasmus warned him not to become too familiar with his charges. He insisted that a measure of authority must be maintained at all times. Furthermore, he recommended that the schoolmaster imitate the methods that mothers use in the earliest training of their infants:

As she prattles baby language, stirs and softens baby food, stoops and guides the tottering steps—so will the master act in things of the mind. Slowly is the transition made to walking alone, or to eating solid food; the tender frame is thus carefully hardened. In exactly the same manner instruction is at first simple, taught by the way of play, taught by degrees. The sense of effort is lost in the pleasure of such natural exercise: insensibly the mind becomes equal to harder tasks.[54]

In proposing instruction for boys, beginning at the age of four, Erasmus was speaking to all parents, rich as well as poor: "If they be poor men, the more need have they of learning in order to minister to their deficiency; if they be rich, in order to learn to govern their wealth aright."[55] He saw education as a means of advancing poor children to higher stations in life; and, no doubt, he viewed his own international reputation in the light of his impoverished beginnings.

As though he were addressing Philippe Ariès in the twentieth century, Erasmus perceived of childhood between the ages of four and eighteen in a special way:

Wholly wrong are those masters who expect their little pupils to act as though they were but diminutive adults, who forget the meaning of youth, who have no standard of what can be done or be understood except that of their own minds.[56]

---

[53] *Ibid.*, p. 208.
[54] *Ibid.*, p. 211.
[55] *Ibid.*, p. 210.
[56] *Ibid.*, p. 211. Ariès, on the other hand, observes that "as soon as he started going to school, the child immediately entered the world of adults." See Ariès, *Centuries of Childhood*, trans. by Baldick, p. 154. He also maintains that "the humanists remained

This sixteenth-century view of childhood underscores the unique place of childhood in the evolving development of man—a stage in life intermediary between infancy and adulthood but including youth. Childhood did not terminate at the age of seven, as Ariès would like us to believe, but extended into adolescence. Erasmus' perception of childhood rested partly on his own boyhood and early education, since he was sent to school at the age of four (along with his brother Pieter, who was three years older). His childhood ended abruptly when he entered the monastery at Steyn at age sixteen. No doubt, Erasmus was sent to school at Gouda at so early an age because of his precocity and the fact that his older brother had reached the normal age of entry into school, namely seven.[57]

But Erasmus' perceptions of childhood also grew out of his theology of the sacraments and was rooted in classical tradition. His view of childhood was truly revolutionary in the sixteenth century because he rejected the extended period of coddling that children received until they reached the age of seven. Moreover, he advanced the thesis that the period in life between the ages of four and sixteen was conducive to acquiring virtue and learning in sufficient quantity to resist temptations and sin in later life when the adult assumes full responsibility before God for his actions. He differed from his humanist contemporaries by stressing the existence of a state of childhood that began at birth and extended until eighteen. Erasmus even went so far as to urge fathers to plan the future instruction of their sons in earliest infancy in order to prepare them for a life of service and virtue:

> In face then, of all these serious facts you will not suffer, I do not say seven years, but three days even, of your son's life to pass, before you take into earnest consideration his nurture and future education.[58]

In addition to the sacramental and Erasmian concepts of childhood, the homilies of the Boy-Bishops were rooted in the belief that children who had not yet reached adolescence were closer to God spiritually than adults. Indeed it was because of their natural virtues that children were held up as models for adults:

---

attached to the idea of a general culture spread over the whole of life and showed scant interest in an education confined to children." *Ibid.*, p. 412.

[57] See R. L. DeMolen, "Erasmus as Adolescent," *Bibliothèque d'Humanisme et Renaissance*, 38 (1976), pp. 7–25.

[58] Erasmus, *De Pueris Instituendis*, trans. Woodward, p. 222.

... young babes, which are symple, wythowt gyle, innocent, wythowt harme, and all pure wythowt corruption, as few above the age of childer are, and as all ought to be, and of necessitie must be if thei intend ther salvacion according to the wordes of Christ. . . . "Love litill ones, therfor, and learn of them how you may have an entre into the kyngdom of heavyn."[59]

Partly in an effort to insure the belief that children were simple, innocent, and pure, the church established the feast of the Holy Innocents as Childermas Day on December 28. Children were to be honored in all of the churches in token of "the innocent childer which shed ther bloud for the person of the most pure innocent child Jesus."[60]

The child-bishop who spoke to the parishioners at Gloucester on December 28, 1558 (from a text written, no doubt, by his schoolmaster), underscored the need to reform "corrupt maners, which are dissonant and disagreable with the incorrupt maners of childer" if they desired to "loke for the kyngdom of heaven."[61] He spoke directly to the adults present in the cathedral, urging them to

Considre well the nature of innocent childer, and yow shall perceive in them no maner of malice, no envy, no disdayne, no hurtfullness, no synfull affection, no pride, no ambition, no singularitie, no desyre of honor, of riches, of carnalitie, of revenginge, or quittyng evyll for evyll; but all the affections quiet, in all pacience, in all simplicitie, in all puritie, in all tractableness, in all obedience, in all humilitie, and in all innocency, and no such synfull affections reigning in them as commynly rageth in men and women of years.[62]

Despite his injunction that adults should imitate children, the author of this sermon insisted, according to Catholic tradition, that not all children were innocent: "Well, well! all is not gold that shynes, nor all are not innocents that beare the face of childer."[63] It was the responsibility of

---

[59] *Two Sermons Preached by the Boy Bishop at St. Paul's . . . and at Gloucester . . .* , ed. Nichols, p. 15.

[60] *Ibid.*, p. 19. This feast was overlooked by Ariès, who insisted that "in the Middle Ages there were no religious festivals of childhood, apart from the great seasonal festivals which were often pagan rather than Christian." See Ariès, *Centuries of Childhood*, trans. Baldick, p. 125. See also R. L. DeMolen, "*Pueri Christi Imitatio:* The Festival of the Boy-Bishop in Tudor England," *Moreana*, 45 (1975), 17–28.

[61] *Two Sermons Preached by the Boy Bishop*, ed. by Nichols, p. 20.

[62] *Ibid.*, p. 21.

[63] *Ibid.*, p. 25.

schoolmasters as "tertios parentes" to discourage youths from "touching vice and vicious maners, and to bolden and corage them in all probitye and vertue, and vertuose maners."[64] Discipline was important for all children. It should not be ignored under the pretense that it might stifle a child's initiative.

In contrast to the polemical tone of the 1558 sermon, the 1495 Boy-Bishop sermon is moralistic.[65] The author urged his listeners to reject "the pleasure of the worlde" and to acquire child-like virtues. The 1495 sermon divides the life of a boy into three parts: infancy, which extends from birth to seven; childhood, from seven to fourteen, and youth, from fourteen to eighteen. The first age is one of bliss. An infant is neither corrected nor beaten. He is subject to no laws and may do whatever he pleases. The freedom of infancy ends at childhood when boys are sent to school. In this "growynge age" there is no "fawte that he doth but he is punysshed."[66] Childhood is succeeded by youth or adolescence, when the teen-ager is won to goodness or lost to lewdness.

In addition to the two English sermons of the Boy-Bishop that have survived, Erasmus wrote his *Concio de Puero Jesu* about 1512, that is shortly after John Colet founded St. Paul's School. Erasmus composed his sermon specifically for "a chylde vnto chyldren."[67] He characterized children as an amalgam of "foolishness," "simplicity," and "pureness": "Howe be it there is vniuersally in the very age of chyldren a certayne natyve and naturall goodnes and as it were a certayne shadowe and ymage of innocencye; or a hope rather and dysposition of a goodnes to come; a softe mynde, and plyable to euery behauour; shamefastnes [modesty], which is a good kepar of innocencie; a wytte voyde of vyces; brightnes of bodye; and as it were a flower of a floryshyng worlde."[68] It is this plethora of virtues that Erasmus exhorts his young listeners to imitate: "And if we can not folowe the man [Jesus], let vs chyldren

---

[64] *Ibid.*, p. 27.

[65] *Ibid.*, p. 12. See Edward F. Rimbault's introductory essay in this same volume where he states that "According to Dr. Dibdin this must have been printed before the year 1496, as the soul of Bishop Kemp is prayed for in it, who died in 1489; and his successor Hill in 1495 or 1496" (p. xxxv).

[66] *Ibid.*, p. 7.

[67] Erasmus, *Erasmi Concio De Puero Iesv: A Sermon on the Child Jesus* [1512?], ed. by J. H. Lupton (London, 1901), p. 20.

[68] *Ibid.*, p. 23.

folowe the chylde [Jesus]."⁶⁹ Erasmus recognized the practicality of identifying in the minds of children for the purpose of imitation the image of the divine Christ Child rather than the figure of the adult Christ.

Erasmus also argues that since the world corrupts it were far better for a child to remain at home or attend a nearby school until he reached adolescence. Erasmus reminds his listeners that Christ did not leave home until he was twelve years of age ("at suche a tendre age of childehood"⁷⁰) in order to lecture to the learned men in the Temple. In a letter to Justus Jonas, dated September 16, 1519, Erasmus described the prominent place of the Child Jesus in the classroom of St. Paul's School:

> Over the high master's chair is a beautifully-wrought figure of the Child Jesus, seated, in the attitude of one teaching; and all the young flock, as they enter and leave school, salute it with a hymn. Over it is the countenance of God the Father, saying HEAR YE HIM: an inscription added at my suggestion.⁷¹

Erasmus held up the image of the twelve year-old Child Jesus as a model for imitation. He expressed a similar theme in one of his five hymns for St. Paul's School (titled *Carmen iambicum: sub persona pueri Jesu praesidentis Scholae Coleticae*): "Know Me First, boys, and strive after pure manners; then add to these God-fearing literature."⁷² But his sermon on the Child Jesus expresses it best, emphasizing the great dignity of children:

> Great is than the mysterie of a chyld, great is the mysterie of chyldhode, wherin Jesus so greatly was delyted. Let not vs then despyce our age, whiche that true praysour and estemer of thynges hath made so much of. Onely this one thynge: lette vs gyve our deuour [duty] that we may be suche chyldren as Jesus loveth. Surely he loueth innocent and harmelesse chyldren, redy and apte to learne, and symple. . . .⁷³

---

⁶⁹ *Ibid.*

⁷⁰ *The first tome or volume of the Paraphrase of Erasmus vpon the Newe Testamente* (London, 1548), sig. e₃.

⁷¹ Erasmus, *The Lives of Jehan Vitrier . . . and John Colet*, ed. J. H. Lupton (London, 1883), pp. 27–28.

⁷² Cornelis Reedijk, *the Poems of Desiderius Erasmus* (Leiden, 1956), pp. 304–305. See a parallel thought in "The Whole Duty of Youth," *The Colloquies of Erasmus*, ed. Thompson, p. 34. Though James H. Reiger, "Erasmus, Colet, and the Schoolboy Jesus," *Studies in the Renaissance*, 9 (1962), 188, insists that "these poems are patently the work of a man who does not understand children. . . ," the poems themselves do not bear him out.

⁷³ Erasmus, *Erasmi Concio De Puero Iesv*, ed. by Lupton, p. 20.

It is hoped that the preceding evidence of childhood in the sixteenth century will be read as a corrective to Ariès, who would like us to believe that the period between seven and fourteen was indistinguishable from adulthood before the seventeenth century. Ariès' insistence that children were incomplete or defective adults contrasts sharply with Erasmus' idealization of the state of childhood. Far from wishing a speedy end to childhood and the early assumption of adult responsibilities he stressed the unique importance of this time of life. Throughout the Renaissance, humanists recognized that the ages of man were not subject to whim but to basic intellectual, physical, spiritual, and emotional changes that took place at definite stages of human development. For Erasmus, preadolescence was the key to success in the later stages of life. Based on his own boyhood experiences, his understanding of the sacraments and Scripture, and his knowledge of the classics, Erasmus argued persuasively for a pivotal place for the child in the Renaissance household. Above all, as a humanist-reformer, he did not "forget the meaning of youth" in the sixteenth century:

> In all other departments of life we may succeed in recovering what we have lost by neglect. Time, however, when once it has flown by—and it flies very quickly— obeys no summons to return. There is no such miracle as a fountain of perpetual youth: no physic which can make old men young again. Of time, then, let us always be sparing; of youthful years most of all, for this is the best part of man's life, the most profitable, if it be rightly guarded.[74]

Perhaps, it would not be inappropriate to end this chapter by recognizing Erasmus of Rotterdam as the guardian of childhood in the sixteenth century because he insisted that a holy and productive life could be achieved by all if it were begun in one's formative years.

---

[74] Erasmus, *De Pueris Instituendis*, trans. by Woodward, p. 219. The recently edited Lisle letters confirm Erasmus' position that the sixteenth century stressed the importance of childhood. See the introduction to *The Lisle Letters*, ed. by Muriel St. Clare Byrne (Chicago, 1981), 1, pp. 87–89.

CHAPTER SEVEN

The Expression of Love in the Oeuvre of Erasmus

I may be able to speak the languages of men and even of angels, but if I have no love, my speech is no more than a noisy gong or a clanging bell. I may have the gift of inspired preaching; I may have all knowledge and understand all secrets; I may have all the faith needed to move mountains—but if I have no love, I am nothing.

1 Corinthians 13:1–3

I

THE first five years of the sixteenth century were active ones for Erasmus. He had published the first edition of the *Adages* in 1500, the *Enchiridion Militis Christiani* in 1503, and his edition of Lorenzo Valla's *Annotations on the New Testament* in 1505. By 1505 his program of reform was in full swing. Nevertheless, while living in London at the end of 1505, Erasmus took time to look backward at the origins of his *philosophia Christi*. When he asked Franciscus Theodoricus, a fellow canon, to collect his earliest letters for publication, he was conscious of the message which they contained and their relationship to his own spiritual transformation and appeal for religious renewal:

> I beg you, dear Franciscus, by the affection we entertain for each other and for your happiness' sake, which is as precious to me as my own, to devote yourself entirely to the Holy Scriptures. Go through the ancient commentators. Believe me, either the road to blessedness lies this way for us or we shall never attain to it.

Scripture and the Church Fathers would serve as the bed rock for his *philosophia Christi,* and he urged everyone within his reach to study these sources of blessedness.

Since Franciscus Theodoricus was living at Steyn after Erasmus' departure about 1493, it was obvious that Erasmus wanted him to collect his Steyn correspondence: "especially those written in some quantity to Cornelis of Gouda, in very large numbers to my friend Willem, and a few to Servatius. Scrape together all you can, from anywhere you can, but do not send them except by a messenger named by me."[1]

Although the Steyn correspondence, composed between 1486 and 1489, was never printed in Erasmus' lifetime, with the exception of *Allen,* 26 and 29, it is a remarkable collection of thirty-two letters. Erasmus recognized in the opening decade of the sixteenth century that his correspondence was an integral part of his works when he expressed a desire to have them published. It is my intention to show in part one that Erasmus attempted through his letters at Steyn to fulfill the biblical injunction to "love your neighbor as you love yourself" (Matthew 22:40) while pursuing studies that would lead to his ordination in 1492, and in part two to demonstrate how he applied his concept of love while living outside the monastery.

In the earliest letter that has come down to us, Pieter Winckel represents those individuals who had benefited from Erasmus' misfortunes during his adolescence by aggrandizing themselves at the expense of his inheritance. It is instructive because it provides insight into the conditions that surrounded Erasmus' entrance into the religious life of a Canon Regular of St. Augustine about 1486.[2] His brother Pieter and Servatius Roger actively thwarted Erasmus' efforts to foster the concept of love in the religious community which he was compelled to join.

Letters 2 through 32 in the Steyn correspondence were written to individuals who were close enough to Erasmus to be regarded as

---

[1] *The Correspondence of Erasmus,* tr. by R. A. B. Mynors and D. F. S. Thomson (Toronto: University of Toronto Press, 1974—), vol. 2, p. 100; *Allen,* 187. Hereafter cited as *CWE* with volume and page numbers. I have also provided the number of the letter that is found in *Opus Epistolarum Des. Erasmi Roterodami,* ed. by Percy S. Allen, H. M. Allen, H. W. Garrod *et al.* (Oxford: Oxford University Press, 1906–1958); hereafter cited as *Allen.*

[2] Contrary to P. S. Allen and the *CWE,* I have argued that Erasmus' letter to Winckel was written at Steyn. See my article on "Erasmus as Adolescent" in the *Bibliothèque d'Humanisme et Renaissance,* 38 (1976), pp. 9–10. David Knowles notes in *The Religious Orders in England* (Cambridge: Cambridge University Press, 1959), 3, p. 148, that Erasmus' "entry into religion was neither wholly spontaneous nor wholly spiritual in motive...." J.-B. Pineau, on the other hand, calls into question the claim of Erasmus that he was forced into the monastery as a child. See his *Érasme: Sa Pensée Religieuse* (Paris: Les Presses Universitaires de France, 1924), p. 1. I prefer to follow Charles Béné's decision to support 1469 as the year of Erasmus' birth and 1487 as the year of his entrance into the monastery at Steyn. See Béné, *Érasme et Saint Augustin* (Geneva: Librairie Droz, 1969), p. 24.

extensions of his family. He referred to Elisabeth, for example, as "dearest sister in Christ" and observed that "if then I can by no means rival you in devoted acts of friendship, still I need never to be outdone in the answering of your love and your letters."[3] At the same time, he chastised his brother for failing to write to him and inquired: "Where is your early good will towards me and the ardent brotherly affection which you once had for me?"[4] In a pleading tone, he tried to persuade Pieter to reciprocate his love for him: "If you desire to know what I am about, I love you intensely, as you deserve; your name is on my lips and in my heart; I think of you and dream of you and speak of you often with my friends. . . ."[5]

Erasmus became most distressed with his relationship with Servatius about 1487 because it failed to be of equal intensity. Erasmus described him to his brother as having a nature which "makes everyone love him."[6] Erasmus assumed that the more he expressed love for Servatius the more he would receive in return, but Servatius disappointed him:[7] ". . . what is it that makes you so hard-hearted that you not only refuse to love him who loves you so well but do not even regard him with esteem? Are you of so inhuman a disposition as to love those who hate you and hate those who love you?"[8]

Servatius at first encouraged and later rejected Erasmus' offer of a relationship based on mutual love. Erasmus outlined the obligations that both would have to accept if their love for one another would endure. "These are the proofs of a true love": "First of all, that friends must feel reciprocal good will; second, that neither should have secrets from the other; again, that each should be glad to help the other; that each should participate in the other's joy and in his sorrow; that they should think of themselves as sharing reciprocally all their thoughts, their plans, and in a word, their lives."[9]

---

[3] *CWE*, 1, 3; *Allen*, 2.
[4] *CWE*, 1, 4; *Allen*, 3.
[5] *CWE*, 1, 5; *Allen*, 3.
[6] For a discussion of the similarities between the *Imitatio Christi* and the *Philosophia Christi*, see my "The Interior Erasmus" in *Leaders of the Reformation*, ed. by R. L. DeMolen (Selinsgrove/London/Toronto: Susquehanna University Press/Associated University Presses, 1984), 11–42.
[7] *CWE*, 1, 5; *Allen*, 3.
[8] *CWE*, 1, 9; *Allen*, 7.
[9] *CWE*, 1, 13; *Allen*, 8.

The statutes of his congregation permitted Erasmus and Servatius to converse only infrequently. As a result they communicated through letters. A total of nine letters, written about 1487 to 1488, from Erasmus to Servatius have survived; those written by Servatius have not been preserved.

Erasmus spent approximately seven years in the monastery of the Canons Regular at Steyn (about 1486 to 1493), following the rule of St. Augustine and the statutes peculiar to the congregation of Sion which was Steyn's motherhouse. Although emotionally drained from the experiences preceding his entrance into the religious life, he strove to effect a reform among the canons at Steyn, based on a careful reading of the rule of St. Augustine. In the process he attacked the statutes governing the congregation, eliciting the disapproval of his prior and resulting ultimately in his departure from Steyn about 1493. It will be the purpose of this chapter to place the thirty-two letters that have survived from his experiences at Steyn in their proper context, showing that Erasmus had tried to fashion a community of canons that would return to the spirit of the rule of St. Augustine as it was laid down by the great church father in the fourth century.

St. Augustine had developed a community life for his followers that was based on love and firmly anchored in Scripture.[10] He prescribed that his clerics were to live together "one in mind and one in heart" (Acts 4:32) and to honor God in one another, because "each of you has become the temple of the living God" (2 Corinthians 6:16). St. Augustine, following St. Paul, insisted that love "is not self-seeking" (1 Corinthians 13:5); that "the way of love is exalted above all other ways" (1 Corinthians 12:13). He also admonished: "Do not let your love for one

---

[10] In his edition of the works of St. Augustine (Basel, 1528–29), 1, pp. 591–92, Erasmus questioned the authorship of the rule of St. Augustine, noting that the Bishop of Hippo probably wrote the rule specifically for women and not men: "quanquam probabile est eam non clericis, sed feminis esse scriptam. . . ." See J. P. Migne, ed., *Patrologiae cursus completus . . . series latina* (Paris, 1844–64), 47, c. 237. Richard Du Mans, O.F.M., criticized Erasmus' position in his *Antidotum contra Erasmi censuram in regulam Divi Augustini* (Paris, 1541). Luc Verheijen, O.S.A., also challenged the claim by Erasmus in *La Règle de Saint Augustin* (Paris: Études Augustiniennes, 1967) where he attributes the rule of St. Augustine to him about 397. See the introduction to *The Rule of Saint Augustine,* ed. by Tarsicius J. Van Bavel, O.S.A., and tr. by Raymond Canning, O.S.A. (London: Darton, Longman and Todd, 1984), pp. 3–8; hereafter cited as *The Rule of Saint Augustine,* ed. Van Bavel.

another remain caught up in self-love; rather, such love must be guided by the [Holy] Spirit."[11]

Despite the emotional quality of his language, Erasmus' relationship with the canons at Steyn was purely platonic and was designed to promote literary studies. Erasmus' plan of reform was based on both Scripture and the example of St. Jerome and St. Augustine, and was intended to lead to moral perfection. Erasmus reminded Servatius Roger that "you know my character well enough and are not unacquainted with my nature,"[12] but Servatius' reserve made a close relationship with Erasmus impossible. Later on, when Servatius was elected prior at Steyn, he insisted that Erasmus return to the monastery, silently concurring, no doubt, with Erasmus' perception that Erasmus was of upright character. To Franciscus Theodoricus, Erasmus revealed his program of reform: "So please see that you govern your way of living according to my precepts; for, if you set out on that journey with no guide, you may easily lose your way."[13]

In drafting his *philosophia Christi*, Erasmus was obviously indebted to Holy Scripture and to the Church Fathers, but he was also indebted to the rule of St. Augustine to which he was bound by vows after 1488. Erasmus became aware of the writings of St. Augustine after he entered the novitiate of the Canons Regular at Steyn. It was then that he decided to effect a reform of the religious life of the Canons Regular, based on the rule of the founder, in which love and community were intertwined and inseparable. Writing to Servatius about 1487, he underscored his efforts to forsake his personal misfortunes in order to eliminate the pain of a brother in Christ:

> Although I who seek to give you consolation am rather myself in need of it, not only because there seems no kind of disaster left which I do not daily encounter but also because for some time past I have endured no greater or harsher misery than your particular troubles, still it is my very special love for you, sweetest Servatius, that has caused me to forget my own pain and to attempt to heal yours.[14]

---

[11] *The Rule of Saint Augustine*, ed. Van Bavel, pp. 22–23.
[12] *CWE*, 1, 15; *Allen*, 9.
[13] *CWE*, 1, 16; *Allen*, 10.
[14] *CWE*, 1, 7; *Allen*, 5. In his letter to Johann Maier von Eck (15 May 1518), Erasmus admitted that during his adolescence he preferred St. Augustine to St. Jerome: ". . . Augustine was the author I read first of them all, and now reread daily as often as need arises." *CWE*, 6, 33; *Allen*, 844.

In keeping with Galatians 6:2, Erasmus was mindful that you must "bear one another's burdens, and thus you will fulfill the law of Christ."

For St. Augustine, good community life was nothing more than the practice of love. His rule of some dozen printed pages directed attention to the building of relationships of love. According to Tarsicius J. Van Bavel, O.S.A., "it is in any case clear that Augustine does not conceive community as an institution or a structure. . . but rather as a network of dynamic relationships between people."[15] Furthermore, St. Augustine paid no attention to asceticism as a way to achieve holiness, nor did he prescribe a particular habit or time schedule. While living at Steyn, Erasmus sought to establish bonds of love with his brother, with Servatius Roger, Franciscus Theodoricus, Cornelis Gerard, Willem Hermans, Sister Elisabeth, and several laymen—persons who were living both within and without his monastery. Erasmus' plan of reform would transcend the physical setting of Steyn and incorporate all those who were within his network of correspondents. His pen was the link that bound the members of his network to a life of mutual sharing.

The intensity of Erasmus' language remains consistent in his earliest correspondence. He loves his fellow canons and correspondents as much as he loves his own brother. He refers to Franciscus Theodoricus as "the half of my soul,"[16] to the layman Sasbout as "once your bosom companion,"[17] to Cornelis Gerard as "sweetest" and "dearest,"[18] and to Willem Hermans as "my second self."[19] To an unnamed married friend, he writes: "I love and dream of you";[20] and to another married friend, Jacob Canter, he asks him "to return my affection."[21]

Erasmus strove not only to teach his companion canons how to love one another but encouraged laymen who were his correspondents to do the same. Erasmus' reforming efforts required a recognition of mutual goals, based on the pursuit of classical letters, from which would be culled moral maxims. The rule of St. Augustine observed that living together is meaningless if the community did not seek interpersonal communication. Canons were required to share one another's life, ideas,

---

[15] *The Rule of Saint Augustine*, ed. Van Bavel, p. 46.
[16] *CWE*, 1, 19; *Allen*, 14.
[17] *CWE*, 1, 23; *Allen*, 16.
[18] *CWE*, 1, 32; *Allen*, 20.
[19] *CWE*, 1, 51; *Allen*, 28.
[20] *CWE*, 1, 60; *Allen*, 31.
[21] *CWE*, 1, 62; *Allen*, 32.

and expectations. This is what St. Augustine meant when he wrote: "You live together in the true sense of the word only if you have but one heart" (*Sermon on Psalm* 100, 11).[22] According to Van Bavel, it is St. Augustine's "deepest conviction that, in giving itself, love never diminishes or wanes; on the contrary, through giving itself love grows, and the more people to whom one's love reaches out, the more loving one becomes."[23] Erasmus sought to realize this ideal by encouraging loving relationships among his companions. To Servatius Roger, he implores:

> Indeed, you would have some reason to excuse yourself, if what I were asking of you were something arduous or difficult or wrong. But you yourself are surely aware what it is that I beg of you, inasmuch as it was not for the sake of reward or out of a desire for any favour that I have wooed you both unhappily and relentlessly. What is it then? Why, that you love him who loves you. What is easier, more pleasant, or more suited to a generous heart, than this? I would repeat: only love me, and it is enough for me.[24]

But Servatius remained unresponsive, preferring a superficial external relationship to an intensely internal one.

Unwilling to admit defeat, Erasmus pursued his efforts at reform, arguing for a change of direction in a letter to Servatius:

> Rather try by all means to become such a man that you may triumph in your turn over those who trample upon you, and in this you would already have succeeded if you had obeyed my advice. But as things stand, since there is nothing that does not encourage you to apply yourself to study, neither the subject nor the setting nor the very season, it seems to me that you have incentives enough to cultivate letters.[25]

St. Augustine had also exhorted his followers to correct faults in one another: "If you love the person, you will also correct his faults. Even though you are sometimes obliged to take harsh action, do it out of love for the good of the other" (*Sermons on the First Letter of John* 7, 11).[26]

Although Erasmus eventually failed to convert Servatius to his program of reform, he was more successful with others. To Servatius, he confided: "And, to fire you more keenly, you should know that our

---

[22] *The Rule of Saint Augustine*, ed. Van Bavel, p. 47.
[23] *Ibid.*, p. 49.
[24] *CWE*, 1, 12; *Allen*, 8.
[25] *CWE*, 1, 18; *Allen*, 13.
[26] *The Rule of Saint Augustine*, ed. Van Bavel, p. 85.

friend Gualterus has managed this and is now completely immersed in literary study, and regrets nothing so much as not having begun this long since."[27] St. Augustine had also observed that "the degree to which you are concerned for the interests of the community, rather than for your own, is the criterion by which you can judge how much progress [toward perfection] you have made."[28] Love must compel the individual to step away from himself and move toward another. Love for others is for Augustine the equivalent of love for God.

It was through his letters that Erasmus became a reformer of religious life in the fifteenth century. Writing to Franciscus Theodoricus about 1488, he noted: "for I consider that there is no more pleasant duty in friendship than such an exchange of correspondence."[29] He considered friendship in terms of mutual sharing. Letters between friends would serve as moral prods—as an external means of achieving spiritual progress through the study of secular and Christian literature. To Sasbout, no doubt a former companion at Steyn, he wrote about 1488:

> But as for you, Sasbout, dearest comrade of mine, do be careful not to devote yourself so completely to painting that you cease to care for literature. You are surely aware of what you promised to me when you were on the point of leaving me, and of the condition under which you took the books of poetry away from me, namely that you would dedicate yourself entirely to the love and pursuit of letters. If you take care to keep this promise, you will do something very pleasing for the sake of love I bear you and likely to be a source of great profit and pleasure to yourself. But if you fail to do it, out of disregard for your own well-being, you will deeply sadden me who am as pained by your misfortunes as by my own. . . . I could name to you, had I but the time within the compass of a letter, very many persons, some of them from our own community, who have now at length discovered for themselves the fame conferred by letters and the disgrace incurred by ignorance of them. . . .[30]

In speaking of the benefit of letters, Erasmus was relating classical literature to the spiritual life of the Christian. The moral arguments of the pre-Christian writers added strength and nuance to the teachings of the Church Fathers. Although Sasbout was no longer living at Steyn, Erasmus had not abandoned him. Indeed, he begged him to remain in

---

[27] *CWE*, 1, 18; *Allen*, 13.
[28] *The Rule of Saint Augustine*, ed. Van Bavel, p. 20.
[29] *CWE*, 1, 19; *Allen*, 14.
[30] *CWE*, 1, 22–23; *Allen*, 16.

touch through the medium of letters: "My earnest desire is to have a letter from you, as soon as possible, to tell me how you are, what you are doing, how you feel about these matters, what you want from me, and in fact, anything else that it concerns me to know."[31] Erasmus was clearly the mentor, reserving the right to continue the spiritual development of his former companion.

Erasmus interpreted Augustine's idea of the community of goods broadly to include such spiritual goods as knowledge and virtue. In the rule of St. Augustine, there appears the exhortation: "their hearts should seek the nobler things, not vain earthly appearance."[32] He was also mindful of Augustine's injunction that "sisters and brothers who wish to live in unity of heart should not let their love be tied up in the earth . . ." (Sermon 359, 1–2).[33] John 4:20 is one of St. Augustine's favorite verses: "Whoever does not love his brother whom he sees, cannot love God whom he does not see." For this reason, in chapter one of the rule, concern for others becomes the criterion for determining one's own love for God. To quote Augustine: ". . . to be more precise, the lazy, the indifferent and the nonchalant are not living in love. Do not think that you love your servant just because you refrain from striking him, or that you love your child if you do not bother to teach him discipline, or that you love your neighbours if you never speak to them. That is not love, but weakness" (*Sermons on the First Letter* of John 7, 11).[34]

Writing to Franciscus Theodoricus about 1488, Erasmus raised questions about the sincerity of his friendship and his commitment to reform: "As it is, since your good faith is (I shall be a little censorious here) suspect in my eyes, and the general confusion in affairs is such that one cannot safely trust even the most reliable people, what do you think I should do? Am I to write or keep silence?"[35] Erasmus' overtures of friendship to Servatius were rejected and became the basis for opposition in his community to his reforming efforts. Erasmus summarized the active hostility present in the monastery at Steyn. In a letter to Cornelis Gerard, an ordained canon at a nearby monastery, he noted:

But (oh, the shame of it!) wherever there is a discussion about poetry here, the

---

[31] *CWE*, 1, 23; Allen, 16.
[32] *The Rule of Saint Augustine*, ed. Van Bavel, p. 12.
[33] *Ibid.*, p. 52.
[34] *Ibid.*, p. 60.
[35] *CWE*, 1, 16; Allen, 14.

weapons used in debate are those not of rational argument but of slander and backbiting. If men listened to reason as they should, then scarcely anything would be easier than to persuade them. Where they condemn immoral themes dressed in a brilliant style, I too condemn this; where they blame immoderate devotion to poetry, I too refuse to commend it. But does it follow that we shall have to censure for indecency everything that is wittily expressed or poetic? You at least, accustomed as you are to reading the poets' works, are clearly aware how much the honeyed flow of poetry abounds not only in elegance of style but in gravity of thought and in knowlege of all things. Where there are so many shining virtues, am I to be offended by a few flaws?

Erasmus' religious superiors rejected his study of classical literature as an adjunct to spiritual growth and, in turn, earned his wrath: "But those worthies are only drawing a cloak over their own lack of culture, with the result that they seem to despise what they despair of achieving. If they looked carefully at Jerome's letters, they would see at least that lack of culture is not holiness, nor cleverness impiety."[36] Erasmus' program of reform was based on the examples of Saints Augustine and Jerome, two pillars of the monastic life, but his arguments fell on deaf ears.

Because of opposition to Erasmus' reforming efforts, the young canon was silenced. There are no surviving letters from Erasmus to his brotherhood of correspondents between 1490 and 1494. It was only after his ordination to the priesthood in April of 1492 that he was in a position to seek escape from the monastery at Steyn. At the end of about 1493, Willem Hermans, then resident at Steyn, asked Erasmus: "As for you, what are you doing, reading and writing where you are?"[37] Erasmus had by this time found employment with the bishop of Cambrai. He would spend the years after 1493 seeking to expand upon his program of reform that was begun during his earliest years at Steyn and would survive long after his death in 1536.

II

If there is anyone among you who wishes to be known for his wisdom and learning, he must prove such a claim by the excellence of his life. James 3:13

Aware of St. James' injunction to base one's reputation on the foundation of a holy life, Erasmus' spirituality was an expression of his love for Christ and his fellow Christians. Stripped of the externals

---

[36] *CWE*, 1, 35; *Allen*, 22.
[37] *CWE*, 1, 65; *Allen*, 34.

associated with materialism, he rejected elaborate dress, imposing titles, and flowery speech. He thought of himself as a practitioner of an interior holiness that rested on dedication to learning; and he exercised his priestly ministry through the printed word rather than the pulpit. He was committed to returning to the purity of the Gospel message, unencumbered by the scholastic debates of the intervening centuries. As Augustin Renaudet expressed it: "L'essentiel de la philosophie chrétienne . . . consiste à concevoir que toute notre espérance repose en Dieu, qui nous accorde gratuitement ses dons par l'intermediaire de son fils."[38]

In his *Precatio Dominica in Septem Portiones Distributa* (1523), Erasmus explained that God the Father had sent his son out of love for humankind.[39] Moreover, he explained that God wished to be regarded as a father rather than as lord or master because He considered us as his children rather than as servants or bondsmen. It was man's duty, therefore, to reciprocate God's love by following the teachings of Christ who taught that we must "love God above all things and love our neighbor and brother no less than ourselves; and that we always show good will and love to our enemy and adversary."[40] In the following year, Erasmus wrote a sermon, *Concerning the Immense Mercy of God*, in which he used the prophet Micah to show us a better sacrifice than the offering of one's body to appease God's wrath:

> I will show you, O man, what is good, and what the Lord doth require of you: 'Above all else to act justly, to love mercy, and to walk humbly with thy God . . .' What is loving mercy? To show kindness even to those who do not deserve it. In his eulogy Paul adds something else. 'If I give my body to be burned,' he says, 'and have not charity, it profits me nothing.' Abraham did a magnificent thing when he was ready to sacrifice the only son whom he loved. But he who gives his body to be burned for the love of God will do a greater thing. Charity is more pleasing to God than even this sacrifice. For what is charity to one's neighbor but mercy?[41]

---

[38] Augustin Renaudet, *Érasme: Sa Pensée Religieuse Et Son Action D'Après Sa Correspondance (1518–1521)* (Paris: Librairie Felix Alcan, 1926), p. 11.

[39] See *A devout treatise vpon the Pater noster*, tr. by Margaret More Roper and ed. by R. L. DeMolen in *Erasmus of Rotterdam: A Quincentennial Symposium* (New York: Twayne Publishers, 1971), p. 105.

[40] *Ibid.*, p. 108. The English has been modernized by me.

[41] *De Immensa Dei Misericordia* was translated by John P. Dolan in *The Essential Erasmus*. A Mentor Book (New York: New American Library, 1964), p. 40; hereafter cited as *Dolan* with page number.

If man truly loves God he will love his neighbor, and he will be loved in turn by Christ.

Henricus Glareanus (1488–1563) wrote on 5 September 1516 that he loved no one more dearly than Erasmus because through him he came to know Christ, "to imitate Him, to worship Him, to love Him."[42] No doubt, he was referring to the *Enchiridion*, which was drafted as a blueprint for holiness in 1501. It was designed as a manual that would help every reader to achieve what Glareanus had thanked Erasmus for giving him. The *Enchiridion* expressed the germ of Erasmus' concept of love which he would elaborate on, again and again, in the years after its publication in 1503: "To overcome evil with good is to emulate the perfect charity of Christ Jesus."[43]

The choice of a religious vocation remained uppermost in the mind of Erasmus even after his release from the monastery at Steyn. He remained critical of religious orders which emphasized ceremonies ("a kind of Judaism") at the expense of Christ's teachings or which enticed youngsters to join their ranks on the basis of fear rather than love. "This only I suggest: that you not define holiness by what you eat, by ritual, or by any visible object. . . ." If a religious order exhibits the "true likeness of Christ" then Erasmus urged the recruit to join it. But, on the other hand, if "there are no men around you whose society improves you," he counseled them to withdraw and to turn to the writings of the saints, prophets, and apostles, and to Christ's teachings. Above all, he urged his reader to meditate on St. Paul day and night "until you commit to memory every word."[44]

Erasmus was especially critical of the efficacy of religious habits. He insisted that God will recognize the truly religious person by the purity of his soul. In a letter to Martin Lipsius (5 September 1528), Erasmus recalled that "in the fifth canon of my *Enchiridion* I had stated that it was no great thing to be buried in the cowl of St. Francis and that the habit would have no value unless one had imitated Francis' life."[45] Erasmus believed that Francis was holy because he imitated the life of Christ, and

---

[42] *CWE*, 4, 69; *Allen*, 463.

[43] *The Enchiridion of Erasmus*, tr. and ed. by Raymond Himelick (Bloomington: Indiana University Press, 1963), p. 197.

[44] *Ibid.*, p. 199.

[45] Translated by Marcus A. Haworth, S.J., in *Erasmus and His Age: Selected Letters of Desiderius Erasmus*, ed. by Hans J. Hillerbrand. Harper Torchbooks (New York: Harper and Row, 1970), p. 218; *Allen*, 2045. Hereafter cited as *Hillerbrand* with page number.

not because of his dress, appearance, or diet. At the same time, in the following year, he wrote to Ludwig Baer (30 March 1529) that "I have never given my approval to those monks who leave their order without serious reason and without papal authorization. In fact, I have consoled or encouraged many who were wavering in their vocation."[46] It is clear that Erasmus did not disapprove of the religious life per se. He simply opposed excessive or exclusive emphasis on certain external aspects of it.

In a sarcastic vein, Erasmus observed in *The Praise of Folly* that Paul had "lived a life of perfect charity, but he neither distinguished it nor defined it with sufficient dialectical precision in the first epistle to the Corinthians, chapter 13"[47] to satisfy the carping scholastic theologians. Substituting human traditions for Christ's precepts, the majority of religious orders "think one heaven is hardly a fitting reward for such merits." In an autobiographical aside that takes us back to his adolescence, Erasmus revealed that

> Long ago, not speaking obliquely in parables but quite openly, I promised my Father's inheritance not to hoods, or trifling prayers, or fasts, but rather deeds of faith and charity.[48]

Corporeal things, such as religious habits, or memorized formulas of prayer, or denial of food, cannot serve as substitutes for "invisible things" in man's quest for eternal life. Erasmus insisted that the "pious strive with all their hearts to reach God himself" through contemplation and the rejection of the body and worldly wealth.[49]

Moreover, Erasmus observed in his *Modus Orandi Deum* (1525) that it was "not the quantity but the quality of prayer that made a man pious and faithful before God."[50] Wealth and honors were singled out by Erasmus as deterents to holiness. Writing to Duke George of Saxony (12 December 1524), he admitted that he had refused both: "As far as wealth is concerned, I have enough to feed my poor little body; besides honors

---

[46] *Ibid.*, 224; Allen, 2136.

[47] Translated by Clarence H. Miller in *Desiderius Erasmus: The Praise of Folly* (New Haven: Yale University Press, 1979), p. 90; hereafter cited as *Miller* with page number.

[48] *Ibid.*, p. 100.

[49] *Ibid.*, p. 134.

[50] *Desiderii Erasmi Roterodami Opera Omnia*, ed. Jean LeClerc, 10 vols. (Leiden, 1703–06), 5, 1129D–1130D. Hereafter cited as *LB*. The translation is my own.

on a man of my health and age is like putting a pack-saddle on an ox or a load on an old broken-down horse; he would fall under it."⁵¹

Erasmus even urged his reader to reject the love of children, parents, and friends "except insofar as they can be assimilated to that highest part of the mind, so that a father is no longer loved simply as a father . . . but as a good man whose personality projects a shining image of that highest mind of all. . . ."⁵² Any external things that separate the individual from God, even love for one's family, must be laid aside for "that highest Good which gathers all things to Himself."⁵³

Furthermore, Erasmus noted that Plato had expressed the notion "that the madness of lovers is the height of happiness. For a person who loves intensely no longer lives in himself but rather in that which he loves." Once the individual rejects the world and his own body, he will be in a position to "be absorbed by the highest mind of all."⁵⁴ And having achieved union with God, he shall be rewarded with unspeakable joys (1 Corinthians 2:9). It was Erasmus' purpose in writing *The Praise of Folly* "to promote morality;"⁵⁵ and in order to proclaim "the praises of love . . . ," "I assumed a mask to play this part," that is Dame Folly.⁵⁶

Writing to the theologian Maarten van Dorp in 1514, Erasmus tried to persuade him to pursue such studies that will lead him to true happiness: "for my eagerness is no less than my love for you . . . and my love is as strong as my interest is boundless."⁵⁷ When he penned his *Paraclesis* in February of 1516, Erasmus discarded the mask that he wore in *The Praise of Folly* and donned the robes of the theologian. Though a doctor of theology himself, he addressed the *Paraclesis* to more than fellow theologians, such as Dorp. He wrote it for all Christians: "Only a very few can be learned, but all can be Christian, all can be devout, and—I shall boldly add—all can be theologians."⁵⁸ Erasmus believed that any man who preaches the message of the Gospel, who exhorts, incites, and en-

---

[51] *Hillerbrand*, 180; *Allen*, 1526.
[52] *Miller*, 135.
[53] *Ibid.*, 137.
[54] *Ibid.*, 136.
[55] Erasmus to Maarten van Dorp (c. September 1514) was translated by C. H. Miller. See *Miller*, 143.
[56] *Ibid.*, 145.
[57] *Ibid.*, 163.
[58] Translated by John C. Olin in *Desiderius Erasmus: Christian Humanism and the Reformation,* ed by John C. Olin. Harper Torchbooks (New York: Harper and Row, 1965), p. 100; hereafter cited as *Olin* with page number.

courages others to live by it, is himself a theologian. Erasmus capsulizes his view of the theologian when he observed: "To me he is truly a theologian who teaches not by skill with intricate syllogisms but by a disposition of mind, by the very expression and the eyes, by his very life that riches should be disdained, that the Christian should not put his trust in the supports of this world but must rely entirely on heaven. . . ."[59]

Albert Dürer captured this characterization of the worthy theologian when he produced his woodcut portrait of Erasmus in 1526. Erasmus appears absorbed in thought. Concentrating on things eternal, he works to further the mission of his ministry, preferring a standing to a sitting position in order to speed up the process. Dürer skillfully blends the products of his mind, his books, with the symbol of his priestly chastity, the lilies of the valley, which are positioned so prominently on his writing table. It is not an exaggeration to insist that this woodcut (in its many states), like the books that he wrote, served as a testimonial to the rich interior life that characterized the prince of theologians. The Dürer woodcut also draws attention to the duty of the Christian theologian which Erasmus emphasized in the *Paraclesis:* "to persuade us to lead here an angelic life, free from every stain, this indeed is the duty of the Christian theologian."[60]

Erasmus himself was aware that the preacher of the Gospel, whether lay or cleric, must also obey it: "Who loves me, Christ says, keeps my word. . . ."[61] In a letter to Thomas Cardinal Wolsey (18 May 1519), Erasmus pleaded his sincerity: "Christ's displeasure ever be my lot if I do not wish whatever I may possess of ability or literary skill to be entirely dedicated to Christ's glory, to the catholic church, and to sacred study."[62] Writing to Felix (possibly Peter Phoenix of Dôle) on 21 February 1528, Erasmus also revealed his devotion to the Virgin Mary: "My devotion to the Virgin is obvious from the two prayers which I published some time ago: the *Paean* and the *Obsecratio,* and also from the new Mass which I recently published with the approval of the Archbishop of Besançon [in 1523]."[63]

---

[59] *Ibid.*, p. 98.
[60] *Ibid.*
[61] *Ibid.*, 99.
[62] *CWE,* 6, 372; Allen, 967.
[63] Hillerbrand, 212; Allen, 1956. The name of the Mass is: *Virginis matris apud Lauretum cultae Liturgia.* The other two works are the *Paean in genera demonstratiuo Virgini marti dicendus* and the *Obsecratio ad eandem semper gloriosam.* See *LB,* 5. The archbishop of

Having published the *Enchiridion* in 1503, Erasmus occasionally received both compliments and complaints from his readers concerning its efficacy. One such double-eged salvo stung him enough that he repeated it in a letter to Paul Volz, dated 14 August 1518:

> But then again I am often made uncomfortable by the pointed comment of a learned friend some time ago, humorously uttered, but I fear with as much truth as it had humour, that holiness of life is more noticeable in the book than in its author.

Erasmus was conscious that his plan of holiness was difficult to achieve since it required a rejection of the allurements of this life. He expressed dismay further on in his letter to Abbot Volz, complaining that the dedicatee himself had not profited from it: "so far is he from tearing himself away from life at court that he is plunged more deeply in it every day. . . ." As for his own sanctity, Erasmus admitted that he too had not succeeded in attaining it:

> And yet I cannot altogether regret this work [*Enchiridion*], if it encourages so many people to the pursuit of true piety. Nor yet do I feel myself open to attack from every quarter if I do not live up as I should to my own precepts. For one thing, it is an element of goodness to have a sincere desire to be good, nor do I think that one should reject a heart that is sincerely devoted to such thoughts, although its efforts are sometimes unsuccessful.

What is more important, Erasmus maintained that repeated efforts are often necessary to achieve true piety:

> This must be one's first purpose all one's life long, and repeated attempts will one day succeed. A man who has readily learnt the way has a good part of a complicated journey already behind him.[64]

As the author of a treatise on spirituality, Erasmus wanted his readers to know that the path to perfection required endurance and patience, and that he was making only slow progress in his quest for holiness. At the same time, he hastened to add that "the good life is everybody's business"[65] even if they cannot attain perfection, since Christ intended it

---

Besançon was Antoine de Vergy (d. 1541). For a thorough examination of this letter, see Georges Chantraine, S.J., *"Mystère" et "Philosophie Du Christ" selon Érasme*. Bibliothèque de la Faculté de Philosophie et Lettres de Namur (Namur and Gembloux, 1971).

[64] *CWE*, 6, 73; Allen, 858.
[65] *CWE*, 6, 74: Allen, 858.

to be accessible to all: "not beset with impenetrable labyrinths of argument but open to sincere faith, to love unfeigned, and their companion, the hope that is not put to shame."[66] Faith, hope, and charity were the means that Christ prescribed for achieveing a good life in this world. Erasmus also maintained that belief in Christ's teachings must be voluntary and sincere. In a letter to Jean de Carondelet (5 January 1523), he underscored the importance of understanding Scripture: "What is coerced cannot be sincere, and what is not voluntary cannot please Christ."[67]

Erasmus thus envisioned two ways of life. The higher life of perfection was available to saints alone, but a "good life" was available to all. Once the individual has "drunk in the spirit of Christ," he begins to be free. It is true charity that marks the good life for it "takes all things in good part, endures all things, refuses nothing, obeys those who are set over it, not only if they are kind and accommodating but even if they are difficult and harsh."[68]

Even the founders of religious orders, St. Benedict, St. Francis, and St. Augustine, desired "to live with friends who joined them willingly a life according to the teaching of the Gospel in liberty of spirit." External circumstances forced them to draw up constitutions that prescribed, among other things, food and clothing. At the same time, they "were afraid that, as often happens, more importance might be ascribed to the constitutions of human origin than to the Gospel. They had a horror of riches; they avoided honours, even in the church."[69] For Erasmus the perfection of Christ is in the soul and not in what persons wear or eat or in the particular rules of religious orders. He expressed it best in *The Education of a Christian Prince* in 1516:

> But on the other hand, do not think that Christ is found in ceremonies, in doctrines kept after a fashion, and in constitutions of the church. Who is truly Christian? Not he who is baptized or anointed, or who attends church. It is rather the man who has embraced Christ in the innermost feelings of his heart, and who emulates Him by his pious deeds.[70]

---

[66] *CWE*, 6, 74–75; *Allen*, 858.
[67] Hillerbrand, 169; *Allen*, 1334.
[68] *CWE*, 6, 87; *Allen*, 858.
[69] *CWE*, 6, 88; *Allen*, 858.
[70] *The Education of a Christian Prince (1516)*, tr. and ed. by Lester K. Born (New York: Columbia University Press, 1936), p. 153.

Christianity is lived interiorly and is reflected exteriorly through good deeds.

Christ also promised peace to those who loved one another "as I have loved you." Erasmus recalled this promise in his *Complaint of Peace,* which was published in 1517, and asked his readers to repeat the passage:

> Do you hear what He leaves us? Does He bequeath horses, an army, an empire, riches? No, none of these things. What then? He leaves peace—peace with His friends, peace with His enemies.[71]

In his *Paraphrases on Romans* 13: 4–8, which likewise appeared in 1517, Erasmus noted that "even if love satisfies others, it never satisfies itself but always heaps up service upon service." Moreover, he insisted that if man loves his neighbor he has automatically fulfilled the terms of the Mosaic law. On the other hand, "if love is absent, no laws, however many, suffice."[72] Sincere love also anticipates the needs of others and does not wait for one to be asked.

In a spirit of reform, Erasmus called on his readers to "cast off the shadows of our former life" and "imitate him [Christ] whom you have drunk in."[73] Erasmus goes on to characterize Christ as chastity, sobriety, peace, and love. Faith in Christ's teachings makes even the ungodly righteous.

Throughout his correspondence Erasmus reflected on the frailty of human life. He also claimed that he was becoming more and more free of the fear of death and the desire for life.[74] To Bishop Fisher he wrote on 23 October 1518: "Christ our Saviour will one day grant that things may go better."[75] But such an admission did not mean that he had abandoned his goals. On 24 April 1519, Erasmus wrote to Jan Becker of Borssele in which he concluded his letter with a reaffirmation of his earthly mission in conformity to the will of God:

> Desire for money has never possessed my mind; the burden of reputation I will gladly lay down if I can. I am not tired of life nor do I desire it; whenever Christ,

---

[71] *Dolan,* 184.

[72] Translated by John B. Payne, Albert Rabil, Jr., and Warren S. Smith, Jr., in *New Testament Scholarship: Paraphrases on Romans and Galatians,* ed. by Robert D. Sider, *CWE,* 42, 76.

[73] *Ibid.,* 77.

[74] Erasmus to Beatus Rhenanus, 15 October 1518, *CWE,* 6, 126; *Allen,* 867.

[75] *CWE,* 6, 166; *Allen,* 889.

my commanding officer, calls me hence, I shall willingly and promptly leave my allotted post in the body, in reliance on him.[76]

At the same time, Erasmus faced the attacks of his adversaries with determination and constancy. Writing to Elector Frederick of Saxony on 14 April 1519, Erasmus defended his position and observed:

> Whoever accuses another man of heresy ought himself to display a character worthy of a Christian—charity in correction, mildness in finding fault, a fair and open mind in passing judgment, and no haste in coming to a decision. As none of us is free from error, why are we so merciless in pursuing other men's fault?[77]

Erasmus remained cautious in his confrontations with critics and tried to refrain from making judgments about the decisions of others. In a letter to Jan Šlechta (23 April 1519), he answered his opponents with resignation and acceptance of the inevitable:

> As I hope for the love of Christ, I swear I am more sorry for their case than for my own. For I find support in a good conscience and in favourable judgment of men of good will; for no mortal man has yet had the good fortune to please everyone all the time.[78]

Erasmus practiced the art of moderation or, as he called it, "polite restraint" in a letter to Luther, dated 30 May 1519. Here he mentioned that his position was in keeping with "how Christ brought the world under his sway."[79] He also advised theologians to "keep our minds above the corruption of anger or hatred, or of ambition; for it is this that lies in wait for us when our religious zeal is in full course."[80]

Erasmus firmly believed that his letters served the message of the Gospel by moderating rival factions throughout Europe. He insisted in a letter to Justus Jonas (10 May 1521) that "I desire to be of service not only to the Germans but to the French, the Spanish, the English, the Bohemians, the Russians, and indeed to the Turks and Saracens as well, if possible."[81] On the other hand, though he looked upon Luther and his supporters as a purely local group whose influence was parochial, he wished to protect Luther from extremists and expressed his desire for

---

[76] *CWE*, 6, 327; *Allen*, 952.
[77] *CWE*, 6, 299; *Allen*, 939.
[78] *CWE*, 6, 323; *Allen*, 950.
[79] *CWE*, 6, 392; *Allen*, 980.
[80] *CWE*, 6, 393; *Allen*, 980.
[81] *Olin*, 161; *Allen*, 1202.

Luther's safety further on in his letter to Jonas: "I desired that Luther be loved openly and without danger."[82] He concluded by chastising his own critics whom he believed did not preach Christ as much as they raged against him.

Erasmus' aversion to martyrdom has often been mentioned. Writing to Lorenzo Cardinal Campeggi on 6 December 1520, Erasmus lamented that "others may desire martyrdom; I do not consider myself worthy of that honor."[83] Unless the truth of the Gospel were at stake, Erasmus would avoid the opportunity to take a stand. In a letter to Richard Pace, dated 5 July 1521, Erasmus revealed that "everyone has not the strength needed for martyrdom." He counseled moderation and discouraged extremism: "I believe that even for men of good will this is legitimate, if there is no hope of better things."[84] In refusing to condemn Henry VIII's divorce from Queen Katherine or to disassociate himself from the family of Queen Anne Boleyn, Erasmus has been criticized; but he was in effect simply following his own advice. Although he lauded Thomas More as a martyr to conscience, he himself would never have sacrificed his life in order to oppose a purely human error of judgment. And the same applied to the teachings of Martin Luther. Paraphrasing Ulrich von Hutten in his *Spongia* of 1523, Erasmus admitted of the possibility of martyrdom but not for the cause of Lutheranism:

> Hutten claims that one should even be willing to die for the truth of the Gospel. I too would not refuse to do this if the occasion demanded it. But for Luther or Luther's paradoxes, I am not yet ready to die.[85]

Individual interpretations were not worth dying for and should be better dealt with by ignoring them. Writing to Duke George of Saxony on 3 September 1522, he confessed: "Finally, I have always held the view that this tragedy [spread of Lutheranism] could most effectively be laid to rest by silence." He believed that papal bulls and imperial edicts simply "fan the flames" and do not change people's minds."[86] In his *Spongia*,

---

[82] *Ibid.*, 163; Allen, 1202.

[83] Hillerbrand, 162; Allen, 1167.

[84] Allen, 1218, 32–37. The translation is my own.

[85] Translated by Randolph J. Klawiter as "The Sponge of Erasmus Against the Aspersions of Hutten" in *The Polemics of Erasmus of Rotterdam and Ulrich von Hutten* (Notre Dame: University of Notre Dame Press, 1977), p. 223. Hereafter cited as *Klawiter* with page number.

[86] Hillerbrand, 169; Allen, 352.

Erasmus also underscored the consistency of his position with regard to Luther:

> If anyone can show that I have altered my initial purpose, then let him accuse me of inconsistency! The matter itself, however, proves that I always realize my plans, promoting good letters and endeavoring to restore a purer and simpler theology—and this I shall continue to do as long as I live, whether Luther is my friend or my enemy . . . . Luther will pass away like all the rest of us; Christ, however, remains for all eternity.[87]

He also advised Pope Adrian VI on 22 March 1523 that "I wish I had the abilities you attribute to me for checking this division. I would not hesitate to heal these public ills even at the cost of my own life."[88]

Erasmus felt that it was wise to maintain contact with those with whom we differed. Thus he agreed to write a commendatory preface to Simon Grynaeus' Greek edition of Aristotle, which was published in May of 1531, even though he did not share his religious views. At the same time, he did not become involved in the quarrel between Johann Reuchlin and Johann Pfefferkorn, even though he was on excellent terms with the learned Hebraist.[89] But Ulrich von Hutten saw only cowardice and hypocrisy in Erasmus' effort to remain neutral for the sake of reason and peace, while Erasmus considered Hutten's determination and ensuing actions as a betrayal of the ideals of humanism.

Although a Canon Regular of St. Augustine, Erasmus had received various papal dispensations that permitted him to live outside his monastery at Steyn, to wear a modified version of his religious habit, to hold benefices and ecclesiastical offices, and to make a will. He exercised his own priesthood by drawing attention to the sacred duties and responsbilities of fellow priests. Writing to Balthasar Merklin, bishop of Constance (15 March 1530), he complained of the materialism of certain priests and insisted on a program of reform that would end the scandals associated with certain clerical practices:

> It is only proper that every semblance of petty bargaining be far removed from this Sacrament [of the Altar]. The ministers of this most sacred rite, not only in their gestures, vestments, and words, but also in their whole manner of living, should correspond to the dignity of their office. What great self-control should be

---

[87] *Allen*, 290 and 300.
[88] *Hillerbrand*, 165; *Allen*, 1313.
[89] *Klawiter*, 198.

theirs, what great virtue, purity, contempt for worldly pleasures, and love for divine letters . . . . Let priests realize the exalted dignity of their profession. When they stand at the altar, they have the angels as their ministers.[90]

Virtue, purity, contempt for worldly pleasures, and love for divine letters should be the characteristics of every priest.

In drafting his response to Ulrich von Hutten (*Spongia*) in 1523, Erasmus opened the flood gates to other attacks. In a letter to Jacopo Cardinal Sadoleto, dated 7 March 1531, Erasmus confessed that he was suffering from those criticisms which grew out of his defense of the Catholic Church:

> If you have read my *Diatribe,* or my two *Hyperaspistes* against the violent book of Martin Luther, or my *Spongia* against Hutten, or my pamphlet against Leopold [Leo Judd], or my letter to Vulturius [Gerard Geldenhauer], or my book against the clergy of Strassburg, then your good judgment will clearly perceive how much it is costing me to refuse to withdraw from union with the Roman Church.

At the same time, he tried to be true to Christ's admonition to remain silent in the face of one's attackers: "I will remain silent about those biting letters not worthy of a response [or which the publishers have not yet released]. I will say nothing of the threatening letters penned with poison; I will say nothing of the charges and slanders that were secretly instigated and which could have destroyed the peace of the most lofty-minded person."[91]

In the same letter to Cardinal Sadoleto, Erasmus also revealed his prayer life which was based primarily on the reading of Scripture: "It is of no little importance to utter a prayer at frequent intervals, for that in a marvelous way gives fresh vigor and enthusiasm to the spirit." But he likewise confessed disappointment that his replies to critics took him away from his study of Scripture: "God immortal! How happy would life be if we could banish all disagreement of thought and feeling! Being one at heart we might seek refuge in the fertile fields of Scripture and play in its lovely meadows. . . ." At the same time, Erasmus repeated his own unworthiness to study and comment on Scripture:

> Indeed, I am conscious of my own uncleanness and well aware that I am a very

---

[90] *Allen,* 2284, 155–168. The translation is my own.

[91] *Hillerbrand,* 246; *Allen,* 2443. I have translated the phrase in parenthesis which was omitted by Hillerbrand.

unsuitable and unmanageable instrument for the working of the Spirit in treating matters in which, according to His will, the deep mysteries of a heavenly philosophy are hidden as in some very sacred sanctuary. Therefore, it is not without trepidation that I approach this area. Almost never is this place approached with sufficient reverence except by those who abide there constantly.[92]

Erasmus' spirituality was rooted in his defense of the study of sacred Scripture. The martyrdom of which he felt unworthy took a different form in his life: it would not come as a result of execution, but as a result of a continuous "stream of disasters." In his letters to Cardinal Sadoleto, he confessed:

When God, who has power over all things, gives you suffering, worries, and ill health, who knows if by doing so He is granting you a greater blessing than if He were to offer you a calm, peaceful leisurely life? . . . Amid a continual stream of disasters the only thought in which I find consolation is that this is beneficial for my salvation. God in His unutterable wisdom uses various means to purify men and make them worthy of Himself.[93]

Erasmus insisted, moreover, that we must ask God's help if we expected to achieve lasting results. Writing to Abbot Antoine d'Albon on 1 April 1531, he observed:

But only God has the power to purify the source of all good actions, and He will do so if with sincere and complete trust we take refuge in His mercy. In response to prayer, He will grant to Church leaders a spirit that will prefer Christ's glory to all worldly advantages. To rules He will grant a mind that can rise above riches and honors, revenge and all human passions, and He will grant them a heavenly wisdom that can prevail over all earthly malice. He will grant to priests and monks a true contempt of the world and a love of the Scriptures; He will grant to civil authorities and to the people a fear of Himself.[94]

Prayer will help civil and church leaders, priests, and the faithful to reject this world in order to grow closer to God. But Erasmus was offering more than just spiritual advice to Abbot d'Albon. He was serving as a living example of total reliance on God. Writing to the Senate of Besançon on 26 July 1531, he commented on his own solitary existence. "No one will be put to inconvenience by me, for I have, thanks to the

---

[92] *Ibid.*, p. 247; *Allen*, 2443.
[93] *Ibid.*, 247–48; *Allen*, 2443.
[94] Hillerbrand, 250–51; *Allen*, 2472.

supernal powers, enough to care for my little wants. I have no connection with any sect, and I have no followers, except in common with Christ, nor shall I have, please God."[95]

Four years before his death, Erasmus wrote to the former master general of the Dominicans, Tommaso de Vio of Gaeta (Cardinal Cajetan) on 25 July 1532, promising to delete from his works any insults of a personal nature which have given offense to individuals or religious orders:

> I have also decided to collect all those passages in my writings which openly attack the slanders and condemned teachings of certain individuals; then secondly, with regard to questionable passages I plan to explain or revise them so thoroughly that hereafter my works will not contain any abusive remarks directed at the name of any individual or order.[96]

Erasmus expressed genuine concern that his works might have offended others and thus violated Christ's precept on charity. But he did not abandon his criticism of religious orders per se. In an introspective letter to Charles Utenhove, dated 9 August 1532, Erasmus repeated his opposition to the efficacy of religious habits and revealed the appearance of St. Francis in a dream:

> They think that I am angry with St. Francis just because I have denounced those men who promise heaven to all who are buried in a Franciscan habit. Recently St. Francis appeared to me in a dream after midnight; his face was calm and friendly. He thanked me for having publicly announced the correction of those passages which he personally had always detested. . . .[97]

Erasmus also insisted that he was not only purifying the rule of St. Francis but that he had the approval of the saint. Erasmus continued: "and he counted me as one of the friends of the Order . . . . As he walked off, he . . . said: 'Keep fighting valiantly; soon you will be one of mine.'"[98]

Erasmus rejected the religious habit as a meaningless external. He exhorted Franciscans to imitate the virtues of their founder, which he considered the foundation of perfection. St. Francis referred to these virtues as "the Seraphic six wings." According to Erasmus:

---

[95] *Allen*, 2514, 11. 25–28. The translation is my own.
[96] Hillerbrand, 267; *Allen*, 2690.
[97] *Ibid.*, 267; *Allen*, 2700.
[98] *Ibid.*, 267–68; *Allen*, 2700.

The first is perfect obedience; the second, evangelical poverty; the third, spotless chastity; the fourth, deep humility; the fifth, a peace-loving simplicity; and the sixth, seraphic charity.

Erasmus recalled in his dream that St. Francis had bid farewell to him with the words "soon you will be one of mine," because Erasmus believed that he was actively pursuing the seraphic wings of perfection in his own life. These six virtues were the basis of Erasmus' spirituality, and he challenged all Franciscans to attain them:

If only they would all carry these virtues around with them in their hearts as they do in their pockets. In that case, men of intelligence and not just weak little females would embrace them as angels of peace.[99]

Charity was the sixth and highest of the virtues that St. Francis laid down as steps to perfection; for without it, the other virtues could not be obtained.

In his desire to achieve reunion with Protestantism, Erasmus wrote *On Mending the Peace of the Church* in 1533, his swan song, so to speak, to Christian unity. In it he repeated the idea that piety must be acquired in stages: "Piety has its steps, too, as does man's life span."[100] "Where does he do this?," Erasmus asked, "in his heart." There are external steps as well, but as Erasmus reasoned they "are not useful unless they are disposed in our hearts." There are, moreover, levels of perfection in this life, and some are content with a lower level. Erasmus noted: "not to live by rapine is a step toward devotion. Not only to restore ill-gotten goods but to give your possessions to the poor for the love of Christ is a step higher."[101] Love of neighbor as a reflection of our love of God is a continual theme in the works of Erasmus:

It is hardly possible in this life to avoid little failings, yet with God's help we can avoid serious sin, provided we have a deep love of God and our neighbor. This should be the basis on which we should center our actions.[102]

Within a year of his death, Erasmus wrote to Damião de Goes (18 August 1535) that he was asking God to take him away from "this mad world" and noting that "if my writings have helped anyone to attain true

---

[99] Ibid., 268; Allen, 2700.
[100] Dolan, 364.
[101] Ibid., 365.
[102] Ibid., 381–82.

piety I am glad."[103] The kind of piety that Erasmus referred to was based on Christian charity. He expressed it best in his *De Contemptu Mundi* which was written at Steyn but did not appear in print until 1521:

> Indeed true love somehow was the effect of making us grieve more bitterly for a friend's misfortune than for our own, of making us more anxious for his wellbeing than for our own, in short, of making a man love his friend more than himself.[104]

It should no longer surprise the reader that the theme of Christian charity which is expressed here was composed while Erasmus was a Canon Regular of St. Augustine at Steyn. Indeed, it grew out of his efforts to reform the monastery, based on his reading of the rule of St. Augustine. Both in tone and spirit, it is fully compatible with the Steyn correspondence and helps to make sense of those emotional letters that have baffled so many and have led others to some unfortunate interpretations.[105]

---

[103] *Allen*, 3043, 17–21. The translation is my own.

[104] *The Contempt of the World* was translated by Erika Rummel in the *Spiritualia*, ed. by John W. O'Malley, S. J., *CWE*, 65 (in press).

[105] See, for example, Nelson H. Minnich and W. W. Meissner, "The Character of Erasmus," *The American Historical Review*, 83 (1978), 598–624, and A. L. Rowse, *Homosexuals in History* (New York: Macmillan, 1977), 6–10.

CHAPTER EIGHT

Erasmus' Commitment to the Canons Regular of St. Augustine

By the northwest coast of England . . . there's a college of canons, to whom, however, the Latins add the title of Regulars: an order midway between monks and the canons called Seculars. You tell me of amphibians, such as the beaver. Yes, and the crocodile. But details aside, I'll try to satisfy you in a few words. In unfavorable matters, they're canons; in favorable ones, monks.

Erasmus, *Colloquies* (1526), tr. Craig R. Thompson

ERASMUS offered this observation of the Canons Regular of St. Augustine in the colloquy "A Pilgrimage for Religion's Sake."[1] Filled with bite and insight, it reflects Erasmus' understanding of the apostolate of the order which he formally joined about 1487. The Canons Regular of St. Augustine, also known as the Austin Canons, performed many of the duties of secular priests. They served parishes, taught in schools and colleges, and served as chaplains. At the same time, they enjoyed a community life based on the rule of St. Augustine. Neither wholly active nor fully contemplative, they were in Erasmus' view, 'amphibians.'[2] It is important to recall that Erasmus remained a member of the Austin Canons throughout his adult life. His life-style harmonized with the spirit of the Austin Canons even though he lived outside of their monastic walls. This fact has not been noted, although it may be occasionally inferred in some of Erasmus' biographies. Many of them have assumed that when he set aside his religious habit in 1517, he ceased

---

[1] 'A Pilgrimage for Religion's Sake' (1526), *The Colloquies of Erasmus*, ed. and tr. Craig R. Thompson (Chicago, 1965), p. 292.

[2] There is a brief discussion of the active ministry of the Austin Canon in J. C. Dickinson, *The Origins of the Austin Canons and Their Introduction into England* (London, 1950), p. 196. Also see Dom David Knowles, *The Religious Orders in England* (Cambridge, 1955), 289, 292–293.

to be an Augustinian Canon; but such was not the case.³ To substantiate this point and to clarify the nature of Erasmus' commitment to the Austin Canons will be the dual purpose of this chapter.

Erasmus entered the religious life of the Austin Canons at Steyn (in Holland) 'voluntarily but not freely'⁴ about 1486. He argued that his vocation had been promoted under pious pretenses by greedy guardians, and, therefore, doubted that he had a true calling. Nevertheless, when he was about seventeen, he professed solemn vows (about 1487), and in succeeding years advanced to the priesthood. Following his ordination on April 25, 1492, Erasmus remained at Steyn, leading the life of a choir canon and digesting selected morsels from the monastery's library. For at least one more year, he seemed satisfied with the Austin Canons. He read widely in the classic and patristic literature and developed a special appreciation of St. Augustine and St. Jerome. Inspired by his confreres, he even wrote a treatise in defense of monasticism, which he called *On the Contempt of the World*.⁵

Deeply religious, Erasmus reflected the piety of his former teachers in Deventer and 's Hertogenbosch. These members of the Brethren of the Common Life were disciples of Christ who sought to imitate the Prince of Peace and to cultivate a spirit which we have called the *Devotio Moderna*.⁶ Yet, at the same time, Erasmus also came under the spell of

---

³ Although there are many examples, I call attention to the following two: John J. Mangan wrote: "In a word, of the three vows of chastity, obedience, and poverty which he [Erasmus] took at the time of his religious profession [1487], he had now by the Pope's dispensation been relieved of the latter two, and was henceforth regarded as a simple priest, with no regular duties, and subject nominally to the Bishop of Utrecht who had ordained him." See Mangan, *Life, Character and Influence of Desiderius Erasmus of Rotterdam* (New York, 1927), 2, 53. George Faludy repeats the error: "In April 1517 he revisited England, staying this time in Ammonio's house. In a ceremony at Westminster Abbey he received absolution from his friend, and at one stroke the nightmare of 30 years was ended: he was released from his vows as an Augustinian canon (though not of course as a priest)." See Faludy, *Erasmus of Rotterdam* (London, 1970), p. 167.

⁴ Erasmus to [Gerard Geldenhouwer] (ca. April 2, 1524). See P. S. Allen, ed., *Opus Epistolarum Des. Erasmi Roterodami* (Oxford, 1924), 5, 427. 24.

⁵ *De Contemptu Mundi* was begun in 1489 but was not published until 1521. For a discussion of the work in terms of 'suasoria' and 'dissuasoria,' see Roland Bainton, *Erasmus of Christendom* (New York, 1970), pp. 14–23.

⁶ For two conflicting interpretations of the origins and history of the *Devotio Moderna*, see R. R. Post, *The Modern Devotion* (Leiden, 1968), and Albert Hyma, *The Christian Renaissance: A History of the Devotio Moderna*, 2nd ed. (Hamden, Conn., 1965).

Renaissance humanism. At Steyn, he read voraciously in the classics. Torn between the emphasis on piety in the *Devotio Moderna* and the growing secularism in Italy, he set his confused mind to work on the *Book of the Antibarbarians*.[7] Written in the form of dialogues, the tract expresses Erasmus' continuing respect for monasticism as an ideal, but records a strong attraction to humanism as well. In pursuit of humanism, Erasmus sought to end his monastic confinement. A year after his ordination, he discovered an episcopal patron who was willing to free him from community life. Erasmus accepted an appointment in 1493 as Latin secretary to Hendrik van Bergen, the bishop of Cambrai. When the bishop's proposed trip to Italy, where he had hoped to be invested as a cardinal, failed to materialize, Erasmus feared that he would be required to return to Steyn and there resume the regular life to which he had developed an aversion. But his fears were groundless. The worldly bishop of Cambrai, taking pity on the brooding cleric, assured his deliverance by sending him off to France for advanced study in theology. Filled with enthusiasm, Erasmus enrolled at Montaigu College within the University of Paris in 1495.

Having been compelled by social and financial considerations to enter the religious life, and having somewhat later discovered the satisfaction of scholarship, Erasmus felt justified in leaving the cloister in order to pursue an advanced degree. But in so doing, he neither renounced his vows nor severed his relationship with the Austin Canons. At the University of Paris, Erasmus remained a professed canon of the monastery at Steyn. Writing to Lambertus Grunnius in the third person (ca. August 1516), Erasmus recalled:

It must be understood, however, that none of these steps were taken except by the permission of the Provost of the Order, both domestic and general, and finally with the acquiescence of the whole Society. And although his conscience was free, and he knew that he was not bound by any enforced vow, yet he so far yielded for the time, partly to his own natural bashfulness, which was so excessive as to be often a misfortune to him, and partly to the invincible scruples

---

[7] *Antibarbarorum Liber* was first composed about 1495, rewritten about 1519, and first published in 1520. See Albert Hyma's edition and discussion of the work in *The Youth of Erasmus*, 2nd ed. (New York, 1968). Also see Kazimierz Kumaniecki's definitive Latin text of the *Antibarbarorum Liber* in *Opera Omnia Desiderii Erasmi Roterodami* (Amsterdam, 1969), 1, 1–138.

of unenlightened and superstitious persons, that he abstained from changing his dress, although invited to do so by his Bishop.[8]

Faithful to "the invincible scruples of unenlightened and superstitious persons," Erasmus continued to wear the religious habit of the Austin Canons, adjusting its color and style to the customs of the countries he visited, from 1495 to 1506. In the latter year, while on his first visit to Bologna, he encountered difficulty because of the similarity of his white habit (scapular) to that of the physicians who were caring for the victims of the bubonic plague. Not realizing that he might be mistaken for a physician, he moved about freely until challenged by two men who thought that he was deliberately exposing others to the dreaded disease. Erasmus makes it clear that as a result of this experience, he was forced to adopt the dress of a secular priest during his stay in Italy.

In laying aside the habit of the Austin Canons, Erasmus opened himself up to severe criticism. He summed up the criticism in his 1516 letter to Grunnius:

Good heavens, what a disturbance has arisen out of a matter of no consequence at all! This exclamation will shock some foolish people who think the whole sum and substance of religion consists in the dress. I admit that this should not be lightly cast aside. And yet the Carthusians often change theirs for that of a merchant in order to travel more safely to synod; and our Canons, either for the sake of study or on occasion of a journey, change or hide their distinctive garment without special permission, and without incurring any censure. For there is not the same scrupulosity about this linen vestment as about others; for the so-called Canons formerly were not monks, and now they are an intermediate class: monks where it is an advantage to be so; not monks where it is not.[9]

It is clear that Erasmus saw the Austin Canons as a new breed of religious priests whose active life occasionally necessitated a dispensation from the habit. Erasmus himself set aside his habit in Italy, and later in England, because he felt it endangered his life and encumbered his scholarly activities. In his letter to Servatius Roger (July 8, 1514), Erasmus wrote frankly of the reasons which prompted him to set aside his habit:

In my case it was put away in Italy [1506–09] by compulsion, to save me from being killed; and afterwards in England [1509–14], because it was not tolerated

---

[8] Erasmus to Lambertus Grunnius, fictitious papal secretary [August 1516], *The Epistles of Erasmus,* tr. Francis M. Nichols (New York, 1904), 2, 356.

[9] *Ibid.,* p. 359.

there, when I should have much preferred to wear it. To resume it afresh now would beget more scandal than was created by the original change.[10]

He also underscored the point that the 1506 dispensation, which he had received from Pope Julius II, would automatically excommunicate him if he cast aside his habit in order to "mix more freely among secular persons."[11] Erasmus dispensed with his habit only when the need arose. He appears almost fanatical about adhering to the regulations of his clerical state. It is also important to remember that he sought the dispensation before he set aside the habit of the Austin Canons.

On the other hand, Margaret Mann Phillips has argued that "surely the fundamental reason for his adopting the ordinary dress of a secular cleric was his profound distaste for all that pertained to the monastic life."[12] If indeed Erasmus had associated the religious life with the religious habit, Phillips' argument would be tenable; but, as the above quotation quite clearly reveals, Erasmus distinguished between 'religion' and 'dress.'

After receiving his doctorate in theology from the University of Turin in 1506, Erasmus justified his continued absence from Steyn on the grounds that his fellow canons no longer contributed to his advancement. Similarly, in the *Enchiridion* (1503), Erasmus advised the Christian knight to withdraw from human companionship if it proved to be of negative value:

Next, when there are no men around you whose society improves you, withdraw as much as you can from human companionship and converse with the saints, the prophets, the Apostles, and with Christ. Above all, however, make Paul your intimate friend. Him you should always cling to, 'meditating upon him day and night' until you commit to memory every word.[13]

Religion, for Erasmus, was within. It came from a knowlege of the saints and from the reading of Scripture.

Motivated by a desire to insure his further advancement and independence, Erasmus sought formal dispensation from the obligation to reside at Steyn. In his letter to Servatius (1514), he insisted that his reasons for remaining outside of the monastery were legitimate. He presented three

---

[10] Erasmus to Servatius Roger, July 8, 1514. See Nichols, 2, 149.

[11] *Ibid.*

[12] M. M. Phillips, *Erasmus and the Northern Renaissance* (London, 1949), p. 87.

[13] The *Enchiridion* was first published in 1503. See *The Enchiridion of Erasmus*, ed. and tr. Raymond Himelick (Bloomington, 1963), p. 199.

arguments. He began by stating that since he had been compelled to enter the monastery—"a sort of life from which I was alien in soul and body"—he did not feel obligated to remain within its cloister. He also insisted that the monastic life at Steyn was devoid of meaning for him: "in a word, the entire routine of the life, from which, if you take away the ceremonial, I fail to see what you have left that is desirable." Finally, Erasmus referred to the frailness of his health, which could no longer stand up to the rigors of the monastic rule. Despite persuasive arguments such as these, Servatius insisted that he return to Steyn. But Erasmus knew that he would be unable to lead the regimented life of an enclosed religious, and therefore he appealed to Pope Julius II for a dispensation. The Pope granted his request in 1506, but the dispensation was never used. Apparently the integrity of the document was challenged by his superiors when it was learned that Erasmus had referred to his parents, in his application for the dispensation, as "a single man and a widow."[14] The monastery officials knew full well that Erasmus was the son of a cleric. Too embarrassed to reapply immediately for the dispensation, Erasmus remained under the injunction of his superior to return to Steyn.

From 1506 to 1517, the officials at Steyn periodically brought pressure on Erasmus to resume the life of a professed canon. Erasmus refused. Finally, in 1517, he petitioned Pope Leo X for a dispensation from required residence at Steyn and from the obligation to wear the full religious habit. This time he presented the facts of his illegitimate and illicit birth openly, and he was not challenged. In securing the 1517 dispensation, Erasmus was free to live anywhere he chose, free to obtain independent sources of income, and free to wear a modified form of the habit.[15] But the fact remains that Erasmus continued to be a member of the Austin Canons, subject to its rules and under obedience to its religious superiors. As a professed member of the Austin Canons—he referred to himself as "canonicos regulariter viventes esse monachos"[16] in 1524—he also enjoyed all of the privileges of a member in good standing. For example, the papal decree of 1517 recognized the right of

---

[14] J. J. Mangan published a translation of the 1506 dispensation in his biography, *Life, Character and Influence of Desiderius Erasmus*, 2, 60–61.

[15] For the text of the 1517 dispensation, see Mangan's translation, *ibid.*, 2, 54–56.

[16] Erasmus to [Gerard Geldenhouwer] (ca. April 2, 1524). See *Allen*, 5, 427. 19.

Erasmus to hold the offices of subprior, prior, or abbot, if he were so elected.

In living outside the immediate influence of the community, Erasmus found justification for his way of life. He first expressed his notion of a religious life in the world in his 1514 letter to Servatius:

> How much more in accordance with the sentiment of Christ, to regard the whole world as one household, or as it were one monastery, to think of all mankind as our brethren or fellow-canons, to hold the sacrament of baptism as the highest order of religion, and not to look where a man lives but how well he lives.[17]

Erasmus conceived a plan whereby all mankind would learn to imitate the way of Christ. Religious life was not to be confined behind monastic walls. It was to become the general standard of human conduct. Erasmus repeated this view in a 1518 letter to Paul Volz (August 15). Writing with eloquence and feeling, he asked: "Why do we so limit the profession of Christ, which he wished to extend most widely? If we are moved by splendid appellations, I beseech you, what else is a city but a great monastery?"[18] It was Erasmus' belief that the person who freely practiced his religion was more virtuous than one who obeyed his superior's injunctions. Coercion, which he identified with monastic confinement, was not a worthy stimulus for the sincere Christian. By 1533, Erasmus was able to offer a defense of the traditional monastic life, without detracting from his enthusiasm for a holy life within the city: "such a man may be a monk in the courts of kings, in the halls of government, or in the marts of men."[19] Erasmus never doubted the efficacy of the monastic ideal. It is true that he did find fault with specific monks and certain monasteries, but not with their way of life. Throughout his own religious life, Erasmus sincerely doubted that he had a true vocation, but since he had 'voluntarily' taken the three vows of poverty, chastity, and obedience, he was determined to keep his word.[20] As a Canon Regular of St. Augustine, he remained true to his religious profession in much the same way as he remained true to the authority of the Roman Catholic Church: he was a free and courageous spirit to the very end.

---

[17] Erasmus to Servatius Roger, July 8, 1514. See Nichols, 2, 144.

[18] Erasmus to Paul Volz, August 15, 1518. *Desiderius Erasmus: Christian Humanism and the Reformation,* tr. John C. Olin (New York, 1965), p. 130.

[19] Erasmus to Jan of Heemstede, February 28, 1533. J. J. Mangan, 2, 347.

[20] Erasmus to Servatius Roger, July 8, 1514. See Nichols, 2, 142.

Epilogue

ERASMUS of Rotterdam's spirituality was neither affected nor sentimental. It was based on a careful reading of sacred Scripture and the Church Fathers. As a reformer of the spiritual life, Erasmus outlined a plan of holiness that could be pursued by lay people and clerics alike within the framework of the Catholic Church. His emphasis on a rich interior life at the expense of external ceremonials differentiated him from many Catholic reformers and led to charges during his own lifetime that he was a heretic.

In 1506 while in Paris, Erasmus wrote to his English humanist friend Thomas Linacre in order to refute the rumor that he had died: "In France I have come to life again; for a persistent and widespread story had been in circulation, that Erasmus had departed this life." He continued: "Though as an omen it does not disturb me . . . I now have a foretaste, while I am still alive, of what those who survive me will say about me when I am dead!"[1] Although, perhaps, spoken in jest, this remark by Erasmus reveals a concern about future historical assessments of himself; and a concern it should have been, for no other figure in the past five centuries has been subject to such a variety of opposing perceptions.

The full impact of Erasmus of Rotterdam on his contemporaries has yet to be assessed. Andreas Flitner has opened the way in his *Erasmus im Urteil Seiner Nachwelt* (Tübingen, 1952). For useful studies on the influence of Erasmus after his death, see Marcel Bataillon, *Erasme et l'Espagne* (Paris, 1937) and James K. McConica, *English Humanists and Reformation Politics under Henry VIII and Edward VI* (Oxford, 1965; revised ed. 1968). Moreover, Bruce E. Mansfield has examined critical views of Erasmus between 1550 and 1750; see *Phoenix of His Age: Interpretations of Erasmus c 1550–1750* (Toronto, 1979). A second volume by the same author will cover the period from 1750 to 1970, the quincentenary of his birth.

Because of the success of the Protestant Reformation after Erasmus' death there was little need for his *philosophia Christi* in the late sixteenth century. By 1540 conciliarism had given way to entrenched confessional battles. In contrast, the seventeenth century sought to rehabilitate the image of Erasmus. Jean Le Clerc edited his works (which were published

---

[1] *CWE*, 117; *Allen*, 194.

at Leiden between 1703 and 1706) and expressed sympathy for him but found that he was too weak to become a Protestant himself. Margaret Mann Phillips has neatly summarized the eighteenth-century view of Erasmus "as a rationalist and precursor of enlightened agnosticism"; the nineteenth-century view of him "as an apostle of liberty and peace"; and the twentieth-century view of him as a "symbol of international understanding."[2]

The historical perception of Erasmus in the nineteenth century, as had been the case in the seventeenth and eighteenth centuries, tended to be manipulated in order to support a particular ideological viewpoint. In the nineteenth century, for example, the liberal tradition characterized Erasmus as the precursor of modern religious attitudes, but it could not understand how the same Erasmus who promoted the liberation of the human spirit could support traditional Catholic doctrine.

In the twentieth century writers have tended to perceive Erasmus in one of three ways: (1) as a precursor of the Reformation, but of too weak a personality to openly commit himself to it; (2) as the spokesman for the middle way, neither fully Catholic nor Protestant; and (3) as fully orthodox and committed to the reform of the Christian church from within. Among those subscribing to the first position are Ephraim Emerton, *Desiderius Erasmus of Rotterdam* (New York, 1900); Preserved Smith, *Erasmus: A Study of His Life, Ideals and Place in History* (New York, 1923); John J. Mangan, *Life, Character and Influence of Desiderius Erasmus of Rotterdam*, 2 vols. (New York, 1927); Albert Hyma, *The Youth of Erasmus* (Ann Arbor, 1931; 2d ed., New York, 1968); Christopher Hollis, *Erasmus* (Milwaukee, Wis., 1933) and Johan Huizinga, *Erasmus and the Age of Reformation,* trans. Federik Hopman (New York, 1924). Examples of those adhering to the second position are Augustin Renaudet, *Etudes Érasmiennes (1521–29)* (Paris, 1939); Margaret Mann Phillips, *Erasmus and the Northern Renaissance* (London, 1949), and Roland H. Bainton, *Erasmus of Christendom* (New York, 1969). Finally, examples of those taking the third position are Maurice Wilkinson, *Erasmus of Rotterdam* (New York, 1921); Louis Bouyer, *Erasmus and His Times,* trans. Francis X. Murphy (Westminster, Md., 1959); Lewis W. Spitz, *The Religious Renaissance of the German Humanists* (Cambridge, Mass., 1963); and E. E. Reynolds, *Thomas More and Erasmus* (New York, 1965).

[2] M. M. Phillips, *Erasmus and the Northern Renaissance* (New York: Collier Books, 1965), p. 11.

Ephraim Emerton's turn-of-the-century biography views Erasmus as a critic of the church who lacked a definite program of reform. According to Emerton, Erasmus was a vain man whose ambition prevented him from siding with Luther. John J. Mangan's psychological insights have led him to the same conclusion as that of Emerton: "There is not the slightest doubt that had Erasmus had the courage to go over to Luther he would have carried with him the greater part of the scholars of Germany at least" (392). Preserved Smith's biographical study of Erasmus endorses this opinion but also insists that Erasmus was a champion of rational Christianity, who saw religion as an ethical concern and who sought to reduce its emphasis on dogma. Erasmus refused to join the Protestant reform because "his interests emphasized the cause of learning and theirs the cause of dogmatic religion, and . . . he both distrusted and feared a popular rebellion, evidently verging more and more toward violence" (325). Given his personality, Smith argues that he could not have done otherwise. For Albert Hyma, Erasmus' character was largely determined by the first twenty years of his life. By the time he left Steyn, Erasmus was the "typical humanist" and "flattery, fame, and honor deteriorated his character" (150, 212). Like Hyma's, Johan Huizinga's portrait of Erasmus is based on an examination of his complex and withdrawn personality. He traces Erasmus' weak character to his illegitimate birth, the death of his parents during his adolescence, his forced entry into the monastery at Steyn, and his rejected craving for love from Servatius Roger, a fellow canon. Huizinga concludes that Erasmus simply did not have the courage of a Luther, a Calvin, or a Loyola: "In that robust sixteenth century it seems as if the oaken strength of Luther was necessary, the steely edge of Calvin, the white heat of Loyola; not the velvet softness of Erasmus . . . ." (189). Writing from a similar point of view, Christopher Hollis attributes Erasmus' failure to take a more militant stance against Luther to character defects and lack of moral courage. Furthermore, he portrays Erasmus as an insincere flatterer who was motivated by avarice, and as a hypocrite who criticized others for the very vices that belonged to him.

The second view of Erasmus emphasizes his role as the developer of a *via media*. Augustin Renaudet devotes attention to Erasmus' plan for "le troisième Eglise" between 1521 and 1529. He argues that Erasmus was the initiator of a rationalist spirituality and as such was a forerunner of modernism. Like her mentor, Renaudet, Margaret Mann Phillips champions a case for Erasmus as the spokesman of the "middle way," which was not only distinct from Catholicism and Protestantism but separated the mind and heart. She claims that Erasmus was dedicated to "the furthering of one great cause—the setting of the wisdom of the ancients at the service of the interpretation of Christianity and the betterment of man" (44). She also insists that Erasmus held fast to his belief in the *philosophia Christi* during the heated debates with Luther and his followers. Far from exhibiting weakness, Phillips believes that he showed incredible fortitude: "If Erasmus had been weak he would surely have fled for refuge to one camp or the other; as it was he stubbornly maintained his central position to the end." See Phillips, "Some Last Words of Erasmus," in *Luther, Erasmus and the Reformation: A Catholic-Protestant Reappraisal,* ed. John C. Olin (New York, 1969), 91. Like Phillips, Roland H. Bainton pictures Erasmus as the "battered liberal" who stressed an inward religion to such an extent that he interiorized his belief and was not, therefore, fully orthodox. He argues that Erasmus' concern for peace and consensus within the church kept him from becoming a Protestant.

The last group of biographers stresses Erasmus' orthodoxy. One of the earliest was Maurice Wilkinson, who writes that "Erasmus never wavered in his Catholicism," even though he refused to "be partisan of a bland obscurantism" (22–23). Nevertheless, Wilkinson sees Erasmus chiefly as a scholar rather than a reformer because he was "constitutionally and intellectually incapable of leading a popular movement" (65). Less critical of the personality of Erasmus is the assessment by Louis Bouyer, who contends that Erasmus' *philosophia Christi* was radically opposed to Protestantism because of its emphasis on faith translated into a life of practical charity. Though opposed to outward forms, on the one hand, and faith alone, on the other, Erasmus held up the ideal of faith and charity, which became the position of the Council of Trent later on in the century. Bouyer also insists that Erasmus' theology "not only in its use of critical methods, but in its realistic application of a sense of history to the thought and the life of primitive Christianity . . . represents . . . for the first time . . . the use of principle and method entirely adequate to effect a really fruitful renewal of Catholic faith and theology" (174). Despite this positive view, Bouyer seems not to understand Erasmus' periods of discouragement or his need for withdrawal and compares him unfavorably with the "saint of humanism," Thomas More. A far more positive view of Erasmus is to be found in the study by Lewis W. Spitz, who presents Erasmus as the developer of an undogmatic Christocentric spirituality that was faithful to the *traditio* of Christian antiquity: "The reform which he envisioned was a reform in the sense of a union of the Scriptures, the Church Fathers, *humanitas* and the *bonae litterae* within the Church. . . . Erasmus was perfectly orthodox and 'correct' on all matters of dogma" (204, 226). Finally, E. E. Reynolds stresses Erasmus' orthodoxy and maintains that his contacts with such saintly men as Colet, Fisher, Warham, and More were proof of his own interior piety.

Erasmus has been the victim of more distortion and misunderstanding than any other great figure of his age. His originality and the uniqueness of his position must account for the diversity of judgments and the disagreements among scholars which his life and thought have engendered. Erasmus was not a man of his age in that he did not represent any of the contemporary schools of thought nor any national or party interests. His ideas for the reform of the church, of individuals, and of society were truly universal in scope and ageless in their appeal. Therefore, it was inevitable that in an age of bitter partisan loyalties, Erasmus would be misunderstood by both sides of the Reformation controversy. Each succeeding generation has seen in Erasmus a reflection of its own limited viewpoint and interests. Only recently have scholars begun to judge Erasmus on his own terms and to restore to its proper place of importance the uniqueness of Erasmus' role as both a reformer and a fully committed, orthodox Christian. Perhaps this new perspective on Erasmus is partially a reflection of hindsight, an attempt to see Erasmus as a forerunner and prophet of the recent reforms in the Catholic Church. Yet Erasmus' reform program, with its emphasis on an inner renewal through a return to the primitive traditions of the church and to the uncorrupted sources of Scripture, is the essence of genuine reform in any age. In the short run, Erasmus may have been blind to the dangers posed by Luther's challenge and the need for the Catholic Church to take a strong and uncompromising stand. But in the long run, the wisdom of Erasmus' stance, his vision of a ". . . purified Church living according to the spirit of the Gospel, a Church of simplicity and charity informed by the true wisdom of Jesus Christ"[3] stands fully vindicated.

Erasmus dedicated his life and work to the accomplishment of this vision. His consistency, his independence, his refusal to yield in the face

---

[3] Robert E. McNally, S.J., Introduction to *Luther, Erasmus and the Reformation: A Catholic-Protestant Reappraisal,* ed. John C. Olin *et al.* (New York: Fordham University Press, 1969), 11–12.

of bitter opposition, all lead to the conclusion that Erasmus was a man of courage and of deep religious faith, whose strength of character and devotion to high ideals were rare in this age and, indeed, in any other.

Selected Bibliography

I. *Bibliographical Guides:*
   Van der Haeghen, Ferdinand, *Bibliotheca Érasmiana: Répertoire des Oeuvres d'Érasme,* 3 vols. (Nieuwkoop: B. De Graaf, 1961, 1972); reprint of Ghent 1893 edition.
   Margolin, Jean-Claude, *Quatorze Années de Bibliographie Érasmienne, 1936–1949* (Paris: J. Vrin, 1969)
   ____, *Douze Années de Bibliographie Érasmienne, 1950–1961* (Paris: J. Vrin, 1963)
   ____, *Neuf Années de Bibliographie Érasmienne, 1962–1970* (Paris: J. Vrin, 1977)
   Bibliographie Internationale de l'Humanisme et de la Renaissance (Geneva: Librairie Droz, 1965—)

II. *Primary Sources: Latin*
   Opus epistolarum Desiderii Erasmi Roterodami, ed. P. S. Allen et al. 12 vols. (Oxford: Clarendon Press, 1906–1958); hereafter *Allen*
   Omnia opera Desiderii Erasmi Roterodami. In progress (Amsterdam: North-Holland Publishing Co., 1969—); hereafter *ASD*
   Erasmi Opuscula, ed. Wallace K. Ferguson (The Hague: Martinus Nijhoff, 1933)
   Desiderii Erasmi Roterodami Opera Omnia, ed. Jean LeClerc. 10 vols. (Leiden: Van der Aa, 1703–06); reprinted by Hildesheim: G. Olms, 1961. Hereafter *LB*
   The Poems of Desiderius Erasmus, ed. Cornelis Reedijk (Leiden: E. J. Brill, 1956)
   Luc Verheijen, O.S.A., *La Règle de Saint Augustin.* 2 vols. (Paris: Études Augustiniennes, 1967): includes Latin text

III. *Primary Sources: English*
   Collected Works
   Collected Works of Erasmus. In progress (Toronto: University of Toronto Press, 1974—); hereafter *CWE*
   Erasmus. Documents of Modern History, ed. Richard L. DeMolen (London: Edward Arnold, 1973)
   The Essential Erasmus, trans. and ed. by John P. Dolan (New York: New American Library, 1964); hereafter *Dolan*
   Erasmus and His Age: Selected Letters of Desiderius Erasmus, trans.

by Marcus A. Haworth, S.J., and ed. by Hans J. Hillerbrand (New York: Harper and Row, 1970); hereafter *Hillerbrand*

The Epistles of Erasmus, trans. by Francis M. Nichols. 3 vols. (London: Longmans, Green and Co., 1901–1918)

Christian Humanism and the Reformation: Selected Writings, trans. and ed. by John C. Olin (New York: Harper and Row, 1965); hereafter *Olin*

Erasmus and Cambridge: The Cambridge Letters of Erasmus, trans. by D. F. S. Thomson (Toronto: University of Toronto Press, 1963)

Erasmus and Fisher: Their Correspondence 1511–1524, trans. by Jean Rouschausse (Paris: J. Vrin, 1968)

Individual Works

Erasmus, *Dialogue Ciceronianus*, trans. by Izora Scott in *Controversies over the Imitation of Cicero* (New York: Teachers College Press, 1910)

The Colloquies of Erasmus, trans. by Craig R. Thompson (Chicago: University of Chicago Press, 1965)

Erasmus, *A playne and godly exposytion or declaration of the commune crede [Symbolum Apostolorum]*, trans. by William Marshall (London [1534]). STC 10504

Erasmus, *Comparison of a Virgin and a Martyr*, trans. by Thomas Paynell (London, 1537) and ed. by William J. Hirten (Gainesville, Fla.: Scholars' Facsimiles & Reprints, 1970)

Erasmus, *A Little Treatise of the Manner and Form of Confession*, anonymous trans. (London [1535?]). STC 10498

Erasmus, *De Contemptu Mundi*, trans. by Thomas Paynell (1533) and ed. by William J. Hirten (Gainsville, Fla.: Scholars' Facsimiles & Reprints, 1967)

Erasmus, *On Copia of Words and Ideas*, trans. and ed. by Donald B. King and H. David Rix (Milwaukee, Wisc.: Marquette University Press, 1963)

Erasmus, *Preparation to Death*, anonymous trans. (London, 1538), STC 10505

Erasmus, *Concerning the Aim and Method of Education*, trans. by William H. Woodward (Cambridge: Cambridge University Press, 1904)

Erasmus, *The Education of a Christian Prince*, trans. by Lester K. Born (New York: Columbia University Press, 1936)

Erasmus, *The Handbook of the Christian Soldier,* trans. by Raymond Himelick (Bloomington: Indiana University Press, 1963)

Erasmus, *De Libero Arbitrio,* trans. and ed. by E. Gordon Rupp et al. in *Luther and Erasmus: Free Will and Salvation* (Philadelphia: Westminster Press, 1969)

Erasmus, *The first tome or volume of the Paraphrase of Erasmus vpon the Newe Testamente,* ed. by Nicholas Udall (London, 1548). STC 2854

Erasmus, *A devout treatise vpon the Pater noster,* trans. by Margaret More Roper and ed. by Richard L. DeMolen in *Erasmus of Rotterdam: A Quincentennial Symposium* (New York: Twayne Publishers, 1971), 104–124

Erasmus, *The Praise of Folly,* trans. by Hoyt H. Hudson (Princeton: Princeton University Press, 1941); trans. by Clarence H. Miller (New Haven: Yale University Press, 1979); trans. by Betty Radice and with notes by A. H. T. Levi (Harmondsworth, Middlesex: Penguin Books, 1971)

Erasmus, *A ryght excellent sermon and full of frute and edificacyon of the chylde Iesus,* anonymous trans. (London, c. 1536). STC 10509

Erasmus, "The Sponge of Erasmus Against the Aspersions of Hutten," in *The Polemics of Erasmus of Rotterdam and Ulrich von Hutten,* trans. by Randolph J. Klawiter (Notre Dame: University of Notre Dame Press, 1977)

Erasmus, *The Lives of Jehan Vitrier . . . and John Colet,* trans. by J. H. Lupton (London: George Bell & Sons, 1883), 1–47

Kempis, Thomas à, *The Imitation of Christ,* trans. by Richard Whitford (c. 1530) and ed. by Harold C. Gardiner, S.J. (New York: Doubleday and Co., 1955)

The Rule of Saint Augustine: Masculine and Feminine Versions, trans. by Raymond Canning, O.S.A., and ed. by Tarsicius J. van Bavel, O.S.A. (London: Darton, Longman, and Todd, 1984)

IV. *Primary Source: French*

Erasmus, *Declamatio de pueris statim ac liberaliter instituendis,* trans. and ed. by Jean-Claude Margolin (Geneva: Librairie Droz, 1966)

V. *Secondary Sources*

Allen, Percy S., *Erasmus: Lectures and Wayfaring Sketches* (Oxford: Clarendon Press, 1934)

Ariès, Philippe, *Centuries of Childhood: A Social History of Family Life,* trans. by Robert Baldick (New York: Random House, 1965)

Aston, Margaret E., "The Northern Renaissance," in *The Meaning of the Renaissance and Reformation,* ed. by Richard L. DeMolen (Boston: Houghton Mifflin, 1974), 71–129

Auer, Alfons, *Die Vollkommene Frömmigkeit des Christen* (Dusseldorf: Patmos, 1954)

Augustijn, Cornelius, *Erasmus en de Reformatie* (Amsterdam: H. J. Paris, 1962)

Bainton, Roland H., *Erasmus of Christendom* (New York: Charles Scribners Sons, 1969)

_____, "The Paraphrases of Erasmus," *Archiv für Reformationsgeschichte,* 57 (1966), 67–75.

Bataillon, Marcel, *Érasme et l'Espagne: Recherches sur l'histoire spirituelle du XVIe siècle* (Paris: Librairie E. Droz, 1937); second ed., *Erasmo y España,* 2 vols. (Buenos Aires, 1950)

Béné, Charles, *Érasme et Saint Augustin* (Geneva: Librairie Droz, 1969)

Bentley, Jerry H., *Humanists and Holy Writ: New Testament Scholarship in the Renaissance* (Princeton: Princeton University Press, 1983)

Bierlaire, Franz, *Les Colloques d'Érasme: réforme des études, réforme des moeurs et réforme de l'Église au XVIe siècle* (Paris: Societé d'Édition "Les Belles Lettres," 1978)

Bietenholz, Peter G., "Erasmus and the German Public, 1518–1520: The Authorized and Unauthorized Circulation of his Correspondence," *The Sixteenth Century Journal,* 8 (1977), 61–78

Bouyer, Louis, *Erasmus and His Times,* trans. by Francis X. Murphy (Westminster, Md.: Newman Press, 1959)

Boyle, Marjorie O'Rourke, *Christening Pagan Mysteries: Erasmus in Pursuit of Wisdom* (Toronto: University of Toronto Press, 1981)

_____, *Erasmus on Langauge and Method in Theology* (Toronto: University of Toronto Press, 1977)

_____, *Rhetoric and Reform: Erasmus' Civil Dispute with Luther* (Cambridge, Mass.: Harvard University Press, 1983)

Callahan, Virginia W., "Andrea Alciati's View of Erasmus:

Prudent Cunctator and Bold Counselor," *Acta Conventus Neo-Latini Sanctandreani* (1982), ed. by I. D. McFarlane (Binghamton, N. Y.: Medieval and Renaissance Texts, 1986), 203–10

Calvazza, Silvano, "La Cronologia degli 'Antibarbari' e le Origini del Pensiero Religioso di Erasmo," *Rinascimento,* 25 (1975), 141–79

Chantraine, Georges, S.J., *Érasme et Luther: libre et serf arbitre* (Paris: Editions Lethielleux; Namur: Presses Universitaires de Namur, 1981)

―――, *'Mystère' et 'Philosophie du Christ' selon Érasme* (Namur and Gembloux: DuCulot, 1971)

Colledge, Edmund, O.S.A., "Erasmus, the Brethren of the Common Life, and the Devotio Moderna," *Erasmus in English,* 7 (1975), 3–4

Colloqvivm Erasmianvm (Mons: Centre Universitaire de l'État, 1968)

Coppens, Joseph, ed., *Scrinium Erasmianum,* 2 vols. (Leiden: E. J. Brill, 1969)

Davis, Kenneth R., "Erasmus as a Progenitor of Anabaptist Theology and Piety," *Mennonite Quarterly,* 47 (1973), 163–78

DeMolen, Richard L., "Ages of Admission to Educational Institutions in Tudor and Stuart England," *History of Education,* 5 (1976), 207–19

―――, "Childhood and the Sacraments in the Sixteenth Century," *Archiv für Reformationsgeschichte,* 66 (1975), 49–71

―――, "Erasmus as Adolescent," *Bibliothèque d'Humanisme et Renaissance,* 38 (1976), 7–25

―――, "Erasmus' Commitment to the Canons Regular of St. Augustine," *Renaissance Quarterly,* 26 (1973), 437–43

―――, ed., *Erasmus of Rotterdam: A Quincentennial Symposium* (New York: Twayne Publishers, 1971)

―――, "Erasmus of Rotterdam in Profile," *Erasmus of Rotterdam: A Quincentennial Symposium,* ed. by R. L. DeMolen (New York: Twayne Publishers, 1971), 15–28

―――, "Erasmus on Childhood," *Erasmus of Rotterdam Society Yearbook Two* (1982), 25–46

―――, ed., *Essays on the Works of Erasmus* (New Haven: Yale University Press, 1978)

———, "First Fruits: The Place of *Antibarbarorum Liber* and *De Contemptu Mundi* in the Formulation of Erasmus' *Philosophia Christi*," *Melanges Érasme,* ed. Jean-Pierre Massaut (Liège: Université de Liège, 1987), in press

———, "The Interior Erasmus," *Leaders of the Reformation,* ed. by R. L. DeMolen (Selinsgrove: Susquehanna University Press/ London and Toronto: Associated University Presses, 1984), 11–42

———, "*Opera Omnia Desiderii Erasmi:* Rungs on the Ladder to the *Philosophia Christi*," *Essays on the Works of Erasmus,* ed. by R. L. DeMolen (New Haven: Yale University Press, 1978), 1–50

———, "*Pueri Christi Imitatio:* The Festival of the Boy-Bishop in Tudor England," *Moreana,* 45 (1975), 17–28

Devereux, E. J., *Renaissance English Translations of Erasmus: A Bibliography to 1700* (Toronto: University of Toronto Press, 1983)

———, "Some Lost English Translations of Erasmus," *Transactions of the Bibliographical Society.* Fifth Series, 17 (1962), 255–59

De Vocht, Henry, "Erasmiana I and II," *Anglia,* 79 (1962), 319–37

Dickinson, J. C., *The Origins of the Austin Canons and Their Introduction into England* (London: The Church Historical Society, 1950)

Dorey, T. A., ed., *Erasmus* (London: Routledge & Kegan Paul., 1970)

Drummond, Robert B., *Erasmus: His Life and Character,* 2 vols. (London: Smith, Elder and Co., 1873)

Emerton, Ephraim, *Desiderius Erasmus of Rotterdam* (New York: G. P. Putnam's Sons, 1899)

Étienne, Jacques, *Spiritualisme Érasmien et Théologiens Louvanistes* (Louvain: Publications Universitaires de Louvain, 1956)

Faludy, George, *Erasmus of Rotterdam* (London: Eyre & Spottiswoode, 1970)

Ferguson, Wallace K., "Renaissance Tendencies in the Religious Thought of Erasmus," *Journal of the History of Ideas,* 15 (1954), 499–508

Froude, J. A., *Life and Letters of Erasmus* (New York: Charles Scribner's Sons, 1925)

Gerlo, Alöis, *Érasme et ses Portraitistes: Metsijs, Dürer, Holbein.* Second ed. (Nieuwkoop: B. De Graaf, 1969)

Gilmore, Myron P., "*De modis disputandi:* The Apologetic Works of Erasmus," *Florilegium Historiale: Essays Presented to Wallace K. Ferguson,* ed. by J. G. Rowe and W. H. Stockdale (Toronto: University of Toronto Press, 1971), 62–88

____, "Italian Reactions to Erasmian Humanism," *Itinerarium Italicum,* ed. by Heiko A. Oberman with Thomas A. Brady, Jr. (Leiden: E. J. Brill, 1975), 61–115

____, *The World of Humanism* (New York: Harper and Brothers, 1952)

Gleason, John B., "The Birth Dates of John Colet and Erasmus of Rotterdam: Fresh Documentary Evidence," *Renaissance Quarterly,* 32 (1979), 73–76

Godin, André, *Érasme: Lecteur D'Origène* (Geneva: Librairie Droz, 1982)

____, *Spiritualité Franciscaine en Flandre au XVIe Siècle: L'Homéliaire de Jean Vitrier* (Geneva: Librairie Droz, 1971)

Halkin, Léon-E., *Érasme et l'Humanisme Chrétien* (Paris: Éditions Universitaires, 1969)

____, *Erasmus Ex Erasmo: Erasme Éditeur da sa Correspondance* (Aubel: P. M. Gason, 1983)

____, "La Piété d'Érasme," *Revue d'Histoire Ecclésiastique,* 79 (1984), 671–708

Harbison, E. H., *The Christian Scholar in the Age of the Reformation* (New York: Charles Scribner's Sons, 1952)

Haverals, Marcel, "Une Première Rédaction du *De Contemptu Mundi* d'Érasme dans un Manuscrit de Zwolle," *Humanistica Lovaniensis,* 30 (1981), 40–54

Hayum, Andrée, "Dürer's Portrait of Erasmus and the Ars Typographorum," *Renaissance Quarterly,* 38 (1985), 650–87

Hoffmann, Manfred, "Erasmus and Religious Toleration," *Erasmus of Rotterdam Society Yearbook Two* (1982), 80–106

____, "Erasmus on Church and Ministry," *Erasmus of Rotterdam Society Yearbook Six* (1986), 1–30.

____, *Erkenntnis und Verwirklichung der wahren Theologie nach Erasmus von Rotterdam* (Tübingen: J. C. Mohr, 1972)

Hollis, Christopher, *Erasmus* (Milwaukee, Wisc.: Bruce, 1933)

Huizinga, Johan, *Erasmus and the Age of Reformation.* trans. by

Frederik J. Hopman. Letters of Erasmus translated by Barbara Flower (Princeton; Princeton University Press, 1984); first published in 1924

Hyma, Albert, *The Christian Renaissance: A History of the Devotio Moderna.* Second ed. (Hamden, Conn.: Archon Books, 1965)

———, *The Youth of Erasmus.* Second ed. (New York: Russell & Russell, 1968)

Jarrott, Catherine A. L., "Erasmus' Biblical Humanism," *Studies in the Renaissance,* 17 (1970), 119–52

Jortin, John, *The Life of Erasmus,* 3 vols. (London: J. Whiston and B. White, 1758–60)

Kaufman, Peter I., *Augustinian Piety and Catholic Reform: Augustine, Colet, and Erasmus* (Macon, Ga.: Mercer University Press, 1982)

Knowles, David., O.S.B., *The Religious Orders in England,* 3 vols. (Cambridge: Cambridge University Press, 1959)

Koch, A. C. F., *The Year of Erasmus' Birth* (Utrecht: Dekker & Gumbert, 1969)

Kohls, Ernst-Wilhelm, "Das Geburtsjahr des Erasmus," *Theologische Zeitschrift,* 22 (1966), 91–121, 347–59

———, *Die Theologie des Erasmus,* 2 vols. (Basel: Friedrich Reinhardt, 1966)

Kristeller, Paul Oskar, "Erasmus from an Italian Perspective," *Renaissance Quarterly,* 23 (1970), 1–14

Krodel, Gottfried, "Luther, Erasmus and Henry VIII," *Archiv für Reformationsgeschichte,* 53 (1962), 60–78

Levi, A. H. T., "Erasmus and the Humanist Ideal," *Heythrop Journal,* 19 (1970), 243–55

Mangan, John J., *Life, Character, & Influence of Desiderius Erasmus of Rotterdam,* 2 vols. (New York: Macmillan, 1927)

Mansfield, Bruce, "Erasmus and the Mediating School," *Journal of Religious History,* 4 (1967), 302–16

———, *Phoenix of His Age: Interpretations of Erasmus c. 1550–1750* (Toronto: University of Toronto Press, 1979)

Margolin, Jean-Claude, ed., *Colloquia Erasmiana Turonensia* (1969), 2 vols. (Toronto: University of Toronto Press, 1972)

———, *Érasme par lui-même* (Paris: Éditions du Seuil, 1965)

McConica, James K., C.S.B., *English Humanists and Reformation*

Politics under Henry VIII and Edward VI. Rev. ed. (Oxford: Clarendon Press, 1968)

_____, "Erasmus and the Grammar of Consent," *Scrinium Erasmianum,* ed. by Joseph Coppens (Leiden: E. J. Brill, 1969), 2, 77–99

Meissinger, Karl A., *Erasmus von Rotterdam,* Second ed. (Berlin: Albert Nauck, 1948)

Mesnard, Pierre, *Érasme ou le Christianisme Critique* (Paris: Éditions Universitaires, 1967)

_____, "La *Paraclesis* d'Érasme," *Bibliothèque d'Humanisme et Renaissance,* 12 (1951), 26–42

Mestwerdt, Paul, *Die Anfänge des Erasmus* (Leipzig: Rudolph Haupt, 1917)

Minnich, Nelson H., and W. W. Meissner, S.J., "The Character of Erasmus," *The American Historical Review,* 83 (1978), 598–624

Nulli, Siro A., *Erasmo e il Rinascimento* (Torino: Guilio Einaudi, 1955)

Oelrich, Karl H., *Der späte Erasmus und die Reformation* (Munster im Westfalen: Aschendorffsche, 1961)

Olin, John C. et al., eds., *Luther, Erasmus and the Reformation: A Catholic-Protestant Reappraisal* (New York: Fordham University Press, 1969)

Olin, John C., *Six Essays on Erasmus* (New York: Fordham University Press, 1979)

O'Malley, John W., S.J., "Erasmus and the History of Sacred Rhetoric: The *Ecclesiastes* of 1535," *Erasmus of Rotterdam Society Yearbook Five* (1985), 1–29

Panofsky, Erwin, "Erasmus and the Visual Arts," *Journal of the Warburg and Courtauld Institutes,* 32 (1969), 200–27

Payne, John B., *Erasmus: His Theology of the Sacraments* (Richmond, Va.: John Knox, 1970)

_____, "Toward the Hermeneutics of Erasmus," *Scrinium Erasmianum,* ed. Joseph Coppens (Leiden: E. J. Brill, 1969), 2, 13–49

Pesch, Otto H., *Humanismus und Reformation: Martin Luther und Erasmus von Rotterdam in den Konflikten ihrer Zeit.* Katholische Akademie Freiburg (Munich/Zurich: Schnell & Steiner, 1985)

Phillips, Margaret Mann, *The Adages of Erasmus: A Study with Translations* (Cambridge: Cambridge University Press, 1964)

———, *Erasmus and the Northern Renaissance* (Woodbridge, Suffolk: Boydell and Brewer, 1981); first published in 1949

———, "The Mystery of the Metsys Portrait," *Erasmus in English*, 7 (1975), 18–21

Pineau, J.-B. *Érasme: Sa Pensée Religieuse* (Paris: Les Presses Universitaires de France, 1924)

Post, R. R., *The Modern Devotion: Confrontation with Reformation and Humanism* (Leiden: E. J. Brill, 1968)

———, "Quelques Précisions sur l'Année de la Naissance d'Érasme (1469) et sur son Éducation," *Bibliothèque d'Humanisme et Renaissance*, 26 (1964), 489–509

Rabil, Albert, Jr., *Erasmus and the New Testament: The Mind of a Christian Humanist* (San Antonio: Trinity University Press, 1972)

Reedijk, Cornelius, ed., *Actes du Congres Érasme* (Rotterdam: 27–29 October) (Amsterdam: North-Holland Publishing Co., 1971)

Renaudet, Augustin, *Érasme: Sa Pensée Religieuse et son Action d'Après sa Correspondance 1518–1521* (Paris: Alcan, 1926)

Reynolds, Ernest E., *Thomas More and Erasmus* (London: Burns & Oates, 1965)

Rieger, James A., "Erasmus, Colet, and the Schoolboy Jesus," *Studies in the Renaissance*, 9 (1962), 187–94

Rix, Herbert D., "The Editions of Erasmus' *De Copia*." *Studies in Philology*, 43 (1946), 595–618

Rummel, Erika, "Quoting Poetry Instead of Scripture: Erasmus and Eucherius on *Contemptus Mundi*," *Bibliothèque d'Humanisme et Renaissance*, 40 (1983), 503–09

———, *Erasmus' Annotations on the New Testament: From Philologist to Theologian* (Toronto: University of Toronto Press, 1986)

———, *Erasmus as a Translator of the Classics* (Toronto: University of Toronto Press, 1985)

Saward, John, *Perfect Fools: Folly for Christ's Sake in Catholic and Orthodox Spirituality* (Oxford: Oxford University Press, 1981)

Schottenloher, Otto, *Erasmus im Ringen um die humanistische Bildungsform* (Munster im Westfalen: Aschendorff, 1933)

Screech, M. A., *Ecstasy and the Praise of Folly* (London: Duckworth, 1980)

Scribner, R. W., "The Social Thought of Erasmus," *Journal of Religious History*, 6 (1970), 3–26

Smith, Preserved, *Erasmus: A Study of His Life, Ideals and Place in History* (New York: Harper and Brothers, 1923)

Snyder, Lee Daniel, "Erasmus on Prayer: A Renaissance Reinterpretation," *Renaissance and Reformation*, 12 (1976), 21–27

Sowards, J. Kelley, *Desiderius Erasmus* (Boston: Twayne Publishers, 1975)

Spitz, Lewis W., *The Religious Renaissance of the German Humanists* (Cambridge, Mass.: Harvard University Press, 1963)

Telle, Emile V., *Érasme de Rotterdam et le Septième Sacrement* (Geneva: Librairie E. Droz, 1954)

Tentler, Thomas N., "Forgiveness and Consolation in the Religious Thought of Erasmus," *Studies in the Renaissance*, 12 (1965), 110–33

Thompson, Craig R., "Erasmus as Internationalist and Cosmopolitan," *Archiv für Reformationsgeschichte*, 46 (1955), 167–95

Thompson, Geraldine M., *Under Pretext of Praise: Satiric Mode in Erasmus' Fiction* (Toronto: University of Toronto Press, 1973)

Thomson, D. F. S., "Erasmus as a Poet in the Context of Northern Humanism," *De Gulden Passer*, 47 (1969), 187–210

Tracy, James D., "Against the 'Barbarians': The Young Erasmus and His Humanist Contemporaries," *The Sixteenth Century Journal*, 11 (1980), 3–22

———, *Erasmus: The Growth of a Mind* (Geneva: Librairie Droz, 1972)

———, "Humanists Among the Scholastics: Erasmus, More, and Lefèvre d'Étaples on the Humanity of Christ," *Erasmus of Rotterdam Society Yearbook Five* (1985), 30–51

———, "On the Composition Dates of Seven of Erasmus' Writings," *Bibliothèque d'Humanisme et Renaissance*, 31 (1969), 355–64

———, *The Politics of Erasmus: A Pacifist Intellectual and His Political Milieu* (Toronto: University of Toronto Press, 1978)

Treu, Erwin, *Die Bildnisse des Erasmus von Rotterdam* (Basel: Gute Schriften, 1959)

Weiss, James W., "*Ecclesiastes* and Erasmus: The Mirror and the Image," *Archiv für Reformationsgeschichte,* 65 (1974), 83–107

INDEX

Abraham, 175
Adolescence, 15–34, 36, 75, 126, 142, 144, 146, 147, 149–54, 160, 162, 177, 201
Adolph of Burgundy, 71
Adrian VI, Pope, 185
Alcalá, 93
Alger of Liège, 73, 102
Allen, P. S., 17, 19, 166
Ambrose, St., 73, 99–102, 112, 139
Amerbach, Boniface, 10
Ammonio, Andrea, 38, 42
Amsterdam, 88
Anglicanism, see Church of England
Anne Boleyn, Queen, 184
Anti-Semitism, 115
Antwerp, 76, 109, 116, 120, 141
Apostles, The, 21, 52, 59, 101, 133, 195
Aquinas, St. Thomas, 102
Arabia, 23
Arianism, 93
Ariès, Philippe, 143–44, 147, 159–60, 164
Aristotle, 91–2, 185
Arnobius, 102
Asceticism, 29
Ascham, Roger, 80
Athanasius, St., 73, 102, 112
Augsburg, 80, 123
Augustine, St., xii, xiv, xvi, 2, 26, 33, 73, 99–102, 112, 129–30, 135–41, 168–74, 181, 190–91

Baechem, Nicolaas, 93
Baer, Ludwig, 94, 99, 104, 105, 177
Baerland, Adriaan, 77
Bainton, Roland H., 20, 61, 200
Baptism, xii, 147–52, 197
Barbier, Pierre, 109
Basel, 7, 9, 12, 71, 76–80, 93–96, 99, 109, 115–16, 120, 124, 131
Basel, bishop of, 96, 99, 101
Basil, St., 73, 102, 112
Bataillon, Marcel, 199

Batt, Jacob, 10, 69, 72, 81, 134–37
Beatus Rhenanus, xiii, 10, 59, 66, 76–7, 109
Beda, Noel, 93
Benedict, St., 140, 181
Benedictines, 63–5, 133, 136
Bergen, Antonius van, 107, 133
Bergen, Hendrik van, xiii, xiv, xvi, 2, 16, 33, 39, 80–1, 130–31, 136–7, 174, 193–94
Bergen-op-Zoom, 80–1, 131–34, 137
Bernard, St., of Clairvaux, 30, 139
Besançon, archbishop of, 179
Besançon, Senate of, 187
Bible, see Scripture
Bibliotheca Belgica, 84
Bibliotheca Erasmiana, 116
Bibliothèque d'Humanisme et Renaissance, xii
Blount, William (Lord Mountjoy), 4, 5, 83
Boece, Hector, xv, 72, 126
Bohemians, 183
Boleyn, Thomas (Viscount Rochford), 54
Bologna, 80, 194
Bonaventure, St., 102
Boner, John, 122
Boner, Severin, 122
Boner, Stanislaus, 122
Book of Hours, 57
Bostius, Arnoldius, 33
Botzheim, Johann von, 71, 85, 105, 112, 142
Bouyer, Louis, 200, 202
Boy-Bishop, 160–63
Boyle, Marjorie O'Rourke, 35
Boys, xvii, 4, 44, 74–5, 90, 109–12, 120–22, 145–46, 163
Brabant, 80, 105
Brethren of the Common Life, 1–3, 18, 35, 39, 115, 125, 158, 192
Briaert, Jan, 92, 96
Bruges, 100
Bucer, Martin, 117
Budé, Guillaume, xvii, 44, 74, 84–5, 90, 95

[217]

Bullock, Henry, 99, 100
Busch, Lubbert ten, 50
Byddell, John, 108

Caius, Thomas, 108
Cajetan, Cardinal, 188
Calvin, John, xiv, 201
Cambrai, bishop of, see Hendrik van Bergen
Cambridge, University of, 6, 7, 73
Campeggi, Lorenzo, 118, 184
Canons Regular of St. Augustine, xi, xiii, xvi–xviii, 2, 3, 15–23, 31–35, 39, 41, 64, 65, 69–71, 79, 125–41, 146, 147, 160, 166–73, 185, 190–97
Canter, Jacob, 170
Canterbury, 99
Capito, Wolfgang Faber, 37, 71, 74, 92, 95, 99
Cardinal, 34, 193
Carmelites, 93, 133–35, 139
Carondelet, Jean de, 103, 181
Carpi, 93
Carranza, Sanctius, of Miranda, 93
Carthusians, 56, 99, 133, 141, 194
Carvajal, Louis de, 93
Catholic Church, 65, 148–50, 186, 197, 199–03
Catholics, 66, 118, 154, 161, 200–01
Cato, Publius Valerius, 74
Chantraine, Georges, xi
Charity, see love
Charles I, King, 41, 91, 92, 106, 109
Childermas Day, 161
Childhood, xviii, 143–64
Christ, Jesus, xi, xiv, xv, xviii, 2, 7, 9, 11, 13, 34, 37–45, 49–65, 70–73, 83–92, 95, 101–05, 112–18, 123–24, 133–37, 142, 149–51, 162–63, 169, 174–76, 179–82, 186, 197, 203
Christendom, 11, 32, 74, 101, 102, 107, 118, 124
Christiana Respublica, 7
Christianity, xiv, 1, 8, 13, 46, 82, 85, 88–91, 94, 102, 114, 182, 201, 202

Christians, 66, 87, 98, 105, 110, 113, 137, 139, 181, 183
Chrysostom, St. John, 63, 73, 99–04, 112
Church, The, 11, 67, 83, 94, 95, 100, 101, 118, 147, 148, 202, 203
Church Fathers, xv, xvii, 26, 47, 50, 63, 73, 75, 83, 84, 94, 97, 99, 102–05, 112, 116, 130, 136, 141, 165, 168, 169, 172, 192, 199, 202
Cicero, xi, xii, 30, 33, 35, 91, 119–20
Cistercians, 133, 139
Classics, xi, xv–xvii, 2, 7, 23, 24, 29, 33–36, 42, 50, 71, 72, 80–6, 92–6, 103, 114, 128–36, 141, 142, 146, 157, 170, 172, 192, 202
Cleves, duke of, 119, 120
Clichthove, Josse van, 93
Colet, John, xvi, 4, 7, 40, 43, 73, 89, 90, 96, 97, 107, 120, 162, 203
Colledge, Edmund, 50
Cologne, 63–5, 120–21
Comenius, Johann Amos, 120–21
Communion, see Eucharist
Confessor, 58–63, 134
Confirmation, 147–53
Conrad, Willem, 134–37
Constance, 72, 185
Cranmer, Thomas, 152
Credo, 9
Cursius, Peter, 93
Cyprian, St., 63, 73, 100–02, 136, 139
Cyril, St., 99, 101, 112

D'Albon, Antoine, 187
Death, 20, 21, 34, 56, 58, 65, 79, 109, 123, 189
De Hegen, Berta, 21, 126, 141
Deloynes, François, 104–05
Deventer, 1, 2, 15, 18, 24, 39, 50, 192
Devil, 20, 56, 115, 150, 153
Devotio Moderna, xi–xviii, 2, 35–6, 46, 50, 52, 126, 192
Divine Providence, 107
Dominic, St., 135
Dominicans, 133–39, 188

INDEX

Dorp, Maarten van, 44, 89, 92, 96–7, 178
Dürer, Albrecht, 9, 10, 36, 65, 179
Du Moulin, François, 58
Dutch (language), 5, 66, 84, 93, 105, 121

Education, 4, 72, 91, 111, 120–22, 144, 156
Edward VI, King, 108
Elijah, 135
Elisabeth, Sister, 15, 17–8, 25, 127, 167, 170
Elizabeth I, Queen, 153
Elyot, Thomas, 120
Emerton, Ephraim, 201
England, xvi, 4, 6, 8, 11–2, 40, 67, 152, 191, 194
England, Church of, 108, 152–54
English (language), 84, 116, 121, 138, 183
Enlightenment, 1
Episcopius, Nicolaus, 82
Erasmus, Works, Individual
  Adages, xvii, 5, 72, 82–4, 165
    Dulce bellum inexpertis, 52, 83, 91
  Against the Pseudoevangelicals of Strasbourg, 93
  Annotations on the New Testament, xiv, 93, 95
  Apologiae, xvii, 69, 73, 92–6, 133
  Book of the Antibarbarians, xviii, 2, 73, 79–82, 92, 125–26, 131–37, 141, 193
  Catalogus Lucubrationum, 24
  Colloquies, xvii, 4, 8, 9, 72, 109–12, 151, 191
  Comparison of a Virgin and a Martyr, 63–5
  The Complaint of Peace, 8, 52, 72, 105–07, 182
  Concerning the Immense Mercy of God, 175
  De Contemptu Mundi, xviii, 2, 16, 30, 125–26, 137–41, 190, 192
  Dialogue on the Ciceronian, 72, 119–20
  Discourse on the Freedom of the Will, 9, 73, 93, 116–19, 123, 186
  Epistles, xiv, xvii, 11, 16–32, 36, 72, 75–9, 96, 127, 129, 166–74, 190
  Handbook of the Christian Soldier (Enchiridion), xvii, 4, 46, 49, 50, 53, 72, 84–6, 93, 96, 137, 141–42, 165, 176, 180, 195
  Hyperaspistes, 93, 117, 186
  The Instruction of a Christian Prince, 8, 54, 72, 75, 90–2, 96, 181
  Manner and Form of Confession, 58–63
  Method of True Theology, 72, 101, 112–14
  Modus orandi Deum, 177
  Novum Instrumentum, xvii, 8, 49, 93, 96–02, 107–08, 112
  Novum Testamentum, 101–02
  Obsecratio, 179
  On Civility of Manners for Boys, 72, 121–22
  On Copia of Words and Things, 7, 72, 89–90, 120
  On the Instruction of Boys, 72, 120–21, 154
  On Mending the Peace of the Church, 189
  On Preaching, 72, 122–24
  On the Prohibition of Eating Meat, 93
  The Our Father, 114–16, 175
  Paean, 179
  Paraclesis, xv, 97–8, 178–79
  Paraphrases of the New Testament, 10, 73, 93, 107–09, 182
  Poetry, xv, 11, 23–4, 126
  The Praise of Folly, xiv, xvii, 6, 44, 53, 72, 86–9, 92, 94, 96, 177–78
  Praise of Marriage, 92
  A Sermon on the Child Jesus, 162–63
  Sponge to Wipe Away the Aspersions of Hutten, 93, 184, 186
  Virginis matris apud Lauretum cultae Liturgia, 179
Erasmus of Rotterdam Society, xiv
Eucharist, xii, 56–7, 107, 147–54, 185
Euripides, 5
Europe, 5, 8, 34, 106, 116, 137, 143–44, 183
Eustace of Sichem, 93
Exegesis, xv, 4, 114
Extreme Unction, 147–48

Faith, 63, 117, 133
Family, 143, 155–56, 167, 178
Ferdinand, Archduke, of Austria, 109
Ferguson, Wallace K., 17, 25, 107
Ferrara, 80
Ficino, Marsilio, 120
Fisher, John, xiii, 6, 12, 40, 99, 113, 123, 182, 203
Flitner, Andreas, 199
Folly, 6, 54, 88, 178
Foxe, Richard, 70, 99
France, 3, 4, 11, 43, 193
Francis, St., of Assisi, 135, 141, 176–77, 181, 188–89
Francis I, King, 92, 106
Franciscans, 70, 85, 88, 93 133–36, 188–89
Frederick, Elector, of Saxony, 183
Free will, 9, 61
Freiburg, 12, 54, 70, 99
French (language), 80, 84, 86, 104, 121, 147, 183
Friars, 70, 133–37, 140
Friars Observants, 56
Froben, Jerome, 13, 80, 82
Froben, Johann, 7, 9, 76–8, 96, 109, 115, 120, 131

Gaguin, Robert, 39, 80, 120
Galen, 155
Galleria Nazionale, 10
Gay, Peter, 1
Geldenhauer, Gerard, 186
Gellius, Aulus, 37, 134
George, Duke, of Saxony, 177, 184
Gerard, Cornelis, 17, 23–31, 39, 71, 125, 128–31, 146, 166, 170, 173
Gerard, Gerard, 1, 15, 20–1, 32, 38, 41, 127
Gerard, Pieter, xvi, 1, 16, 20–2, 32, 38, 127, 160, 166–67, 170
German (language), 84–5, 105, 121, 183
Germany, 8, 11, 43, 201
Gerson, Jean de, 60
Gillis, Peter, 10, 76
Glareanus, Henricus, 176

Gleason, John B., xiii
God, xi, xiv, 6, 13, 33, 36–7, 45–8, 51–63, 66, 81, 95, 107, 114–17, 121, 124, 160, 172, 175–78, 187–89
Goes, Damião de, 124, 189
Gospel, see Scripture
Gouda, 1, 17, 18, 141, 160
Grace, xi, 116–17, 150, 154
Greek (language), xvi, xvii, 4–8, 50, 69, 73, 81, 86, 96–03, 110, 112, 120, 185
Gregory, St., 24
Grimani, Domenico, 99, 108
Grocyn, William, 4
Groote, Gerard, 125
Grunnius, Lambertus, 18, 22, 25, 30–31, 130, 140, 193–94
Grynaeus, Simon, 185

Halkin, Léon-E., xiv
Hampton Court Palace, 10
Hebrew (language), 71, 92, 103, 112–13, 185
Hemsdonck, 76
Henry VIII, King, 5, 12, 41, 92, 106, 184
Henry of Burgundy, Lord of Veere, 121
Heresy, 93–4, 105, 183
Hermans, Willem, 25, 28, 130–31, 134, 166, 170, 174
Herodotus, 91
Herwagen, Johann, 78
Hilary, St., 73, 99, 102–03, 112
Historiography, 65, 199–03
Holbein, Hans, the Younger, 10, 12, 36, 65
Holland, 8, 192
Hollis, Christopher, 200–01
Holy Innocents, 161
Holy Land, The, 106
Holy Orders, 148, 193
Holy Spirit, 11, 48, 56–60, 117, 133, 169, 187
Huizinga, Johan, 200–01
Humanism, Italian, xiv, 1, 2, 114, 185, 193
Humanists, xiv, 4–7, 12, 40, 74, 80,

INDEX

104, 115, 119, 124, 134, 144, 150, 157, 160, 164, 201
Hutten, Ulrich von, 93, 184, 186
Hyma, Albert, 31–2, 200–01

Imitation of Christ, The, xii, xvi, 35, 39, 41, 49, 52, 66
Irenaeus, St., 73, 102
Iscariot, Judas, 21, 85
Italy, 2–6, 11, 193–94
Ithaca College, xi

Jacob's ladder, 124
Jan of Heemstede, 141
Jerome, St., xiv, xviii, 2, 7, 26, 73, 97, 99–05, 112–13, 129–30, 135–36, 141, 169, 174, 192
Jerusalem, 112
Jews, 115, 176
Jodocus, the physician, 134–36
Johannes of Louvain, 88
John, Elector of Saxony, 116
John, Master, 86
John III, King, 103–04, 124
Jonas, Justus, 140, 163, 184
Judd, Leo, 186
Julius II, Pope, 140, 195–96

Katherine, Queen, 184
Kempis, Thomas à, xvii, 35, 39, 66
Knowledge, xv, 46–7, 70, 86, 103, 121, 132–35, 149, 155, 158
Koch, A. C. F., xiii
Kohls, Ernst-Wilhelm, xiii

Lactantius, 73, 102
Laski, Jan (II), xiii
Lateran Councils, 99, 133, 148–49, 151
Latin (language), 2–4, 7–8, 50, 69, 73, 75, 81–6, 89, 100–03, 109–12, 116, 120, 122, 127, 134, 193
Latomus, Jacobus, 92, 96, 113
Laurinus, Marcus, 100
Law, 6
Law, Canon, 145–46
Le Clerc, Jean, 199

Lee, Edward, 92, 96
Lefèvre d'Etaples, Jacques, 92, 95–6
Leiden, 125, 200
Leo X, Pope, 21, 32, 38, 41–2, 64, 97, 99, 103, 106, 140, 196
Le Sauvage, Jean, 105
Lice, Robert de la, 123
Liège, University of, xi, xii
Linacre, Thomas, 4, 65, 199
Lipsius, Martin, 176
Livy, 91, 135
London, 4, 6, 7, 65, 95, 109, 165
López de Zuñiga (Stunica), Diego, 93, 96
Lopsen, 23, 125
Louvain, 76, 85, 93, 112–13, 138
Louvain, University of, 44, 69, 92
Love, xviii, 13, 33, 37, 53, 56, 62–5, 103, 114, 127, 165–90, 202
Low Countries, 4, 9
Loyola, St. Ignatius, 201
Lucian, 5, 72, 87
Luther, Martin, xiii, xiv, 8, 9, 20, 45, 57, 61, 69, 93, 101, 111, 117–18, 153, 183–85, 201, 203
Lutherans, 93, 118, 184

Machiavelli, 8
Mangan, John J., 200–01
Mansfield, Bruce E., 65, 199
Manutius, Aldus, 5
Margaret (mother of Erasmus), 1, 15, 20–1, 32, 38, 127
Margaret, Lady (Beaufort), 6
Mariolatry, 63
Martens, Thierry, 76–7, 141
Martyrs, 82
Mary, Virgin, 24, 37, 179
Mass, 42, 48, 58, 62
Massaut, Jean-Pierre, xi, xii
Matrimony, 148
Maximilian I, Emperor, 92
McConica, James K., 56, 199
Merklin, Balthasar, 185
Metsys, Quentin, 10, 12, 36, 65
Middle Ages, The, 129
Miller, Clarence H., xii
Mombaer, Jan, 33
Monarchy, 8

Monasticism, 2, 3, 29, 30, 33, 137–42, 192–93
Monks, 93, 129, 133–36, 141, 177, 191
Montaigu College, 3, 128, 193
More, Thomas, 4, 10, 12, 40, 86, 99, 202–03
Morin, Jean, 124
Mosaic law, 110, 182
Mountjoy, Lord, see William Blount

Nazianzen, St. Gregory, 102, 112
Netherlands, The, 11
New Testament, 7, 8, 91, 96–12, 120
  Acts, 92, 108, 168
  Corinthians, 93, 165, 168, 177–78
  Galatians, 170
  Hebrews, 92
  St. James, 174
  St. John, 93, 105, 108–09, 173
  St. Luke, 105, 108
  St. Mark, 108
  St. Matthew, 105, 108, 166
  St. Paul, 105
  Romans, 93, 97
New York, xi
Nicene Creed, 63
Northern Renaissance, xiv, 13
Noviomagus, Gerardus (Geldenhouwer), 93

Oecolampadius, Johann, 99
Old, John, 108
Old Testament, xvi, 105, 113, 120
  Ecclesiastes, 91
  Isaiah, 105
  Proverbs, 91
  Psalms, 105
  Wisdom of Solomon, 91
Olin, John C., xii, 96
Origen, 12, 63, 73, 97, 101–02, 112
Oxford, 4

Pace, Richard, 80, 184
Pacifism, 8
Paganism, 71
Palermo, 103

Papacy, xviii, 62, 106, 184–85, 196
Paris, xvi, 3, 4, 40, 82, 85, 99, 109, 120–21, 142, 199
Paris, University of, 3, 4, 89, 92, 109, 126, 128, 134, 193
Parliament, 153
Patristics, xii, xiv, xv, 5
Paul, St., xi, xii, 37, 51, 87, 93, 95, 97–8, 107–09, 168, 175–76, 195
Paul III, Pope, 34
Paynell, Thomas, 138
Peace, 91, 101, 105–06, 119, 182, 185, 192
Penance, 57–63, 147–54
Peter, St., 37, 110
Petrarch, 13
Pfefferkorn, Johann, 185
Philip of Burgundy, 86, 105
Philippi, Johannes, 82
Phillips, Margaret Mann, 8, 195, 200–02
Philology, xiv, xvi, 5, 107
Philosophia Christi, xi, xiv–xviii, 4, 11, 35–7, 40, 41, 49, 58, 69–142, 165, 169, 199, 202
Philosophy, 7, 81, 84, 116, 120, 157, 175, 187
Phoenix, Peter, of Dôle, 179
Pico della Mirandola, 120
Piety, xi, xvii, 9, 38, 40, 46, 50–1, 70, 72–5, 81, 88, 92–5, 100, 103–04, 111, 114, 122, 124, 129, 133–36, 141–42, 180, 189, 190
Pio, Albert, 93
Plague, bubonic, 16, 20, 65, 142, 194
Plato, 91, 178
Plautus, 5
Pliny, 134
Plutarch, 5, 72, 91, 120
Poetry, 80, 81, 111, 112, 126, 128
Poland, 122
Poppenruyter, Johann, 85, 86
Portugal, 103, 124, 151
Post, R. R., xiii
Prayers, 46, 47, 53, 63, 114, 153, 177, 179, 186, 187
Preachers, 72, 122–24, 134
Predestination, 61
Premonstratensians, 129
Priesthood, xiii, xiv, 2, 3, 39, 41, 42,

INDEX

58, 59, 65, 130, 135, 139, 168, 185–86, 192, 195
Printing, xvii, 69, 76
Protestantism, 11, 61, 117, 119, 150, 152, 189, 199
Protestants, 66, 111, 151, 154, 200–01
Pucci, Antonio, 101–02

Quintilian, 134

Rabil, Albert, Jr., xii
Rationalism, xiv
Recusants, 153
Reedijk, Cornelis, 24
Reform, church, 8, 38, 199
Reformation, The, 65, 148, 200, 203
Reisch, Gregor, 99
Religious life, 16–22, 30–34, 41, 55, 64–5, 89, 125, 135–42, 145–47, 193, 197
Renaissance, 1, 2, 7, 13, 143–44, 157, 160, 164, 193
Renaissance Quarterly, xii
Renaudet, Augustin, xi, 175, 200–01
Reuchlin, Johann, 185
Reynolds, E. E., 200, 203
Rhetoric, 35, 80–1, 111–12
Riario, Raffaele, 99
Rochester, bishop of, xiii, 12
Roger, Servatius, 20, 23–28, 46, 72, 89, 97, 126–30, 140, 166–73, 194–97, 201
Rome, 3, 10, 43, 143
Rotterdam, 1, 23, 35, 37, 58, 66, 67, 114, 124, 144, 154, 164, 199
Rummel, Erika, xv
Russians, 183

's Hertogenbosch, 2, 15, 18, 21, 24, 39, 192
Sacraments, xii, 59, 62, 66, 107, 147–54, 164
Sadoleto, Jacopo, 38, 186
Saint-Omer, 85
St. Paul's Cathedral, 73
St. Paul's School, 7, 89, 162, 163
Salamanca, 93
Sallust, 91

Salvation, 48, 59, 140, 152
Sanctity, xi
Sasbout, 127, 170, 172
Scaliger, J. C., 38
Scholasticism, xvi, 3, 94–5, 102, 177
Schoolmaster, 144–45, 158–62
Schottenloher, Otto, 27, 29
Screech, M. A., xiv
Scripture, xi, xii, xv–xvii, 5, 8, 13, 43, 47–50, 63–4, 83–7, 94, 97–07, 111–18, 123–24, 136, 148, 164–69, 175, 178, 181–87, 195, 203
Sélestat, 132
Seneca, 5, 91, 157
Sermons, 160–63
Sion, 21, 127, 168
Skepticism, 118
Šlechta, Jan, 183
Smith, Preserved, 200–01
Socrates, 110
Sorbonne, 93, 111
Soul, xii, 48, 95, 124
Spain, 151
Spanish (language), 84, 93, 121, 183
Spitz, Lewis W., 94, 114, 200, 202–03
Stadion, Christoph von, 123
Steyn, xi, xiii, xv–xviii, 2, 3, 15–43, 50, 64, 66, 70, 72, 75, 79, 97, 125–30, 134, 138, 141, 160, 165–74, 185, 190–96, 201
Stoicism, xiv, 49
Strasbourg, 93, 116–17, 120
Studia humanitatis, 81, 112, 202
Susquehanna University Press, xii
Sutor, Peter, 93
Switzerland, 11

Ten Commandments, 63
Tentler, Thomas N., 63
Terence, 5, 28–9, 71
Tertullian, 63
Theodoricus, Franciscus, 26, 76, 127, 165, 169–72
Theodoricus of Haarlem, 138–40
Theologians, 44, 71, 81, 86–7, 93–4, 102–05, 113, 134, 177–79, 183
Theology, 3, 75, 84, 94–5, 101–02, 112, 185, 202

Thompson, Craig R., 75, 109–110
Tournehem, 85, 142
Tracy, James D., xii, 27–9
Trent, Council of, 145, 148–50, 202
Tunstall, Cuthbert, 95
Turin, University of, 5
Turks, 106, 183
Twayne Publishers, xii

Udall, Nicholas, 108
Utenheim, Christoph von, 93
Utenhove, Charles, 188
Utrecht, 1, 105

Valla, Lorenzo, 5, 165
Van Bavel, Tarsicius J., 170–71
Van Borssele, Lady Anna, 69
Vernacular languages, 63, 98–9, 121
Villoslada, Richard G., xi
Virginity, 64
Virtues, xv, xvii, 4, 9, 33, 38–41, 45–8, 57–60, 65, 73, 85, 91–2, 129, 132, 150, 156, 160–62, 181, 186

Vitrier, Jean, 85, 133
Vives, Juan Luis, 120
Vlatten, Johann von, 119
Volz, Paul, 133, 136, 142, 180, 197
Vulgate, xviii, 2, 93, 97, 100–01

Warham, William, 6, 99, 203
Watson, John, 73–4, 99
Wilkinson, Maurice, 200, 202
William of Cleves, Duke, 120
Winchester, bishop of, 70
Winckel, Pieter, 17–8, 32, 166
Wittenberg, 9
Witz, Johannes, 81, 132
Wolsey, Thomas, 100, 179
Woodward, W. H., 120

Xenophon, 91

Yale University Press, xii
York, archbishop of, 92